DO THE HUMANITIES CREATE KNOWLEDGE?

There is in certain circles a widely held belief that the only proper kind of knowledge is scientific knowledge. This belief often runs parallel to the notion that legitimate knowledge is obtained when a scientist follows a rigorous investigative procedure called the Scientific Method. Chris Haufe challenges this idea. He shows that what we know about the Scientific Method rests fundamentally on the use of finely tuned human judgments directed toward certain questions about the natural world. He suggests that this dependence on judgment in fact reveals deep affinities between scientific knowledge and another, equally important, sort of comprehension: that of humanistic creative endeavour. His wide-ranging and stimulating new book uncovers the unexpected unity underlying all our efforts – whether scientific or arts-based – to understand human experience. In so doing, it makes a vital contribution to broader conversation about the value of the humanities in an increasingly STEM-saturated educational culture.

CHRIS HAUFE is the Elizabeth M. and William C. Treuhaft Professor of the Humanities and Chair of the Department of Philosophy, Case Western Reserve University. He is the author of *How Knowledge Grows* (2022) and *Fruitfulness* (2024).

DO THE HUMANITIES CREATE KNOWLEDGE?

CHRIS HAUFE

Case Western Reserve University

Shaftesbury Road, Cambridge CB2 8EA, United Kingdom

One Liberty Plaza, 20th Floor, New York, NY 10006, USA

477 Williamstown Road, Port Melbourne, VIC 3207, Australia

314–321, 3rd Floor, Plot 3, Splendor Forum, Jasola District Centre, New Delhi – 110025, India

103 Penang Road, #05–06/07, Visioncrest Commercial, Singapore 238467

Cambridge University Press is part of Cambridge University Press & Assessment, a department of the University of Cambridge.

We share the University's mission to contribute to society through the pursuit of education, learning and research at the highest international levels of excellence.

www.cambridge.org
Information on this title: www.cambridge.org/9781316512500

DOI: 10.1017/9781009067508

© Chris Haufe 2023

This publication is in copyright. Subject to statutory exception and to the provisions of relevant collective licensing agreements, no reproduction of any part may take place without the written permission of Cambridge University Press & Assessment.

First published 2023

Printed in the United Kingdom by TJ Books Limited, Padstow, Cornwall

A catalogue record for this publication is available from the British Library

Library of Congress Cataloging-in-Publication Data
NAMES: Haufe, Chris, author.
TITLE: Do the humanities create knowledge? / Chris Haufe, Case Western Reserve University, Ohio.
DESCRIPTION: Cambridge, United Kingdom ; New York, NY : Cambridge University Press, 2023. | Includes bibliographical references and index.
IDENTIFIERS: LCCN 2023000035 | ISBN 9781316512500 (hardback) | ISBN 9781009067508 (ebook)
SUBJECTS: LCSH: Humanities – Philosophy. | Knowledge, Theory of. | Science – Philosophy.
CLASSIFICATION: LCC AZ101 .H39 2023 | DDC 001.301–dc23/eng/20230123
LC record available at https://lccn.loc.gov/2023000035

ISBN 978-1-316-51250-0 Hardback

Cambridge University Press & Assessment has no responsibility for the persistence or accuracy of URLs for external or third-party internet websites referred to in this publication and does not guarantee that any content on such websites is, or will remain, accurate or appropriate.

*For my mother, who never cared whether the humanities
created knowledge as long as I was happy*

and of the knowledge of humanism, it is enough that you be able to cite the evidential example and the exemplar.
Abdullah ibn 'Abbas (d. 68 AH/687–88 CE),
cousin of the Prophet Muhammad

Contents

Preface		*page* ix
Acknowledgments		xi
1	Introduction	1
2	What Would the Community Think?	17
3	Canon and Consensus	36
4	Knowing What Matters	71
5	In Defense of How Things Seem	107
6	Reading What Lies Within	137
7	Humanities Victorious?	161
8	Of Interest	178
9	The Hoax and the Humanities	205
10	Conclusion	233
References		237
Index		247

Preface

I am writing this from inside a box. The walls of this box are adorned with the most resplendent scenes, sprawling vistas that only become more enticing the more carefully one studies them. The corners are neat and square, like the gorgeous cellar dug by Mike Mulligan and his steam shovel, Mary Anne, in Virginia Burton's classic children's book, *Mike Mulligan and His Steam Shovel* (Mary Anne). Mike and Mary Anne never left that cellar. And why would they? It contained all they would ever need: a roaring fire, hot coffee, probably some flapjacks or something. Anything else would just be frills – foam on the sea, possessed neither of stability nor of real substance.

A lot of people say that there is no safe harbor outside the box; only darkness and confusion. It is either the box or anarchy. Sometimes, though, and with enormous effort, I'm able to poke my head through some freshly patched drywall to look at things as if from outside. To my astonishment, the goings-on out there appear in many ways to be remarkably similar to what happens inside the box. Moreover, the outer surface of the box looks nothing like those beautifully ornamented walls with their corners neat and square; it's a bloody mess. Although it's clearly very strong and stable in certain places, it is jagged and disjointed. There are leaks and huge, gaping holes. Some are being furiously plugged, while others just sit there encircled by workmen who are not at all sure what to do. And by no means does it go on forever. At most, there are half-formed plans to extend it. The grounds are littered with the remains of what looks like old decor, which is weird, because I don't remember anyone saying anything about redecorating. I just assumed those resplendent scenes had always been there.

My box is the notion that the only kind of knowledge is scientific knowledge, and this book is an attempt to rescue a sense of epistemological order that exists outside the box. I'm not convinced I want to leave my box. I think there are good reasons to stay tucked cozily in the sumptuous epistemic triumphs of the last 350 years. I do *not* think that they are overwhelmingly good, and I do not think that the garden variety reasons for staying inside are the good ones. At the very least, I sympathize with the desire to stay in the box, because it appears to be the only box in town. But I have never liked "only game in town" arguments. They are unwholesome. One feels dirty after having made such an argument. And one feels suspicious and abused after having such an argument used against him.

As humanists, we owe it to our disciplines and to the broader human culture to explain how the humanities produce knowledge. We owe it to ourselves. I know lots of humanists who subscribe to the notion that knowledge is what the sciences are for. They are convinced that, for all their scholarly efforts, they do not generate knowledge. I aim to show that this conviction rests on a mistaken conception of what knowledge is. Others have lately made appeals to the authority of "lived experience" and of "other ways of knowing." It will not come as news to these humanists that such appeals have largely not been taken seriously. Their dismissal is motivated partly by this mistaken conception of knowledge, be it latent or manifest. But it is also grounded in the fact that the content of these alternative conceptions has been left unworkably opaque. My purpose here is to provide a kind of structure or template that can be used to elaborate that content in a way that clarifies the coherence of these appeals.

Whatever your background, I hope you will read this with an open mind about the humanities *and* about the natural sciences. My conception of scientific knowledge is derived not from philosophers in search of the pristine orderliness which they are convinced must lie at the foundation of scientific inquiry, but from practicing scientists who seemed to worry that the true essence of the scientific adventure was being occluded by a well-intentioned enthusiasm for fortifying the citadels of reason. Most people, including many scientists, do not consider themselves to be partisans of the idea that scientific knowledge is the only species of knowledge worth the name. If you find yourself, as I once did, deeply skeptical about the prospects for humanistic knowledge, though, it might be because you subscribe to this thesis. If you find the question, "Do the Humanities Create Knowledge?" to be incoherent or pitiable, you *definitely* subscribe to this thesis. Maybe we should subscribe to it. Maybe there's really nothing outside the box. Let's have a proper look.

Acknowledgments

Of the many debts I have incurred through writing this book, the deepest of them are owed to Philip Kitcher, Peter Vickers, and my wife, Maysan Haydar. Each of them read the entire manuscript, offered precious feedback, and showed a disturbing convergence of opinion on what needed to change. I hope that I am asked to return the favor. I hope that I am equal to the task.

The early murmurings of my interest in writing a book about the epistemology of the humanities began at the University of Rochester's Center for the Humanities, where I was a fellow during the academic year 2018–2019. My time there and my conversations with Will Miller, Chris Rovee, and the Center's director, Joanie Rubin expanded my view of the humanities in ways that would otherwise not have been possible.

Case Western Reserve University has been a wonderful and supportive research environment from the moment I arrived, as has our Baker-Nord Center for the Humanities, which has hosted several talks on material that follows and provided financial support for research materials and for the book's indexing. I have benefitted from many conversations on the issues covered herein with my colleagues Michael Clune and Aviva Rothman, both of whom seem to me to understand the humanities at a very deep level. Many conversations with Cyrus Taylor enriched my understanding of the cultural and practice of science immeasurably. Jeremy Bendik-Keymer read the entire manuscript and pointed me to a variety of connections with deeper social and moral issues.

Much of this book was conceived of and written during an extended visit from the historian of science Omar W. Nasim to Case Western as the Hildegarde and Elbert Baker Visiting Scholar in the Humanities. Prof. Nasim was a crucial interlocutor and advisor on virtually every major issue I address here. Many thanks go to Hilary Gaskin, the philosophy editor at Cambridge University Press who brought this book into being and who offered valuable encouragement and suggestions; and to Nicola Maclean who oversaw the book's production.

A different sort of acknowledgment is due to my children, Zayd, Sinan, and Layla. They have endured endless exhortations (not always in the gentlest of tones) to make the best use of their free time while they have it, and to avoid the endless avalanche of ephemera that threatens to bury things of real value and sweep away our opportunities to pursue them. While their futures are, to a large degree, wide open, they are being reared in a culture which breeds into its young a sense that time spent on the humanities could be better spent on less interesting things. They are not fooled. I am proud of them. I am proud of who they will become. I hope this book will steady them as they set out on the all-too-short road to adult life.

CHAPTER 1

Introduction

In the nearly perfect movie, *Office Space*, some business consultants are brought in to a software company to trim a little fat. As part of that process, employees are called to meet with the consultants, to more or less interview for the job they already have. During one of these meetings, a guy named Tom with a job that clearly did not need to exist becomes irate, spluttering about this and that in a desperate plea for relevance before his inevitable exposure as a superfluous, and thus expendable, accoutrement.

The world is full of Toms. We hope that we are not among them. Sometimes this is because we do not want to lose our jobs. Tom's protests in *Office Space* were focused on preserving his livelihood. Often enough, though, we simply lament the prospect that other people might not value what we contribute ... and that they might be right to do so. We lament this prospect, not because we think we deserve their respect or recognition, but because we don't want to waste our time. Moment by moment, I feel the crushing threat of wasted time bearing down on me. I hear the echoes of Tom's futile, self-serving outburst as I try to tell myself that what I do is important.

The book you are reading is the result of an extended meditation on the question of whether the humanities produce knowledge. And I do mean *extended*. For half of my life, I have tried to work out for myself what it is exactly I do with the time I spend reading, writing, and talking to academics across a wide range of disciplines. When I describe this pattern to people outside of academia, they often burst out laughing; this frequently happens during interactions with natural scientists as well. My own children are pretty much convinced that I do nothing all day long. The way in which I and most other humanists work simply does not comport with their image of what knowledge production looks like. And the fact that I'm literally wearing a tweed jacket as I write this probably doesn't help, either.

Their image of knowledge production comes from the natural sciences. They have a clear sense of what it means to produce knowledge because research in the natural sciences has produced concrete results that we can use to make stuff. Thanks to the natural sciences, my iPhone can accurately predict local temperature changes in ten-minute increments. Thanks to the natural sciences, we have developed increasingly powerful and efficient energy alternatives to fossil fuels. For many of us, the awe-inspiring concrete achievements of modern science have made the difference between life and death, between joy and grief. My son, a type 1 diabetic, has an insulin pump that can predict high blood sugar and provide compensatory insulin so that he can basically lead a normal life. The world owes the natural sciences a humbling debt for the development of the COVID-19 vaccine. In the soaring words of Richard Dawkins, "Planes fly. Cars drive... It works, bitches."[1]

To complement these tangible and often personally meaningful results, we have also been treated to a highly refined schematic representation of *how* they have been achieved – the Scientific Method: observation, hypothesis, experiment, analysis, and conclusion. Boom! Knowledge accomplished. In addition to being easy to grasp, there is something very intuitive about the process encapsulated here. Its essence is to think and to check, with some bespoke add-ons for the purposes of ensuring that the "checking" part is worthwhile. Thinking and checking are reflexes of the mind. The Scientific Method gives voice to those mental impulses, trains them a bit, and crowns them as the Royal Road to knowledge land. Hence, it is not merely that science works. It is that we understand why it works. Indeed, we understand why it *should* work. By disciplining and extending certain built-in habits of the mind, the Scientific Method allows us to learn about the world in a way that asks very little from us in the form of fundamentally novel behavior. Perhaps the Scientific Method is simply a natural stage in the development of humanity's relentless quest to acquire knowledge. Perhaps it is the ultimate stage.

It has long been fashionable in many circles to deride the notion of the Scientific Method – not just the canonical version I laid out above but the very idea that there is an identifiable method according to which scientists structure their investigations. There is some justice in these criticisms. Yet it would not be difficult to accurately model a great many actual scientific investigations as if they were following this template, at least at a very general level. That is to say, there is something right about

[1] www.youtube.com/watch?v=0OtFSDKrq88. Last accessed March 2, 2022.

how the schematic Scientific Method portrays the nature and the spirit of scientific investigation. Were we to show that schematic representation to the likes of Galileo, Newton, Boyle, and countless researchers who lived before the emergence of the concept of *the Scientific Method*, they would doubtless instantly recognize the essential process it depicts, as would any practicing scientist of today who had never heard of the Scientific Method. That means something. It suggests that there is a gross pattern to scientific inquiry, and that scientists have seen themselves in that schematic depiction of science precisely because it accentuates the salient features of real scientific investigation.

The problem, I think, is that this schematic depiction elides an enormous amount of detail, detail which, were it to be widely appreciated, would almost certainly effect "a decisive transformation in the image of science by which we are now possessed" (Kuhn 1962, 1). Indeed, the volume of stuff it does not talk about is so copious that I actually need to divide it into two categories. First, each of the model's components – observation, hypothesis, etc. – represents an incredibly complex and confusing phenomenon. Thus, to say that, for example, observation is part of the Scientific Method is to make a claim that appears to be as clear as day but is in fact very poorly understood (see, e.g., Hacking 1981; Daston 2008). For instance, Nasim (2013) provides compelling evidence that the practice of drawing nebulae in nineteenth-century astronomy was *part* of the observation process, not simply an *aid* to observation. Rudwick (1972) shows how early attempts to draw fossils forced Renaissance naturalists to focus on representing certain features, without any knowledge of whether those features were biologically or taxonomically significant. What is more, each of these components "has a history," as they say; that is, each of them becomes part of the Scientific Method through a complex historical process, a process which might have gone in another direction. It took a long time for the use of hypotheses to be viewed as an acceptable way to do science. The eighteenth-century physicist Georges-Louis Le Sage endured widespread resistance to his use of hypotheses in trying to understand the nature of gravity (Laudan 1981). Charles Darwin was roundly criticized for the *Origin*'s liberal use of hypotheses (Hull 2003). *Darwin.* In addition, the form that many of these components take in our time would have been unrecognizable to our predecessors. To a contemporary scientist, "analyzing data" often just means running it through Stata or some other off-the-shelf statistical package. Newton never used Stata, because Newton didn't have a computer. Also, he didn't have statistics. In sum, to the extent that the schematic depiction of science is accurate, it is woefully underspecified, and that underspecification significantly affects how we understand scientific knowledge and its place in human culture. In particular, it suppresses the massive role of human judgment in the development of scientific knowledge.

That brings us to the second category. The traditional portrayal of the Scientific Method leaves out entirely what is in my opinion truly distinctive about scientific inquiry – namely, its social dimension. Observation, hypothesis, experiment, analysis, and conclusion – none of it amounts to much in the hands of a single individual, even when perfectly executed. Scientific knowledge is not the conclusion one draws from his properly carried-out scientific methodology. It is a social sausage-making process, during which groups of similarly inclined but often antagonistic scientific charcutiers select the finest cuts from the world's prize-winning pigs, applying a prescription-strength dewormer before surgically slicing them to bits and packing them in the highly elastic but appropriately constrictive intestinal casing of publication, so they can be smoothly digested by members of the community. This social dimension is what distinguishes the *idea* of a single person from the *knowledge* of a community. But the Scientific Method doesn't even mention this. It invites us to conceive of scientific knowledge as the output of a single Cartesian investigator. I have no idea why, and I won't speculate. Yet, here again, we see the exclusion of a defining feature of scientific inquiry that just happens to center around the necessity of human judgment. Indeed, even to say it is a *defining* feature of inquiry credits the social dimension with too small of a role. I'm sensing a pattern here....

We have concocted a story about how scientific knowledge is acquired that is very satisfying but not very accurate, which is actually pretty ironic if you think about it. That story, because of its generality and its plausibility, has proven to be as seductive as it is resilient. And as the eminent historian of science, John Heilbron has observed, "you do not have to be right to make a revolution. You have to have a plausible and comprehensive programme" (Heilbron 2013, 15). Now, if it were just another innocent seduction, that would be one thing. This dalliance, however, has spawned all manner of poisoned fruit. For, the story of the Scientific Method has precipitated a revolution not only in our conception of scientific knowledge but in the very idea of knowledge itself. In doing so, it has severely undermined our ability to recognize and appreciate other forms of knowledge. Before I present an overview of the specific alternative that interests me, I want to spend some time giving due respect to the forgivable slide from respect for science to disrespect for the humanities.

Introduction

The philosopher of physics Harvey Brown once remarked that anyone who is not mystified by the law of inertia has not properly understood it (Brown 2005, 15). Something similar must be held in relation to the successes of modern science. Looking closely at the intellectual and experimental triumphs of modern science, particularly since the seventeenth century, we are presented with countless manifestations of human genius, creativity, and intellectual fortitude that are truly humbling. For reasons that are understandable but not altogether satisfying, these deeply human struggles are hidden from view by certain constraints imposed on the various forms of science communication – including education and journalism, the vehicles through which most of us make contact with modern science. The actual historical details of a scientific investigation – the undaunted, often spiritually taxing journey from some inchoate sense of confusion to (say) a mathematically precise expression of the behavior of unobservable particles – accentuate the human features of scientific inquiry. They reveal the scientist to be nothing more (or less) than an ordinary person with a dogged commitment to developing some understanding of nature with which she can be satisfied, if only for a moment. As we trace her struggles, we can relate to her passion, her frustration, and her desperate groping for a lifeline by which she can, with effort, momentarily breach the surface of a problem before being plunged back into the depths of befuddlement where light fails to penetrate. We sympathize with her temptation to cut corners and to be too easily convinced by signs of promise. We admire her disciplined refusal to take the easy way out, just as we cringe at the less-than-admirable depths to which she sometimes sinks to outdo her competitors. When afflicted with setbacks, we feel her disappointment. We celebrate her triumphs. In scientific investigation, we find a microcosm of the cognitive and emotional tumult that is human life.

And yet, the intellectual content of this recognizably human struggle is often something that relatively few of us can appreciate. What are Einstein's field equations? What form do solutions to those equations take, and what do they even mean? What are gravitational waves? Why is our ability to detect them significant? How does the "spike protein" facilitate our efforts to inoculate people against COVID-19? And on and on and on. While most of us have encountered these and other terms from the natural sciences, far more (including me) have at most a tenuous grasp of their meanings. Our ability to reflect on them, to turn them over in our minds, to get a feel for them, to understand their implications is even more poorly grounded. We lack the sensibilities that give rise to the mathematician's aesthetic appreciation of the Macdonald equation, described by the polymath Freeman Dyson as "the most beautiful thing that I ever discovered."[2] The simplicity of Schrödinger's equation is lost on us; it was not lost on his fellow physicist Werner Heisenberg. Although none of us finds any difficulty grasping the meaning of the symbol H_2O, the ease with which we can relate to it masks the intimidating cognitive demands of the conceptual and experimental morass that impeded its formulation over much of the nineteenth century (Rocke 1984). We understand that Darwin's theory of natural selection explains adaptation, yet how many of us are tempted by the meaningless suspicion that the theory of evolution is "just a theory"? Our scientific literacy (whatever that means) might be up to par. However, when confronted with demands that require more than a surface understanding, those of us without advanced scientific training or mathematical training – people like me – are essentially alienated from the practitioner's capacity to admire the relentless torrent of cognitive victories which characterizes the history of science and mathematics.

Thus, even if are able to see something of ourselves in the emotional tumult reflected in the finer historical details of scientific inquiry, our capacity to appreciate the significance of scientific achievement is typically quite limited. In this way, we join a venerable lineage of cognoscenti who, not for lack of intelligence, are unable to take part in the pleasure of developments made outside the range of our experience. Archimedes could have fit any living mathematician in his hip pocket. But he would have found our modern approach to measuring the area under a curve to be quite incomprehensible, despite the fact that it would have spared him much exhaustion. Cut off from a community of practitioners due to time, space, or specialization, he would lack the background of accumulated knowledge required to relate to these developments on more than a superficial level (though I suspect he'd get up to speed fairly quickly). To be perfectly forthcoming about my own limitations, following any discussion that goes beyond high school mathematics can quickly go from taxing to hopeless. It can sometimes take several uninterrupted days of concerted effort for me to reconstruct (for teaching purposes) some historically important geometrical proof. If you find yourself unable to list from memory Einstein's field equations, welcome to the club. If you cannot see what Freeman Dyson sees in the Macdonald equation, you're not alone. If the Schrödinger equation strikes you as no less simple than anything else in quantum mechanics, I feel your pain. Our paths diverged long ago from those who went on to the kind of training that results in a connoisseur's esteem for scientific achievement.

[2] www.ias.edu/ideas/2015/dyson-concinnitas. Last accessed March 5, 2022.

Introduction

The corollary to all this is that those with training in the natural sciences and in mathematics often have a keen sense of the significance of these triumphs as well as, albeit somewhat less frequently, the struggles that went into achieving them. And although the outcomes can be exhilarating for practitioners, most science is extremely tedious and boring. No psychologically normal human would elect to endure for a span of a few minutes the sorts of things on which many scientists spend the best years of their graduate students' lives. The philosopher Robert Paul Wolff reflected on this gulf in an anecdote recalling the occasion of his meeting the entomologist and popular science author, Edward O. Wilson:

> We met in Wilson's office in the Museum. After the usual greetings, he showed me the centerpiece of the office, a large table on which, under a Plexiglas dome, was a bustling, complex ant colony. Wilson banged the side of the table, which set the ants scurrying, and as they poured out of the anthill he pointed out the soldier ants, worker ants, and so forth. I didn't have much in the way of conversation. What can you say about an anthill, after all? So, casting about for something to say, I mused aloud, "I wonder how many ants there are in the entire colony." "Fifteen thousand," Wilson replied. "How can you be sure?" I asked. "I counted them," he said.
>
> There are moments in life when the scales fall from your eyes and you suddenly see clearly something that has hitherto been obscured from view. This was one of those moments. I had from time to time reflected on how different the workaday lives are of people in different corners of the Academy, even though we all call ourselves "Professor." Here was E. O. Wilson, the creator of Sociobiology, who thought nothing at all about counting fifteen thousand ants. Had anyone asked me to figure out the number of ants in an anthill, the farthest I would have gone was watching eight or ten walk by and then guesstimating the rest.
>
> To be sure, philosophers sometimes descend to the level of the particular. But our tendency is to go in somewhat the opposite direction. Confronted with the real world, the reflex reaction of philosophers is to ask about possible worlds. It was clear to me that although we were both professors and authors, Wilson and I led lives so utterly different that no real mutual understanding was likely. It was also clear that however much the world might think of Wilson as the tendentious, controversial author of Sociobiology, his real interest was in those ants.[3]

This is not to deny "the pleasure of finding things out," as the great physicist Richard Feynman put it.[4] That pleasure, however, tends to come in

---

[3] https://robertpaulwolff.blogspot.com/2013/09/what-have-i-been-reading.html.
[4] In needs to be borne in mind that, by any standard, Feynman was an absolute genius; he was such a genius that the title of his biography is literally just *Genius* (Gleick 1992). Perhaps Feynman was not well-acquainted with the humdrum of science, given his use of "the Feynman Method," which his

the moment of insight, not the years-long slog through data, grant applications, disappointment, grant applications, and more data. The ability to achieve anything of real scientific value – to gain access to the delights of discovery – requires a degree of disciplined meticulousness and persistence that most people simply do not have. As the founder of atomic theory, John Dalton expressed it, "If I have succeeded better than many who surround me, it has been chiefly, nay, I may say almost solely from unwavering assiduity." Dalton himself amassed more than 200,000 entries in his meteorological diary (Pennock 2019, 153. See Strevens 2020 for many similar examples). Indeed, novice scientists are often stunned to discover that actual scientific research is not the blazing state of perpetual ecstasy that it is often depicted as being.

Caught between the mind-numbing monotony of actual scientific research and the general inaccessibility of scientific pleasures for most people, we have constructed a handful of convenient yet intuitively plausible distortions of the nature of scientific inquiry that we use to bring scientific knowledge into the consciousness of the nonscientific public. As I write, I am sitting in an auditorium with about 300 little kids (my daughter says more like 150), watching a man in an affected red bowtie and white lab coat boisterously pour liquid nitrogen on stuff to shock and amaze. His grand finale is dropping Cheetos into a bowl of liquid nitrogen and then feeding them to volunteers, to the delight of the entire audience. Professor McInquiry and his Dazzling Display of Wizzbangery are both parts of a tried-and-true method of inviting – or better, *luring* – unsuspecting marks into the scientific adventure through awe-inspiring manipulations of nature's hidden properties. Lying just beneath the surface, these marvels are ready-made vehicles for bringing the pleasures of scientific knowledge to a public that is ill-equipped to appreciate the more recondite versions of excitement to which the practicing scientist hopes to gain access. Because we can all partake in the spectacle of a rehearsed demonstration, and follow along with the explanation of how cold things get smaller and hot things get bigger, it becomes possible to cultivate an appreciation for the majesty of scientific knowledge without any background knowledge, without any particular talent, and without any particular predilection. Professor McInquiry was a hit with audience members of all ages. Wrapping things up, the man in charge of the event tellingly quipped, "He's also available for birthdays and bar mitzvahs."

colleague Murray Gell-Mann characterized in the following way: "Dick's method is this. You write down the problem. You think very hard. (He shuts his eyes and presses his knuckles parodically to his forehead.) Then you write down the answer" (Gleick 1992, 315).

A parallel phenomenon exists in science journalism and in the popularized accounts of science that are published mostly by trade presses. Much of the way science is depicted in these venues is shaped by constraints like that of being interesting to "an old lady on her way to the grocery store," as one science journalist described it to me. Her tongue-in-cheek way of framing this constraint was intended to emphasize that science stories need an audience. They are not aimed at practicing scientists. They must be stories that speak to people from a panoply of backgrounds. In order to do that, you need to either (1) describe something totally amazing or (2) contort the history of discovery into a thrilling yet tidy narrative arc: the low rumble of complication, the promising early efforts, the setback about two-thirds of the way through the story, and the eventual triumph. Each of these strategies is designed to exploit well-known human tendencies – respectively, the love of novelty and the love of a good story. Potent in their own way, such tactics can do for anyone's morning commute or weekend reading what Professor McInquiry can do for your birthday party. They put scientific knowledge into a form that generates an immediate response in pretty much anybody.

The combined force of these publicly accessible distortions is, I think, incredibly powerful. We have perpetuated a base caricature of how scientific knowledge is produced in the form of the Scientific Method. We carefully select the most titillating and mystifying bits of that knowledge for public consumption. And we emphasize the (often illusory) astonishing potential applications of this knowledge. To add to this, there is a vast plenitude of actual applications that are quite legitimately astonishing. Scientific inquiry led to a COVID-19 vaccine in significantly less than a year. Scientific inquiry led to the transistor and the computer. Scientific inquiry has made it possible for my own child to live an essentially normal life through effortless management of his diabetes. Even if we acknowledge the genuinely horrific downstream consequences of some inquiry, we all know that we owe science big time. In this curious melange of legitimate admiration and ill-gotten awe, the idea that scientific knowledge is exemplary of knowledge itself is not a very hard sell. Literary criticism cannot cure diabetes. Philosophy cannot send something to the moon, not even those chimps that were rumored to have come back super-intelligent.[5] Art history cannot reprogram cells to search and destroy. The study of poetry in ancient Rome will not lead to insights into any of the Millennium problems in mathematics. We know that science can or will do these things.

---

[5] *The Simpsons*, Season 5, Episode 15.

And we have a convincing explanation – the Scientific Method – of exactly how science does them. In short, we have a clearly articulated model for understanding how truly stunning triumphs of human ingenuity occur. They occur through *scientific* inquiry.

By contrast, the output of humanistic inquiry, however enjoyable it may be, generally lacks the power to astonish, particularly when it comes to the uninitiated. It consists almost entirely of words on pages – increasingly, on digital pages through which we rapidly scroll. There are no blinding flashes of light. There are no iPhones. There are no high-res three-dimensional computer-generated animations of the processes described by humanists; and if there were, humanists would probably object to them for some reason or other. There is no humanist counterpart to Professor McInquiry. Go ahead, try inviting an art historian to your seven-year-old's birthday party. What a raucous hoot that will be. Unless you can get Anthony Grafton to let the kids ride his book wheel, odds are that this is going to be a very disappointing and embarrassing birthday for your son or daughter.[6] While the humanities are just as capable as the natural sciences at producing that profound sense of wonder and appreciation among connoisseurs, we simply cannot compete with the power of the natural sciences to provide high-potency hits of dopamine to the novices.

But there is more to it than that, and here humanists would appear to bear total responsibility. This second asymmetry concerns the ability of nonspecialists to grapple with the nature, process, and significance of humanistic inquiry. In the natural sciences, the Scientific Method gives nonspecialists the sense that the wonders of science are not just magic. Yes, that sense is based on a way of representing scientific inquiry that is not faithful to loads of significant detail. But there's a word for that: *idealization*. Idealizations are valuable precisely because they afford a kind of cognitive grasp that does not get bogged down in certain particulars. That sense of understanding the process behind the magic, I have argued, has partly fueled the reputation of the natural sciences as having cornered the knowledge market. It makes sense of why science can do all these amazing things. If you take that sense of understanding away, all that is left is the Dazzling Display of Whizzbangery and the technological marvels. As early campaigners on behalf of science well knew, in the absence of an accessible narrative that could capture the process by which these marvels are achieved, the natural sciences were likely to remain in their stature as an

---

[6] www.princeton.edu/~paw/archive_new/PAW06-07/11-0404/features_grafton.html. Last accessed March 7, 2022.

entertaining cabinet of curiosities (Laudan 1993). Thus, before the middle of the nineteenth century, long before the natural sciences could claim responsibility for world-changing devices, popular narratives of scientific progress had solidified the reputation of the natural sciences as knowledge generators *par excellence*. But we do not even have an *idealization* of humanistic inquiry, let alone a fine-grained model that faithfully captures the details. To put it bluntly, *there is no humanities equivalent of the Scientific Method*. There is no model, distorted or otherwise, of how humanistic knowledge is produced. There is no account of how the output of humanistic scholarly endeavor qualifies as knowledge of any kind. This is a serious problem.

To be sure, there is no shortage of books on the *value* of the humanities. Written largely in response to the declining appreciation for the humanities, they tend to be more concerned with the content and effect of ideas that have emerged through the tradition of humanistic thought, rather than with the process by which those ideas are refined and accepted (see, e.g., Nussbaum 2010; Small 2013). While there is much in these efforts to admire, what this approach does not address is the fact that not all ideas are created equal, and that the Scientific Method is now understood to be the all-purpose tool by which we are able to distinguish the ideas that we ought to take seriously from the ideas with which we need not bother. The Scientific Method is how we gain access to *truth*. The profound influence of philosophical and literary ideas, while not to be denied, does not tell us that they are true, and it does not establish them as knowledge. Aristotle's physics was enormously influential; still wrong. How do we know? The Scientific Method. Galileo disproved the Aristotelian idea that heavier objects fall faster by performing an *experiment* involving spheres of different masses dropped from the Leaning Tower of Pisa. Case Closed.[7] Now, where is the experimental evidence for the value of democracy? What predictive successes does John Rawls' theory of justice as fairness have under its belt? How do we even test the hypothesis that love is all you need? We do not need to reject the beauty of any of the results of humanistic inquiry in order to acknowledge the straightforward sense in which those results clearly fail to qualify as knowledge. The seventeenth century gave us modern science. Modern science gave us the tools to distinguish truth from really nice-sounding ideas. But a rogue group of sentimental bookworms chose to ignore those developments and continue playing with words like Aristotle did. Like Thomas Hobbes did. Like Galen did. The humanities today are the contemporary descendants of that group. They are not on the winning side of the history of knowledge.

---

[7] The veracity of this report, first made by Galileo's disciple and biographer Viviani, is widely disputed.

The Enlightenment produced an epistemological vacuum so completely devoid of substance that something as appallingly inaccurate as the Scientific Method had no trouble filling it. Since that time, natural science has continued to shore up its claim to epistemic hegemony through persistent efforts to refine and promulgate its theory of knowledge and by producing certain results that everyone can and should appreciate. Rather than develop an alternative model of knowledge, though, we have watched as more and more territory falls under the ostensible purview of natural science. Consequently, we now live in a time where the humanities are viewed as being constitutionally incapable of producing knowledge because they are not the natural sciences, and in which surveys conducted by evolutionary psychologists are perceived as having more to teach us about love than *Romeo and Juliet*. (Which romantic love measurement framework do *you* find most compelling – the Passionate Love Scale, the Triangular Love Scale, or the Love Attitudes Scale? I just can't make up my mind, although they say the Passionate Love Scale is really "only valid in people who are in a romantic relationship with their loved one," which makes total sense if you really think about it.)[8] Would that Shakespeare had lived in a time awash with such wonders as these. Perhaps then he might have produced something of real value.

1.1 Toward an Epistemology of Disciplinary Knowledge

The mid-twentieth century produced a perspective on scientific knowledge which sort of runs parallel to the Scientific Method and which was almost entirely neglected by theorists of knowledge. I take this alternative tradition to be principally the progeny of four highly original thinkers, who sort into two natural pairings. The first pair: Ludwik Fleck and Thomas Kuhn. The second: Michael Polanyi and Noam Chomsky. Each of these mavericks worked as an empirical scientist before training their sites on questions of knowledge. I'm going to briefly state their respective contributions to this alternative picture of scientific knowledge, before explaining how it is relevant to the problem of knowledge in the humanities.

In *The Genesis and Development of a Scientific Fact* (1935), Fleck, a bacteriologist and physician, shows how the knowledge basis upon which any scientific inquiry rests is an accumulation of ideas that have survived the scrutiny of a scientific community. Scientific facts are those propositions that are accepted by a scientific community as facts as a result of

---

[8] Bode 2021, 4.

this process. Doubtless there are facts that no one knows about. There is a fact about how many dust particles adorn my computer screen. But that sense of *fact* is significantly different from the one employed in the phrase, "scientific fact." To say that some proposition is a *scientific* fact is to say something about a perspective at which a scientific community has arrived after proper scrutiny of some assertion of fact.

The community norms that determine whether a mode of scrutiny is proper, and whether the subject of that scrutiny is warranted, emerge from reflection on the disciplinary import of certain exemplars. So argued Thomas Kuhn, a physicist trained under the Nobel Prize winner John Van Vleck, in an elegant model of a specific historical pattern that many sciences appear to exhibit, described in his famous book, *The Structure of Scientific Revolutions* (1962). Kuhn developed a picture according to which exemplars are used in various ways to govern the process by which certain facts are selected for scrutiny, as well to as to govern the nature of scrutiny itself. In his model, the norms followed by practitioners in the course of scientific inquiry are acquired through training and experience, rather than through explicit instruction as to what the norms are and why they matter. The intensity of this process affects perception, cognition, and language, shaping practitioners into the communicative communities that engage with each other on a variety of levels to produce scientific facts in the sense outlined by Fleck.

Together, Kuhn and Fleck give us a picture of what real scientific knowledge looks like, because they give us a framework for seeing how that knowledge develops at the level of a disciplinary community. Any conception of scientific knowledge that fails to give due consideration to the centrality of the disciplinary community cannot be held to be credible. This is the principal reason why the Scientific Method is so inexcusably inadequate. Without the community component, the Scientific Method is ultimately just another appeal to someone's "lived experience."

The Chomsky-Polanyi pairing is focused on the recognition of a variety of knowledge that was radically out-of-step with the prevailing trends in twentieth-century epistemology. While somewhat idiosyncratic, Polanyi's (1958) *Personal Knowledge* provides an exhaustive catalog of instances of the kind of knowledge that people have but cannot articulate, which he called "tacit knowledge." Many of the instances on which he focuses were inspired by his training as a scientist and his long and distinguished research career in physical chemistry. Perhaps unsurprisingly, these instances of knowledge that derive from the context of scientific practice align precisely with the sorts of considerations which Kuhn portrayed as the principal determinants of the direction of scientific research. Scientists know things that they cannot or do not articulate, things that guide the development of scientific knowledge in profound and explicable ways.

No one who reads Polanyi's book and considers his staggering wealth of examples can fail to come away with the conclusion that propositional knowledge is but a subspecies of human knowledge more generally, and possibly not an overwhelmingly important one at that. What is more, this alternative variety – *tacit knowledge* – does not appear to result from the application of the Scientific Method, or of any explicit "method" at all. Rather, it travels via the same channels as our acquisition of skills and of cultural norms. It requires no explicit instruction. Indeed, attempts to explicate necessarily fall short and systematically mislead. In sum, Polanyi's impressive survey grounds Kuhn's generalizations about the kind of knowledge that scientists derive from exemplars, knowledge which shapes the nature of scientific practice within a community of practitioners.

The last contributor, Noam Chomsky, is the well-known founder of modern linguistics (also known for other stuff). Beginning in the late 1950s, Chomsky revived the ancient practice of systematically probing the value judgments of people who had achieved mastery over a certain body of knowledge, producing a model of that knowledge by constructing a careful mapping of its outer edges (Chomsky 1957).[9] As his principal focus was language, he took an interest in the kinds of utterances that respondents found intuitively unacceptable, even if they could not explain what it was about those utterances that displeased them so. From those objections, Chomskyan linguists formed a kind of negative image of the content of the norms governing speakers' use of language, norms which the speakers themselves could not articulate and of which they in general showed no signs of awareness. These norms are precisely the sort of phenomenon that Polanyi described as tacit knowledge, and Chomsky developed their extraction into a precise experimental research program.

Together, these four distinct components combine to give us a framework for understanding what I'll be calling *disciplinary knowledge*. Disciplinary knowledge consists of knowledge of the norms governing value judgments in a discipline. It is acquired through exemplification rather than explicit instruction. It is typically tacit. And it can be/has been/is studied through deliberate attempts to violate those norms. The humanities have a distinguished history of systematically exploring these tacit norms, one that dates back to long before the Renaissance. Indeed, such explorations

[9] See Sprouse 2020; Ludlow 2013, esp. chapters 1, 3–4.

helped to define humanistic inquiry itself. The humanities, I will argue, produce disciplinary knowledge of human experience.

Humanistic knowledge is deceptively difficult to obtain. The deceptive part lies in the fact that, unlike the exotic formulae and methods of the natural sciences, the humanities overwhelmingly involve reading, writing, listening, and looking. What could be simpler? One needs no special training to look or to listen. Reading and writing are acquired often well before the age of five. What these utterly quotidian practices disguise are the significant differences between a concerto buff and someone with a trained ear, or between a Renaissance art buff and an art historian. These people hear and see things that I do not hear, because for the expert, looking and listening are more than just using your eyes and your ears. They involve cultivated capacities to notice and examine specific features from among the multitude. Of course, the existence of such capacities is the most familiar thing in the world to the practicing scientist; they are quite literally indispensable. They are what make him an expert. They are what enable him to separate the telling phenomena from the surrounding cacophony of nature. Distracted by the incomprehensibility of equations or the high-octane antics of Professor McInquiry, we forget how much of scientific expertise comes from reading and writing, looking, and listening. Or, for chemists before the twentieth century, tasting and smelling (yes, many of them had severe brain damage). We do not consider that dimension of his expertise to be part of scientific knowledge. That needs to change.

I develop a model of disciplinary knowledge over the next four chapters. Chapter 2 concentrates on clearing away a lot of epistemological brush so that we can get a better, more realistic picture of scientific knowledge, one which foregrounds its fundamentally social and disciplinary nature. In Chapter 3, I peel away that surface layer to reveal the role of consensus in the development of disciplinary knowledge. Chapter 4 explains the way in which exemplars factor into the production of consensus. And Chapter 5 describes the cross-disciplinary practice of studying norms by attempting to violate them. This model is as at home in the natural sciences as it is in the humanities, which is just as it should be. For, the model rests on features of inquiry that are common to every group of practitioners that forms a genuine research community. Not every group does, just as the group of people who recognize the superiority of *Office Space* do not thereby constitute a culture (a cult, maybe). These special groups – the disciplines – share more than just a passion. They share a whole world of norms that are specific to their narrow research focus. The sum of these norms is the corpus of disciplinary knowledge. Chapter 6 moves away from concerns specific to practitioners of the humanities to look at how disciplinary knowledge can be extended beyond the context of research to touch the lives of everyone.

Chapter 7 marks an inflection point in our study of the humanities, where we begin the painful process of looking at some of the humanities' current weaknesses and trying to understand what's gone wrong. The model of disciplinary knowledge comes in handy here as well, showing how some of the contemporary threats to humanistic knowledge described in Chapters 8 and 9 can be understood as deviations from the model.

CHAPTER 2

What Would the Community Think?

2.1 The Social Enterprise of Knowledge

In the ideal case, the output of scientific research is knowledge. Lots of research fails to rise to this level. Undoubtedly, there will be thousands of scientific research articles published this year that, for one reason or another, contribute nothing to human knowledge. There will be hundreds of thousands of research hours spent on investigations that yield no insight into nature, or into how to improve our investigation of it. But often enough, and often in astonishing ways, scientific research results in something that we can use to manage our relationship with nature; something on which future generations of researchers can build to refine and extend our general picture of the natural world; something that provides us with understanding. We call this product *scientific knowledge*.

Modern scientific knowledge is traditionally associated with distinctive methods of investigation. Scientific investigation characteristically involves the observation of natural phenomena. Frequently, this includes observing the results of careful and systematic experimentation of one kind or another. These experiments often incorporate the use of instruments specifically designed for producing, observing, and measuring effects. The production, observation, and measurement of certain effects are commonly carried out in relation to a hypothesis. At every step, it is customary for mathematics to play a central and indispensable role as scientists endeavor to clarify their ideas and evaluate them with precision. This specific medley of methods employed in the investigation of nature has, since the early seventeenth century, been associated with science's marked capacity for generating knowledge. We refer to the period marking the beginning of widespread uptake of these methods as "the Scientific Revolution." More than anything, the Scientific Revolution was a revolution in epistemology, a fundamental transformation of our basic conception of what it took to acquire knowledge of the world. Since that time, the use of these methods has been central to our understanding of what allows us to resolve, more or less definitively, the fascinating and multilayered set of puzzles presented by the natural world. An idea rises to the level of scientific knowledge when it solves one or more of those puzzles.

How do puzzles get solved? A natural response to this question is to invoke the use of the methods described above: when we make observations, formulate hypotheses, design experiments to test them, and then analyze the results (ideally, guided by mathematics), we eventually arrive at the solution to our puzzle. The reason that this answer has such a satisfying ring to it is because it is an abstraction of the Scientific Revolution's legacy – and because it is, in part, correct. Our ability to solve natural puzzles of all sorts – including really, really hard puzzles – has increased dramatically since the beginning of the seventeenth century; the methods of scientific investigation deserve much of the credit for that. But not all of it. While the production of scientific knowledge might characteristically *require* the use of certain varieties of investigative approach, it is not *reducible* to the use of those varieties.

Part of the reason we know this is because the history of each of these methods predates the advent of modern science. This historical fact has led some scholars to make the hasty inference that there was no such thing as the Scientific Revolution. If all there was to the emergence of modern science was the emergence of scientific methods, then that inference might hold up. However, during this fascinating time, we also see the diffusion of something distinctly *social*, a spirit or recognition among practitioners that their embrace of this suite of methods places them in relation to each other and to future practitioners in ways that seem to matter for developing a better understanding of nature. This recognition forms the basis of what will evolve into increasingly well-defined *intellectual communities*, of which our modern scientific communities provide instructive examples (to varying degrees).

Groups of this kind are themselves nothing new in the seventeenth century. Intellectual communities can be found in recognizably mature form since antiquity in cultures throughout the world. But, for reasons which I believe are (like the seventeenth century itself) still not very well understood, the intellectual communities that coalesced around scientific methods – and the intellectual cultures which came to define those communities – proved to be remarkably effective at producing knowledge of nature. When this suite of methods combined with a certain set of norms governing a culture of inquiry, something historically unprecedented was achieved. Precisely how or why this happens has proven to be a very difficult question to answer. Nevertheless, one of the most important developments in our understanding of the nature of science has been the scholarly consensus that has emerged around the idea that these communities are essential to the epistemic power of modern science.

Once you start looking at science from this socially oriented perspective, you quickly begin to see a number of ways in which the entire edifice of scientific knowledge – indeed, the scientific enterprise itself – rests on phenomena that are essentially social in nature. To take one example already mentioned, what does it mean to say that an idea becomes knowledge when it solves a puzzle? What I called the "natural response" to this question – the method-centered response – does not work, and the reason it does not work is because an investigation could still check all the "method" boxes and yet fail to be accepted as a solution by members of the scientific community. Another idea might be accepted as a solution despite failing to check several of the "method" boxes. Ultimately, what seems to matter is just whether the community accepts the idea as a solution to the puzzle. The conditions under which it is prone to do so vary across disciplines and across time within a discipline. What remains relatively invariant, though, are (1) the way in which widespread agreement within the research community results in the suspension of debate on an idea's acceptability, (2) the lifting of that suspension in the face of overwhelming pressure on the community to do so, and (3) the way in which widespread agreement *per se* fosters the community's ability to generate more knowledge. Each of these invariants plays a deep and significant role in the production of scientific knowledge. And for each invariant – the status of a puzzle as *solved*, the role of that status in the further development of inquiry, and the eventual erosion of that status – the prime mover is the set of social relations upon which a puzzle's solution ultimately rests.

When we look at the extraordinary achievements of the natural sciences, it is tempting to connect their ability to produce knowledge *per se* to the distinctive suite of methods for which the seventeenth century is credited as midwife. But it's crucial here to disentangle two dimensions of scientific knowledge that become deeply intertwined from around that time, right down to the present day: (1) the specific methods of investigation that practitioners employ as part of their efforts to refine our understanding of nature, and (2) the social mechanisms by which those efforts are weighed and filtered. While the former methods can plausibly be understood to be importantly related to what makes some knowledge *scientific*, they do not, I will show, provide us with an understanding of how some instances of scientific investigation become *knowledge*. The natural sciences produce knowledge. Not necessarily because they do experiments, or because they use precise measurement devices, or because they investigate reality, but because they have developed highly conservative epistemic cultures whose members are overwhelmingly concerned with what the community thinks. My purpose in this chapter is to support this claim as one component of a more general conception of disciplinary knowledge, a species of knowledge of which both the natural sciences and the humanities have historically been able stewards. If we use the natural sciences as a model for what real knowledge looks like, the question, "Do the humanities create knowledge?" turns not so much on the degree to which the humanities employ the Scientific Method, but on the degree to which they take part in the social processes by which disciplinary knowledge is achieved.

2.2 Alternatives to Knowledge

The eminent historian Stefan Collini rejects the notion that the humanities are primarily engaged with the production of knowledge: "…'knowledge' itself is surely less than ideal as a description of what we're after… 'Knowledge' is too easily thought of as accumulated stock, as something that doesn't need to be discovered again and is simply there for anyone who wants to use it." Rather, he suggests:

> [t]he contrast with 'understanding' indicates a lot of what it leaves out or misrepresents, and even a term like 'cultivation' has a claim here, or would do had it not come to be so closely associated with images of affected connoisseurship and simple snobbery….But 'understanding' underlines that it's a *human* activity, and so is inseparable from the people who do it. Notoriously, the possibilities of extending our understanding depend not just on what we already understand, but also on what sorts of people we have become. (Collini 1999, 237)

For Collini, this contrast underlies the distinction between "research" and whatever it is that humanists do:

> It has to be said – and has to be said now more emphatically than ever – that in many areas of the humanities 'research' can be a misleading term. It is difficult to state briefly how work in these areas should be characterized, but…we are at least pointed in the right direction by phrases like 'cultivating understanding', 'nurturing and extending a cultural heritage', and so on …. Publication in the humanities is, therefore, not always a matter of communicating 'new findings' or proposing a 'new theory'. It is often the expression of the deepened understanding which some

individual has acquired, through much reading, discussion, and reflection, on a topic which has been in some sense 'known' for many generations. (Collini 1999, 243)[1]

I imagine that Collini's putative alternative form of scholarly production will resonate with many humanists – as it does with me – because it reflects widely held views about the spirit and function of humanistic inquiry. It also identifies categories – *understanding*, *cultivation*, and *cultural heritage* – which most of us recognize as important and worthy of cultural investment. If our scholarly effort "cultivates understanding" or "preserves cultural heritage," we needn't trouble ourselves over the possibility that the humanities do not create knowledge. Perhaps they even create something more valuable than knowledge. Who would doubt that scholarly engagement with the dialogues of Plato, or the Homeric epics, or Alberti's writings on perspective, or Thucydides' account of the Peloponnesian War, or the Sistine Chapel, will outlast Einstein's General Theory of Relativity, or the Standard Model of particle physics? It is easy to imagine a world three hundred years from now in which, although physical science continues to grow, Einstein's theory is relegated to a footnote, while Plato and Confucius continue to enjoy tens of thousands of references annually. That is a world in which Einstein's theory has been superseded by a framework that better facilitates physical inquiry; we *hope* to see such a world. By contrast, it would seem that for the world to become Plato-free in three hundred years would require a cultural catastrophe of historic magnitude. To envision a world no longer in conversation with the wisdom of Socrates is to envision a profoundly impoverished iteration of human civilization.

For reasons which I articulate throughout the book, I do not think that distancing the humanities from the idea of knowledge is a very promising strategy. One very simple reason why it lacks promise is that the assertion is radically at odds with the history of humanistic inquiry, both in word and in deed. Humanists and their intellectual communities from antiquity to the present typically *do* relate to their scholarly endeavors in ways that are most naturally interpreted as epistemic; this is part of the reason why the social epistemology of the natural sciences appears to offer an intuitive framework with which to guide an examination of humanistic inquiry. Peer-reviewed research journals are a social epistemic phenomenon. Research grant review panels are a social epistemic phenomenon. Academic conferences are a social epistemic phenomenon. Each of these

---

[1] This distinction is endorsed by Small (2013, 2).

institutions is crucial to the development of knowledge in scientific communities. We have a fairly good understanding of how they function to promote the growth of scientific knowledge. As in the humanities, they do so through the social processes that make knowledge *disciplinary*.

Of equal significance is the fact that the kinds of scholarly categories which Collini takes to be distinctive of inquiry in the humanities are *also* serviceable vehicles for capturing the nature of scientific research. Mathematics provides a convincing illustration. It is common within mathematics to search for new ways of proving a theorem that has already been proven. While a new proof of an old theorem is a "new finding" in Collini's sense, that is not what motivates the mathematician's search, nor is it what is valued by the broader community of mathematicians. Instead, what would make the new proof valuable is if it offered us a better understanding of *why* the theorem is true.[2] This is literally how they talk. The focus on well-established theorems as subjects of mathematical research resembles in every way Collini's image of distinctively humanistic research as "expression of the deepened understanding which some individual has acquired, through much reading, discussion, and reflection, on a topic which has been in some sense 'known' for many generations."

This symmetry can also be found across the great works of scientific achievement that are venerated to this day, even outside the confines of scientific communities. Darwin's *Origin*, for example, reports but a few isolated and mostly insignificant "new findings," such as his observations about the ability of seeds to germinate after a long soak in the sea or after having been dried out for ages; there can't be more than a dozen references to such low-level findings in the nearly 500 pages that comprise the *Origin*. And it scarcely bears mention that these findings are in no way the anchor for the *Origin*'s intellectual contribution, nor have they ever been. The *Origin* is at its core a collection and highly persuasive arrangement of facts that had been uncovered by the last few generations of naturalists, along with an articulation of a handful of common-sense principles about selective breeding that had been in practice since who knows when. If ever there was an "expression of the deepened understanding which some individual has acquired, through much reading, discussion, and reflection, on a topic which has been in some sense 'known' for many generations," it is *On the Origin of Species*.[3]

---

[2] See, for example, Tappenden 2005 and Lange 2015.
[3] Ospovat (1981, chapter 4) argues that the bulk of Darwin's scientific research consisted of precisely these activities.

Although it is true that most modern scientific research publications do not take the form of great works of literature in the way that Darwin's do,[4] it is absolutely routine for them to take the form of "the expression of the deepened understanding which some individual has acquired, through much reading, discussion, and reflection, on a topic which has been in some sense 'known' for many generations." I will here offer two more well-known examples, with the promise that further illustrations will be introduced later on in the book. The fact that the sun was somehow the cause of the orbit of the planets around it had been known for a few generations before Newton (Cohen 1985, Chapter 6). Among the first handful of results that Newton proves in the *Principia* is the fact that a body moving in a straight line while simultaneously subject to a continuous impulsive force in the direction of a particular fixed point will trace an ellipse around that fixed point (Proposition 2, Theorem 2). Upon reading this proof, Newton's audience would have been treated to "the expression of the deepened understanding which some individual has acquired, through much reading, discussion, and reflection, on a topic which has been in some sense 'known' for many generations." Those who followed Newton's proof would, in the same sense to which Collini appeals, have found themselves to have gained a deep and profound understanding of the well-known fact of the sun's causal role in producing elliptical orbits.

Again from physics, Einstein's famous 1905 paper, "On the Electrodynamics of Moving Bodies," reports no "new findings," nor does it "propose a new theory." It merely (!) observes a tension between a few fundamental tenets of physical science. I would hesitate to describe it as an "expression of deepened understanding," except in the sense that it deepened our understanding of our own ignorance, which is arguably of greater value. However, Collini's "cultivating understanding" seems entirely appropriate: physicists of the nineteenth century had adopted a number of commitments in different physical contexts which, when brought together by Einstein, enabled them to see clearly that their views had unacceptable consequences regarding the difference between an electrical field and a magnetic field (Renn 2007).

Further illustrations from the history of science could be adduced, but they ultimately would only reinforce a point which I hope has by now been convincingly established – namely, that a qualitative distinction between the cognitive aims of scientific inquiry and those of the humanities is not easily made. The "nurturing, animating, revising, and extending

---

[4] *Descent of Man* (1871) and *On the Various Contrivances* (1862) are beautiful and engaging works.

[of] our understanding" is every bit as central a preoccupation of inquiry in mathematics and the natural sciences as it is in the humanities (Collini 1999, 238). The perception that it is *not* central – let alone so marginal as to constitute a passable metric for distinguishing between scholarly production in the sciences and the humanities – is based on a misleadingly limited conception of what actually goes on in science, one which envisions the essence of productive scientific inquiry to reside in the ahistorical accumulation or "cataloguing" of facts.[5]

Contrast that limited conception with this poignant characterization of inquiry by Collini, in which any practitioner of mathematics or the natural sciences would instantly recognize her own struggle to generate deeper scientific understanding:

> The truth is that there is often work by our predecessors which it may be right neither simply to repeat (even were that strictly possible) nor to repudiate and replace with something else. The proper response may be to acknowledge it, possess it, learn from it, and allow it to inform our understanding. One trouble with this way of putting it is that it may seem vulnerable to the charges of rigidity and passivity: any suggestion of merely handing on our cultural inheritance makes us seem like rather indolent museum curators ... who are sure that everything worth preserving is already in the collection. But this is a misconception of what this kind of understanding involves. For each generation to repossess a cultural inheritance ... is to modify and extend it. Apart from anything else, our understanding has to be different from that of previous generations just because it is ours: we fit it into the framework of other things we understand, we articulate it with our other concerns ... and we restate it in our idiom and for our audience.

Each of the historical examples I provided above is well captured by this account of inquiry. Darwin, Newton, Einstein, along with every other scientist since the seventeenth century, have each taken the work of previous generations, "acknowledged it, possessed it, learned from it, and allowed it to inform their understanding." Far from employing it "rigidly and passively," they "fit it into the framework of things they understood, articulated it with their other concerns ... and restated it in their idiom and for their audience." For instance, Galileo, Newton, and Einstein would each look anew at the phenomenon of an object in free fall. Galileo's understanding of this phenomenon as a physical process is strongly informed by his predecessor and chief antagonist, Aristotle.[6] Newton, with his sights

---

[5] Ibid., 238. "Cataloguing" is another term that Collini employs as an example of what the humanities are *not* about, in contrast to other scholarly endeavors.
[6] Westfall 1971, esp. Chapter 1.

set on an inertial physics, has no use for Galileo's Aristotelian *physical* conceptualization of free fall. Nevertheless, he incorporates Galileo's *mathematical* description of free fall into his new physics, "articulating it with his other concerns," and "restating it in the idiom of" his Second Law of Motion.[7] More than two centuries later, Einstein would reinterpret the phenomenon of free fall – along with the entire edifice of physical science which had been erected upon it – within the framework of relativity, a framework which had grown out of his 1905 attempt to articulate the other concerns mentioned above. It is impossible to see Einstein as repudiating either Galileo's or Newton's work; surely he sees more of himself in them than they would. He "acknowledges it, possesses it, learns from it, and allows it to inform his understanding." He then "modifies and extends it." The observation below, made by Damerow et al. in reference to the period between Galileo and Newton, could with equal justice apply to the transition from Newton's "classical mechanics" to Einstein's mechanics:

> The conceptual development embodied in the transition to classical mechanics cannot be identified with any particular way station and is not to be found in any particular text. It is a process which begins with such figures as Descartes and Galileo and takes shape with the generation of their successors. These disciples or even adversaries read the old problems and arguments from the point of view of their new solutions, thus establishing classical mechanics, because their point of departure was now the concepts as they are implicitly defined within the derivations of the theorems, e.g., the law of free fall. Thus, while for the first discoverer, the law of free fall is achieved by applying and modifying an independently grounded, pre-existing conceptual system, for his disciples it is the law of fall that canonically defines key concepts in a new conceptual system. The very same reading of these theorems that establishes classical mechanics also obliterates the traces of its real historical genesis because the original problems and the concepts involved are now understood within a very different theoretical and semantic framework. But since the successors themselves derive the inherited theorems on the basis of the new concepts, they impute these concepts to the discoverers. (Damerow et al. 1991, 5)

The interesting thing here is that the poignant characterization of inquiry with which I began the previous paragraph is actually Collini's attempt to characterize inquiry in the *humanities*. It is unsurprising that his entirely apt characterization of humanities research so closely matches the description of the conceptual development of classical mechanics, along with

---

[7] Notes the Newton historian I.B. Cohen (1985, 155), "only a Newton could have seen [the Second Law] in Galileo's studies of falling bodies."

countless other episodes in the history of science. The pursuit of scientific knowledge is an intensely historical endeavor, an underappreciated fact in itself and one which partly accounts for the immense power of modern science. Indeed, how could it be otherwise? Were it so ahistorical, each practitioner would be "forced to build his field anew from its foundations" (Kuhn 1962, 13). Although it is true that, as Collini remarks, "the humanities … are inherently 'conversational' subjects," this is equally the case for science. Scientists and mathematicians are in constant conversation with their predecessors, "and conversing … requires a constant, flexible, responsiveness" – precisely the kind of flexible responsiveness we see in the sciences as each researcher picks up the work of previous generations, reinterprets it from within her framework, connects it with her concerns, and restates it for her audience and in her idiom (Collini 1999, 238).

I have made a point of quoting Collini at length because it is important to see how a very capable account of scholarly effort in the humanities is able to function as an accurate and powerful encapsulation of scientific research. That is no accident. We in the humanities have adopted a certain vernacular for describing our creative output, I suspect with an eye toward contrasting our intellectual contribution with that of science for reasons that need no rehearsal (talking about university admin here). I do not believe that the intended contrast holds up to scrutiny, and would further wager that an alternate vernacular designed to facilitate similar ends would meet a similar fate. The problems we face in articulating what is distinctive and valuable about our work are not of the superficial sort that can be solved merely through artful redescription. They are substantive. And they can only be addressed by holding ourselves to a standard that is not designed to ensure our success.

The way we talk about the humanities – or the way in which we attempt to contrast them with the sciences – is a significant problem, one which is rooted partly in our defensiveness about our value in the current culture and partly in widespread ignorance about the nature of science. But it is not the deepest problem we face. That problem, too, can be brought to the fore by once again looking closely at Collini's able description of the humanities. We have seen that, in developing his contrast with knowledge, Collini emphasizes the alternative humanistic production of *understanding*: "Publication in the humanities … is often the expression of the deepened understanding which some individual has acquired"; "the possibilities of extending our understanding depend not just on what we already understand, but also on what sorts of people we have become"; and so forth.

I now want to look at what sort of state of affairs we are asked to envision when we imagine a scenario involving "deepened understanding," or "extended understanding," as well as "what we already understand," etc.

Regarding a publication in the humanities, for example, how could we tell whether it "expresses deepened understanding which some individual has acquired"? For an individual to "acquire deepened understanding" sounds like an achievement of some sort. We're all familiar with the feeling of that kind of achievement. I can remember my wife explaining to me why Darcy concealed his past dealings with Wickham from Elizabeth. For me, understanding that was an achievement. I don't share Jane Austen's social sensibilities; the idea of family honor is not intuitive to me. Also, not so good when it comes to understanding people's emotions. But I got there eventually. As educators, we're often lucky enough to elicit that feeling in our students. I'll never forget the expression on my son's face when he realized why the area of a triangle *had* to be *bh*/2. Now, of course, neither of these events is appropriate for publication intended for an audience of scholarly peers. But not because they fail to qualify as "deepened understanding which some individual has acquired." In fact, it is precisely *because* they are such clear instances of deepened understanding that makes any announcement to the scholarly community unnecessary. We already have a good understanding of why the area of a triangle is *bh*/2. Anyone who is not burdened by my endearing brand of sociopathy is able to appreciate Darcy's reticence. In order to be appropriate for submission to a scholarly audience, there needs to be some outstanding question regarding whether or not the insight I think I've achieved is genuinely plausible. If there is no such question – if, say, Darcy's guarded behavior is a part of "what we already understand" – there's not going to be much demand for me announcing that I've finally caught up with the rest of you. However, if my thoughts do not reflect "what we already understand," then I can hardly claim to have achieved deepened understanding just because I say or think something. Perhaps what I'm expressing is not the acquisition of deepened understanding but rather a misguided, muddled, unenlightened, or superficial reflection. Whether my humanities publication expresses deepened understanding is something that has to be sorted out at the level of the *scholarly community*.

2.3 From Ideas to Knowledge

To begin framing the problem of humanistic knowledge, I want to set out the preliminaries for a distinction that will occupy us in one way or another for the remainder of our discussion. Traditionally – at least, within philosophy – we are prone to contrasting knowledge with "mere opinion" or "mere belief." That contrast has been one of the main foci of epistemology since it was explored with estimable clarity in Plato's *Meno*. Although there is instructive overlap between Plato's (and most epistemologists') conception of knowledge and the kind of knowledge we'll explore over the course of this book, they are nevertheless quite distinct. Whereas the appropriate contrast class with Plato's *knowledge* is "mere opinion," the distinction that concerns us is between knowledge and *ideas*.

In his study of the reception of scientific theories, *Making 20th Century Science*, historian of physics Stephen Brush tells the story of "how theories became knowledge."[8] For Brush, an idea becomes knowledge when that "idea is adopted [/accepted] by the relevant scientific community" (Brush 2015, 3). In Brush's account, an idea is adopted/accepted (henceforth "adopted") when it moves beyond the unruly realm of scientific disputation and into the comfortable dotage of warranted presupposition. His interest lay in understanding the kinds of reasons that tended to motivate members of a community of practitioners to eventually treat some idea as a relatively fixed point with which they ought to make their own research consistent going forward. Although the specific form taken by these motivating reasons is in some sense an artifact of their association with natural science, there are a few instructive lessons that we can derive, both from the goals of inquiry that these motivating reasons seem to service, as well as the conception of knowledge that Brush employs.

The first thing worth observing about Brush's study is that an idea does not need to be "true" in any sense in order to "become knowledge." Neither, interestingly (and relatedly), does the idea need to be *believed* by anyone. All that's required is that the idea come to be *used* by the community's members as part of the more or less uncontested background to research and education in the discipline. Knowledge in this sense and in this context thus differs in important ways from the kind of knowledge possessed by an individual agent who has a true belief that is also justified. To say that I know next week's lottery numbers are going to be 1, 2, 3, 4, and 5 is, in the traditional sense, to say that (a) the lottery numbers *are* going to be 1–5, (b) I believe that they are going to be 1–5, and (c) I have persuasive evidence that they are going to be 1–5 (let's just say I know a

---

[8] In an earlier, unpublished draft which Brush was kind enough to share with me, the book's title was, *How Ideas Became Knowledge*. I assume that my interest in the contrast between ideas and knowledge (or, at least, a certain conceptualization of that contrast) derives from this encounter with Brush's terminology.

guy...).⁹ Satisfying only (a) and (b) won't get me there; that's just a lucky guess, a "mere opinion" which happens to be correct. Nor will satisfying (b) and (c) suffice; I'd just be *wrong*. If anything is incompatible with the traditional Western philosophical understanding of knowledge, it is the notion that someone could know something that is not true.

When we think of knowledge in scientific contexts, however, we need to treat the communal function of scientific knowledge as paramount. And this is a function which ideas can perform whether or not they are true, as well as whether or not they are believed to be true. It is a function which ideas can perform even when there is no persuasive evidence in favor of their truth. This is because the role that ideas play in science depends more on what the community of practitioners *agrees to use* to propel the study of nature than it does on what mind-independent nature is fundamentally like. But, surely practitioners would not adopt an idea unless they believed it to be true, right? Right?! I think it is very far from clear whether that is the case, and I think that lack of clarity says something of profound significance about the peculiar nature of *scientific* knowledge.

Looking across the history of science, we find countless instances of ideas which we would regard as literally false nevertheless serving this communal function. We find practitioners employing ideas which they by their own admission do not believe. And we find them adopting ideas which clearly lack persuasive evidence. None of this makes any sense if we view the adoption of a scientific idea as the adoption of a belief about nature. If, instead, we view the adoption of a scientific idea as the adoption of a *technique* used to *study* nature, we are able to fit a lot more of what researchers do into a coherent picture of knowledge production. In adopting a technique, we do not ask whether the technique is true; techniques are not the sorts of things that can be true. In adopting a technique, we do routinely demand something like evidence – but not evidence of its truth. Rather, we seek evidence of its efficacy. There are better or worse techniques, or techniques which are more or less useful.

Viewed from this perspective, an idea becomes scientific knowledge when members of the relevant community adopt it as part of a general community-wide approach to the study of nature. Prior to that, an idea is, well, just an idea. Peer-reviewed publication of an idea is normally the *beginning* of a process which may or may not eventuate in that idea's

---

⁹ Following Gettier (1963), it is now customary to include a fourth condition to the effect that conditions (1)–(3) could not easily have been otherwise. This reflects Socrates' emphasis on stability in the *Meno*.

becoming knowledge. A peer-reviewed research publication functions as an invitation to members of the scientific community to consider an idea as a candidate for community uptake and, thus, for scientific knowledge. Even if we think that only scientific ideas that are true can be published in peer-reviewed journals, time will tell whether a certain true idea becomes knowledge. Because of the essentially *social* nature of scientific knowledge, each idea – even the *true* ones – must go through a community-level process of determining whether it will serve the communal function performed by scientific knowledge.

Although it has taken a very long time, this thesis – which has been obvious to historians of science over the last century – is gradually beginning to gain a substantial foothold within the philosophy of science. But wherein lies its significance for the question of whether the humanities generate knowledge? I have devoted considerable space to introducing this socially-oriented conception of scientific knowledge for two reasons. First, I believe that it offers a plausible and accessible model for a certain kind of knowledge that is held specifically by research *communities*, regardless of the focus of their research. It thus offers a guide with which we can assess questions related to the research output of humanities disciplines. Humanists produce lots and lots of ideas. I think it is an open question whether, given the nature of contemporary humanities research communities, any of these ideas can be placed on a trajectory that might eventuate in knowledge.

Another advantage relates to the way in which this conception of scientific knowledge is inoculated against some of the frailties that afflict efforts to apply individualistic, proposition-oriented conceptions of knowledge, *mutatis mutandis*, to the context of scientific inquiry. In particular, it avoids the difficulties we encounter when we insist that an idea needs to be true in order to qualify as knowledge. In avoiding this complication, moreover, we remove the temptation to insist on a deal-breaking disanalogy between scientific and humanistic knowledge, based on the supposition that scientific knowledge takes the form of truths about nature, whereas humanistic knowledge takes the form of ... well, something else altogether. I agree that humanistic knowledge, were it to exist, would normally take a form other than that of truths about nature. My primary aim in this book is to explore the question of whether that alternative form can be understood as closely related to the form that we now associate with scientific knowledge, as well as the question of whether a mismatch between these two domains can help us understand something deeper about the peculiar nature of humanistic knowledge.

Thirdly, the community-centered conception of scientific knowledge allows us to connect the idea of knowledge in the humanities with some of the alternatives to knowledge we explored above. For, the process by which ideas become knowledge in science is akin – perhaps, even identical – to the process by which ideas come to constitute items of deeper understanding. Upon initial completion, the idea is submitted to a select group of peer referees. This unrepresentative sample of scholars eventually makes a determination as to whether the idea is fit for declaration to the broader scholarly community, that is, whether it is fit for publication. As with knowledge, the scholarly community's reaction to the idea will determine whether deeper understanding has been achieved. If the idea comes to form part of the framework through which members of the community develop their own ideas – as Darwin's and Einstein's ideas eventually did – then we can assert with confidence that the publication "expresses deepened understanding which some individual has acquired." However, if the idea is rejected, or ignored, it is hard to see upon what basis a verdict of "deepened understanding" could rest. If, after publication, the relevant scientific community rejects the idea as confused or false, or just pays no attention to it, then to nevertheless insist that the idea constitutes deepened understanding is to imply that the community's assent is immaterial to whether understanding is achieved. But if that is the case – if the community's uptake is genuinely irrelevant – then why go through the charade of peer review and publication? Scientific journals do not exist simply for practitioners to express their thoughts and feelings. That is what diaries are for. Scientific journals are intended to function as venues for the proposal and evaluation of ideas at the community level, to see whether those ideas have properties that satisfy the community's norms for adoption. If we embrace a conception of scholarly understanding – or of knowledge – that obviates the need for community-level adjudication, we erase any meaningful distinction between an individual's sense of intellectual satisfaction, on the one hand, and genuine insight.

The notion that community-level adjudication is essential to the acquisition of scientific understanding can be clearly discerned in the development of Darwin's theory of natural selection. Darwin hit upon the basic idea of natural selection in the September of 1838, after reading Thomas Malthus's *An Essay on the Principle of Population*. We know this because he recorded the event in a notebook he was keeping at that time (Ospovat 1981, 61). Darwin published a basic outline of the theory in 1858 in a short paper, with the more carefully elaborated version appearing in 1859 in *On the Origin of Species*. That book, in turn, would go through five subsequent editions, the sixth containing roughly 50% new material as compared with the first. The question we now want to answer is, at what point did someone – *any*one – come to understand how populations of organisms are modified through natural selection, "the preservation of favorable variations and the destruction of injurious variations"?

Part of the difficulty in answering this question lies in the substantive revisions that Darwin would make to the theory between 1838 and 1859, such as his shift from a belief in perfect adaptedness to one of adaptedness relative to conspecifics (Ospovat 1981, Chapter 3). That is probably the most significant update Darwin made to the idea of natural selection *per se*, although other core components of the Darwinian picture – such as how natural selection produces entirely *new* species – would also undergo fundamental rethinking (Kohn 2008). So, if we believe it was Darwin who first understood that populations are modified over time by their environments, that achievement could have occurred as late as 1859ish, when *On the Origin of Species* was completed.

There are a variety of features related to the book's reception that appear to undercut this conclusion. There isn't time to survey the community's responses,[10] but two reactions bear particular notice, given their relevance to the acquisition of understanding. One, which a number of critics seem to have had, was that the projection from domestic breeding practices to a principle governing the modification of wild populations was not valid. If that inference was generally regarded by practitioners as invalid (as indeed it appears to have been), it is difficult to support the claim that Darwin achieved understanding of how populations are modified prior to the publication of the *Origin*. His argument rested on an inferential step that violated accepted norms of scientific inference at the time (Hull 2003). For all anyone had reason to think, he "may be as woefully wrong as Humphrey Belcher, who believed the time was ripe for a cheese cauldron."[11]

The violation of accepted inferential norms exemplifies some of the difficulties we face, because it provides an illustration of a clear sense in which the very meaning of notions such as *knowledge* and *understanding* depend on the existence of community-wide conventions concerned with how to properly conduct inquiry. Despite the intuitive pull of the idea that Darwin achieved genuine insight after reading Malthus (more so in the ensuing two decades), we have to resist this temptation if the scientific

---

[10] See Hull 1973; Engels and Glick 2008; Ruse 1979.
[11] Rowling 2005, Chapter 10.

community's adjudicatory role is to carry any weight. If we think it should carry weight, then we need to at least suspend judgment with respect to the question of whether between 1838 and 1859 Darwin acquired a deeper understanding of how populations of organisms are modified.

Another famous reaction to Darwin's theory provides, I think, a more decisive verdict on the question of what Darwin understood. In 1865, Scottish engineer (and, according to Wikipedia, inventor of the cable car) Fleeming Jenkin, published a review of the *Origin* which was to haunt Darwin. In his review, Jenkin showed that Darwin's suggested mechanism for evolutionary change was fundamentally incompatible with his views about the nature of biological inheritance. In particular, what Jenkin showed was that if one assumes that (1) biological traits are inherited through a "blending" process – rather than in discrete units like genes – and that (2) the variations that provide environmental advantages tend to be "minute," as Darwin claimed, then favorable variations will inevitably be diluted over time and will cease to make a difference to the properties of organisms. In short, the process of evolutionary change that Darwin envisioned was simply not possible. If his image of evolutionary change was known to be self-contradictory, it is far from clear that that image nevertheless amounted to some kind of understanding at the time. The problem that Jenkin raised for natural selection was deceptively difficult, as evinced by the fact that the conceptual waters remained cloudy for roughly sixty years after Jenkin's initial criticism. It was not until the 1920s that the muddle surrounding natural selection and the nature of biological inheritance was sorted out. It took three truly brilliant mathematicians – Haldane, Fisher, and Wright – who, during that process, created modern statistics. Up to that time, the community of naturalists was largely skeptical as to whether Darwin's theory described a coherent process of evolutionary change, and they were right to be so (Gayon 1998). Even after that, it still took another twenty years or so for the majority of practitioners to embrace the idea that, not only was natural selection *possible*, in fact it appeared to be the dominant evolutionary force – the "paramount power," as Darwin had called it (Brush 2009).

I have taken care to describe this historical vignette in some detail because it offers a clear and compelling illustration of the *processual* nature of scientific understanding, a process that in this case begins with a flash of insight in 1838 and ends with a series of publications between 1918 and 1924. The publication of Darwin's views was just one, relatively early and underdeveloped, node in this process. In a certain sense, though, so were the publications of Haldane, Fisher, and Wright; our picture of natural selection is still evolving in fundamental ways.[12] Most importantly, I want this episode to exemplify the way in which the historical trajectory of the process of understanding is dictated in large part by the community of practitioners. This process *could* have stopped with the publication of the *Origin*. But the cogency and publicity of Jenkin's criticisms in particular ensured that that would not happen; Darwin's idea could not and *did* not gain widespread acceptance until the community was convinced that those criticisms had been resolved. And yet, neither do we want to say that Darwin acquired *no* understanding in 1838. After all, it's not for nothing that we call it the *Darwinian* theory of natural selection. But this is as it should be. Given the way in which significant ideas are shaped, refined, reconsidered, and ultimately either transformed or rejected, often over several generations of thinkers, we should expect confusion to arise when we attempt to specify a particular moment or individual out of which understanding emerges. Characteristically, *there is no such moment or individual*. There are communities that undergo identifiable periods of relative equilibrium – not *stasis*, but periods in which members of a field partake of a shared framework for inquiry that encompasses everything from what constitutes an important research question to how specific bits of the natural world behave. "What we already understand" is determined by the elements of this shared framework. "Cultivating understanding," then, is often a matter of drawing out less salient, perhaps tacit, features of that framework and submitting them to the community for consideration.

Rather than test the reader's patience with yet further ways in which the large-scale cognitive aims of the humanities – knowledge, understanding, interpretation, and so forth – parallel those of the natural sciences, I propose to adopt as a working hypothesis that both domains participate in the general cultural form picked about by the term *disciplinary inquiry*. While the many manifestations of this form are as different as the disciplines that serve as its hosts, they exhibit a pleasing generality with respect to the intellectual goals that rational inquiry is perceived to satisfy. It is also, I think, a predictable one. From the moment we are born, we are in search of patterns that can give us insight into a broader system. Although we use these insights to an enormous variety of ends, from the purely cognitive to the doggedly practical, what unites their application is the hope that we can stand upon them to extend our grasp of experience even further.

---

[12] See, for example, Orr 2005. Also Wallace 1991, who chronicles the history of genetic load, a theoretical problem in population genetics that is still not resolved.

There is now overwhelming historical evidence that this practice thrives especially well in communities with very specific properties, modern science being a relatively recent and powerful instantiation of those properties. As I have detailed above, the community's contribution to rational inquiry is indeed so distinctive that the meaning of terms such as *knowledge* and *understanding* have come to be defined partly in terms of communities when used in connection with disciplinary inquiry. It is strange that it has taken us so long to make this dimension of inquiry explicit in our thinking about the nature of knowledge and its cognitive associates. Looking back, it does seem that this was perhaps so obvious to scholars of the premodern era that it could scarcely bear mention. Modern science is in many ways a very late outgrowth of this ancient and widely embraced scholarly tradition. There is a sense in which, rather than being the first of its kind, modern science was a bizarrely delayed application of community-centered principles of intellectual growth to the domain of nature.

Although our understanding of community-driven rational inquiry continues to develop, many of its components have been subject to able scrutiny over the past half-century or so, such that we can now fit them into a reasonably coherent picture of how, in general, intellectual communities advance. And although this picture has been pieced together largely through the historical study of the natural sciences, it is important to appreciate that it need not have been. Had we instead derived our understanding of disciplinary inquiry from ancient intellectual communities (to whom natural science would have appeared as perverse and inadequate in many ways), we would, I believe, have developed essentially the same lens through which we now view the growth of scientific knowledge. It is time that we turned this lens toward the humanities.

CHAPTER 3

Canon and Consensus

3.1 Introduction

Imagine a world, very much unlike our own, in which the material covered in humanities classes is structured predominately around the contents of textbooks; in which the range of available textbooks covers more or less the same content, and in more or less the same order. At the beginning of a given semester, students in humanities classes all over the world will be introduced to the same basic ideas, perhaps framed in slightly different ways depending on who is teaching the class and which introductory textbook they're using. As students move through a humanities curriculum, their shared background continues to expand, such that, by the time they graduate, they have mastered the same body of content and techniques as every other student in their field. Perhaps this tradition has been practiced for several decades, even centuries. Perhaps longer.

There is something about this image that sickens me. It has a zombie-like resonance to it, one that has nothing to do with the specific way I've chosen to present it. The very notion that students all over the world would be fed the same steady, curated diet of ideas – regardless of how tasty and protein-rich they are – feels as if it goes against the entire spirit of and motivation for higher education. How could we possibly do justice to our students without doing justice to the veritable cornucopia of thought available for the mind to feast upon? Or, at the very least, a sampler platter – maybe a tapas menu – which affords them a sense of the variety of creative output of which human thought has demonstrated itself to be capable?

What bothers me even more, though, is that I cannot tell whether the reason that this sickens me is because it is a truly hellish vision, or rather simply because as a humanist trained in twenty-first-century America, I have been enculturated to conceive of the humanities in a very specific, historically contingent way. After all, if the idea of every student learning the same body of content over the course of a four-year process is so irredeemably hellish, why is it *de rigueur* in the natural sciences? Is there something about the humanities in particular that makes this such a loathsome prospect?

The pronounced uniformity of learning in the natural sciences is a symptom of the relatively high propensity of natural science disciplines to strive for and achieve *consensus* on matters of scholarly concern. The culture of consensus that pervades the natural sciences has significant effects on the prospects for scientific knowledge. Indeed, owing to the socially infused conception of scientific knowledge that has become increasingly influential in the past few decades, many scholars have begun to embrace the idea that consensus is an essential component of scientific knowledge – that is, that what it means for knowledge to be scientific is, in part, for it to be an object of consensus among relevant members of the scientific community. We saw this conceptual link exploited by Stephen Brush in the previous chapter, who used the consensus of members of various disciplinary communities as a metric for diagnosing when a scientific idea became knowledge. The philosopher William Lycan hints at a broader scope for the essential epistemic role of consensus when he argues against the existence of philosophical knowledge on the grounds that there are no matters of consensus in philosophy:

> Philosophy has had two millennia in which to put its methods to work, and the thing it has most conspicuously *not* done is produce consensus. There are periods of very wide agreement, but they are pathetically short, and geographically local. (2019, 87)

This suggests that the epistemic centrality of consensus might apply to disciplinary knowledge in general, rather than being restricted specifically to *scientific* disciplines.

I will argue for a version of this edgy thesis in the present chapter. Whether or not it ultimately holds up, though, both the spirit and the existence of consensus shape the intellectual culture of the natural sciences in profound ways. And the nature of some of these effects seems to indicate that disciplines which do not possess a culture of consensus might be unable to produce knowledge. Even if consensus is not bound up in what it *means* to know something, the absence of consensus might nevertheless undermine the prospects for knowledge on account of the *causal* role that consensus plays in the development of disciplinary knowledge.

There are thus multiple routes by which issues surrounding consensus might come to bear on the question of whether the humanities create knowledge. Much of my focus in this book lies in (1) articulating a general conception of the relationship between consensus and disciplinary knowledge, and (2) exploring the kinds of factors that contribute to the absence of consensus – in truth, the absence of a *culture* of consensus – in the humanities. Are these factors endemic to humanistic inquiry itself? Is the absence of consensus in the humanities a virtue? Or is it a recent, remediable perversion that stifles the intellectual culture and mission of the humanities? The thought experiment with which this discussion began derives traction from the widely held intuition that the perpetual state of dissensus that characterizes contemporary humanities disciplines is a badge of honor, a reflection of the redoubtable intellectual courage that has always defined the best of humanistic inquiry. However, both the history of the humanities and the function of consensus in the development of scientific knowledge seem to bear on the soundness of this intuition in ways that matter for the appraisal of contemporary humanities scholarship.

3.2 Consensus in the Natural Sciences

There are a few pernicious myths surrounding the concept of scientific consensus which it will be helpful to dispel, because their influence over our thinking can occlude the potential relevance of consensus to the culture of inquiry in the humanities. The first and most unquestionably annoying of these is that scientific consensus requires the unanimous agreement of qualified experts; call this the Unanimity Condition. One of the reasons to doubt this condition is historical: members of the scientific community are characteristically comfortable declaring consensus despite the continued existence of qualified experts who disagree with the proposition around which consensus has formed. Even among experts, there is such a thing as irrelevant disagreement. One of the main reasons why community-based inquiry is so much more powerful than the isolated musings of individuals is that subjecting ideas to the scrutiny of an entire group helps to buffer the process of knowledge formation against some of the frailties of human rationality. Because we are all subject to these frailties to varying degrees and, moreover, because we often see things from different perspectives, we expect there to be some persistent disagreement even among experts, just by default. This is why practitioners do not need something like a census of opinion in order to gauge consensus, which would undoubtedly show some diversity of opinion even on the most "settled" of scientific issues. Rather, community members are interested in *general* agreement, and – above all – in a trend in which dissent becomes *increasingly uncommon*. As the range of plausible views becomes narrower and narrower, the evidentiary burden for publishing views outside that range becomes commensurately high. Such views are regarded as extraordinary, and extraordinary claims require extraordinary evidence. Disagreements – even by qualified experts – are considered irrelevant when they conflict with the range of plausible positions but lack sufficiently extraordinary backing. There is a lot more that can be said about the demography of consensus (and still more that we simply don't know), but we don't want to get bogged down in all that. The key point is that the Unanimity Condition is a myth, and it is pretty easy to see why it would have to be.

The absence of any need for a census in order to detect the presence of consensus points to another interesting feature of scientific consensus, one which again bears on its appropriateness as a framework for analyzing the epistemology of the humanities. Apart from concerns about what *level* of agreement constitutes scientific consensus, there is the issue of what *sort* of attitude a practitioner needs to exhibit in order to be considered part of the consensus. We know from the absence of any census or voting procedure in science that explicit positive affirmation of some proposition p is unnecessary in order to qualify as party to the consensus that p. Does a practitioner then need to merely *not object* to p? What about a kind of hybrid situation, where she positively affirms a different proposition q which implies p; or, in which she declines to object to q?[1]

Research on the history, philosophy, and sociology of scientific consensus is still in its infancy, so I want to emphasize the tentativeness of my remarks below. With that caution in place, I think the current state of our understanding of scientific consensus licenses the following claims. Above all, what seems to matter is whether a practitioner can safely presuppose p as part of the background for future research – that is, whether she can confidently expect no meaningful objection from members of her research community to the presupposition that p.[2] This could involve either an explicit presupposition that p, as in, "I presuppose that p," or "p is well-established." Or it could involve a tacit presupposition that p, as with an explicit presupposition that q, which implies p (and so on…). In short, whether there is scientific consensus on p requires only the general absence of a predisposition to object to a claim on the grounds that it presupposes

---

[1] Beatty (2017) examines the varying forms of consensus participation in the context of the Intergovernmental Panel on Climate Change (IPCC).
[2] I derive this formulation from Galison's (1987) characterization of "how experiments end."

that p. Now, this obviously leaves a lot of room for different versions of how individual practitioners relate to p psychologically; but that's a good thing. Some community members might enthusiastically affirm p on the basis of direct experience. Others might take their word for it. Or they might simply develop the sense that the community is increasingly accepting of p. Functionally, they come to the same thing, which is that practitioners can confidently premise future research on the presupposition that p without fear of meaningful objection on those grounds.

How might this look in practice? We could take the process by which I composed the preceding paragraph as a simple, easily analyzable case. As I wrote, I chose my words carefully so as to avoid saying anything to which a certain group of scholarly peers could reasonably object, while dismissing potential objections from outside that group as basically unworthy of serious concern (no offense). My filtering process involves two distinct components: (1) a careful, concentrated reflection on what I think is plausible or correct, and on what I think would pass peer inspection based on my professional experience; and (2) a consultation of the relevant scholarly literature in search of countervailing sentiments. As such, I take what I've said about scientific consensus above to be both plausible and consistent with the evidence we've uncovered about consensus so far. I foresee no serious objections to what I've said. And so I henceforth confidently employ it as a presupposition in future research. Whatever objections that future research may invite, they will presumably not be related to the minimal claims I've made about scientific consensus.

We know about as much about how scientific consensus develops as we do about what determines whether a research community has achieved it. But something like the above cannot be that far off, because there are only a handful of sources from which information relevant to a proposition can be effectively derived. Scientists read their primary literature, correspond with colleagues, chat with each other at conferences, colloquia, and associated social engagements, do their own research, and reflect. Through these channels, practitioners develop a sense of what the most reasonable opinion is, given all that is known. It is difficult to make more specific claims than this, in part because of how little research has been done, but also because of the significant amount of scholarly disagreement regarding which of these sources exert the greatest influence and why. Nevertheless, the range of channels by which scientific opinion is communicated and developed should sound familiar to members of any modern research community. There's a good reason for this, and its significance will become increasingly clear as our investigation unfolds.

Removing these myths from the general image of scientific consensus is a necessary step toward seeing whether the concept of consensus in the natural sciences can illuminate anything about the results of research in the humanities. Going forward, it will help to keep in mind that scholarly consensus may manifest itself only through a generalized absence of objection to a given proposition, and that it is compatible with even the dissent of qualified experts. Although each of these notions conflicts with a commonsense conception of consensus, they are both readily discernible features of scientific consensus as we actually find it. This is reminiscent of the point made in Chapter 2 concerning the differences between a commonsense or even a philosophical conception of knowledge *per se*, on the one hand, and *scientific* knowledge, on the other. And we will see yet further ripples of this phenomenon in later chapters – each stemming from the variety of functional roles required of knowledge in disciplinary contexts.

3.3 Consensus beyond Propositions

I began this chapter by conjuring up a hellscape in which students around the world learn the same sequence of ideas drawn from the humanities – a scenario which for some reason is not a hellscape when applied to instruction in the natural sciences. But things are actually considerably weirder than that. In addition to our being totally cool with every student on Earth learning the same science, we're also apparently OK with them all being taught things that we know are technically incorrect. As the Fall semester begins, millions of students across the globe will learn how to model the dynamics of moving bodies using Newton's Laws of Motion – laws which have been known since the beginning of the twentieth century *not* to have, as Einstein put it, "an unlimited domain of validity" (Einstein 1916/2015, 90). Thus, although Newton's laws are useful rules of thumb, they cannot be the true laws of nature. However, that won't stop us from using them to judge student competence in basic mechanics, along with a variety of even more consequential undertakings. Undergraduate programs across the United States, for example, will use proficiency with Newton's laws as part of their approach to preparing applicants for medical school.

Is this just a sick game that physics departments have devised in order to demonstrate their intellectual superiority over their future physicians? Part of me hopes that it is, but these hopes are undermined by the fact that this same approach to education prevails across the undergraduate curriculum, long after pre-meds have exited the course sequence. And it doesn't stop there. The first year or two of graduate training in any natural science will regularly focus on the mastery of an analytical toolkit that has been known for at least a few generations to be not quite correct in one way or another. Moreover, practicing scientists will routinely employ many of the elements in these toolkits in the normal course of professional research.

These habits are hard to square with the time-honored mythology of science education and scientific discovery as the acquisition of an inventory of basic truths about nature. But, when seen in another light, patterns of agreement across the natural sciences become clear illustrations of the nature of scientific consensus and the essential function that it performs in the ongoing process of scientific research. Specifically, by understanding the ubiquitous use of these tools as an index of their widely accepted propriety – rather than practitioners' convergent belief in their truth – we can begin to see the way in which the primary role of consensus in science is to develop and broaden something like a "common language" or "conceptual currency" through which scientific communities engage in the exchange and extension of ideas that have proven particularly useful for the study of nature. Viewed through a lens that shifts the focus away from *correct beliefs* and toward *especially fruitful research techniques*, the near-universality of approaches to science education and research seems both less problematic (if it ever was) and more consonant with the application of research frameworks in the humanities.

This points toward a critical lesson for understanding the epistemology of science: the primary value of widespread agreement in science does not lie in its ability to function as a signal of truth (or probable truth, or approximate truth). Don't get me wrong: scientific consensus *might* indicate the truth of a proposition; it's just that truth *per se* is not what makes a proposition scientifically valuable. Nor is this to say that truth *per se* is not valuable. Whether statements from the scientific community are true clearly matters to lots of people for lots of different reasons. The truth of claims about the probability of global warming, for example, is extremely significant for most of us. But what appears to make scientific consensus valuable for *scientists* is the way in which it substantively facilitates further research.[3] First, it builds a foundation for a community's pursuit of deeper, more refined research questions. On a community-wide scale, the cessation of debate functions as permission to employ a proposition and its implications as (part of) a working hypothesis. As such, the consensus position can function as a platform which helps to legitimize the pursuit of questions that presuppose it and which can contribute to the delegitimization of

---

[3] This point is to be distinguished from the role that consensus might play in serving as the basis for public trust in science, recently examined by Naomi Oreskes (2019). My concern here is the set of epistemic functions that consensus enables among practitioners of some discipline.

views that are in conflict with it. If the consensus proposition is sufficiently general in scope, this may result in a serious restriction on practitioners' perceptions of the set of potentially fruitful avenues for further research. The capacity of consensus to narrow the focus of what counts as legitimate research is central to science's demonstrated power for generating knowledge, a point stressed by Thomas Kuhn more than sixty years ago which still has yet to be treated with the gravity it deserves.

Consensus also enables the pursuit of certain classes of research problems – namely, those with which researchers may previously have had very limited success, but which are made to appear tractable by new means subsequent to the development of consensus. Once an idea becomes widely and unobjectionably applied in research, it can begin to take on a kind of canonical status, which encourages its extension to different sorts of phenomena, perhaps very far removed from those for which it was originally developed. In the same way that technology designed for one function will routinely be repurposed in the service of wholly distinct objectives, an idea can be stretched and contorted in ways that make it amenable for export to alternative sets of problems. The motivation for approaching old problems in this way frequently comes from the success that inspired the consensus in the first place. Researchers look for different though broadly acceptable perspectives on the consensus idea that can be used to widen its range of applicability. This will often involve the use of analogy, metaphor, or some other kind of artful reimagining of the previously successful idea, as in the rise of the idea of inheritance through culture (rather than just biological material) as a way of extending Darwin's theory of natural selection to explain the development of human societies and technologies.[4] The history of each of the natural sciences is densely packed with instances of this inevitability of the research process.[5]

In the same way that consensus on an idea permits the analogical or metaphorical extension of that idea to long-standing problems in the hopes of making much-awaited headway, consensus can also result in the development of new research problems. Once the community of mid-nineteenth century naturalists accepted Darwin's theory of descent,[6] for instance,

---

[4] Of the several scholarly treatments of this phenomenon, I.B. Cohen's (1956) investigation of the influence of Newtonian science on the study of electricity is the most systematic and thorough.
[5] For a classic study, see Hesse (1966). Haufe (2024) explains how this process drives the development of scientific inquiry.
[6] Even by modern standards, this occurred rapidly. Ruse (1979) observes that questions which treated the theory of descent as an established fact began appearing on exams at Cambridge within a decade.

a number of new categories of questions suddenly become salient for the investigation of natural history. Details of geographic distribution, embryonic development, and variation within and across populations (to name but a few) all emerge out of the theory of descent as essential components of scientific explanations of organismal behavior and morphology. Importantly, this question-generating and organizing capacity of the theory was widely held to be its most valuable contribution (Kitcher 1985). And how surprising is that, really? Looking at the publication of the *Origin* after more than one hundred fifty years, it stands out to most of us as the inauguration of the theory of descent with modification through natural selection, an event possibly without a peer in the whole history of scientific thought. But the professional researcher – regardless of discipline – can surely empathize with those of Darwin's contemporaries who celebrated the theory as an engine for producing new research problems on which one has a general sense of how to make progress toward a better understanding of the phenomena, not merely (!) as the enunciation of an extremely deep fact about the world. As fascinating as deep facts about the world are, they are not all equally well equipped to furnish researchers with solvable research problems.

I want to close this section by reviewing some of the basic contrasts that I've attempted to draw between a cluster of commonsense views about the nature and significance of scientific consensus, on the one hand, and those aspects of consensus which, historically, seem to have mattered most to researchers. The first such contrast is between consensus around *propositions* vs. around *frameworks*. Although the specific object of consensus among scientists will frequently be a proposition – for example, "The anomalous magnetic moment of the muon is 0.00116592061(41)" – the functional role occupied by that proposition in a research context is to serve as a framework (or part of a framework) for organizing future research. We might think that the obvious way in which it does this is, say, by ruling out certain scientific models that imply different values for the muon's magnetic moment. As natural and logical as this reaction would be, what we actually see in scientific practice is a bit more complicated – which is precisely what one would expect if a proposition's role as an object of scientific consensus was to become integrated into a framework for further research. In the case of the muon, recent measurements of its magnetic moment prompted theoreticians to return to their mathematical model of particles to see whether they had accurately calculated the muon's theoretically expected magnetic moment in the first place (Overbye 2021). Thus, although there is perhaps consensus on what the actual physical value of the magnetic moment is, the implications of that agreement for future research are nowhere near as straightforward as ruling out a certain class of models as physically impossible. In the event, it has included the search for ways of resolving apparent conflicts between expected and observed values. Those attempts at resolution, in turn, will inevitably prompt further lines of inquiry as theoreticians probe more deeply into the mathematical intricacies of their models. And so on and so forth.

This points to the second set of contrasts: *belief* vs. *use*. When we conceive of an object of consensus as (part of) a framework rather than as a proposition, the focus of practitioners' relationship to that object of consensus shifts away from a sense in which they have converged on a specific *belief* about what nature is like and, instead, toward the sense in which they have converged on a specific *approach* to the study of nature. This allows us to treat consensus propositions as part of the same general family of convergent practices as things like the ubiquitous use of Newtonian mechanics – that is, things that are clearly not doxastic commitments to certain propositions. But it also suggests a concomitant shift in the way we ought to conceive of the value of consensus. We do not judge the value of a practice on the basis of whether it is true or false, but rather on the basis of its demonstrated or expected utility. And a scientific truth is generally only valuable in research contexts insofar as it facilitates further research. All truths are not equally endowed in this regard. Indeed, as modern scientists have always recognized, a cleverly designed falsehood such as an idealization is generally far more useful in terms of generating insight and further lines of inquiry than a literally true description of nature. The scale on which both propositions as well as nonpropositional representations are weighed in the context of research is one that registers something much closer to "capacity for generating further understanding" or "capacity for generating further lines of inquiry" than to "probable truth" or "degree of certainty." Although the latter metrics are particularly important in certain contexts – for example, policy-making – their value in research contexts is limited, tending – like other epistemic values – to be parasitic on how well it facilitates further scientific research.

I have made an effort to draw out these contrasts for two reasons. The first, to which I briefly alluded above, involves debunking a widespread cluster of myths about scientific knowledge which have proven convenient for supporting a marked distinction between the kind of intellectual activity with which the natural sciences and the humanities concern themselves. A great deal of humanistic scholarly effort is self-consciously devoted to the development of a range of plausible perspectives or "interpretive lenses" through which we are invited to process human experience, encoded in historical documents and other artifacts, great feats of creative artistic and literary expression, and the palpable meaningfulness of subjective experience. This activity has fueled a disciplinary self-image that is frequently used to distinguish humanistic scholarly activity from scientific research, with the implicit assertion that the two scholarly domains are by their nature incommensurable. I think this disciplinary self-image is broadly accurate – as accurate as anything of that level of generality is likely to be, given the manifest heterogeneity of humanistic scholarship. My objective in the preceding discussion has been to illustrate some of the ways in which the form, texture, and disciplinary function of scientific knowledge lies much closer to that which exemplifies humanities scholarship than is often supposed.

Recall our examination of the pedagogical role of Newton's Laws of Motion. It will be observed that the universality of this approach to training physicists is not to teach them what the physical world is fundamentally like. It is about giving students a feel for how to approach the challenges that arise when attempting to understand the physical world. Newton's style, exemplified in the 1687 publication of his *Principia*, still serves as the backbone and spirit of problem-solving in physics. When we introduce students to this style, we aim to enculturate them into the tradition of problem-solving that has defined modern physics since the seventeenth century. *Prima facie* differences notwithstanding, I argued above that objects of scholarly research consensus in the natural sciences are of a piece with this pedagogical program. Professional researchers do not need further enculturation; they are focused rather on *expanding* that culture, on extending the scope of the set of interpretive frameworks that define their research tradition. In essence, they seek to contribute to the canon of scientific knowledge. The disciplinary function of consensus is to distinguish between more and less promising ways of doing that. It will sometimes be helpful to focus in part on the probable truth of a proposition in order to make such distinctions. But there are myriad contexts in which some proposition's truth is simply not necessary for concluding that a form of representation to which it is related (e.g., a diagrammatic idealization) constitutes the best available means of moving forward on a given research frontier. By contrast, there are *no* contexts in which the mere truth of a proposition will suffice for advancing research. *Pace* Collini's picture, practitioners of the natural sciences have no interest in sitting atop a mountain of inert facts.

This brings us to the second aim. The image of scientific knowledge developed over the last chapter-and-a-half points to a disciplinary role for scientific consensus which possesses a number of suggestive affinities with the function of canonical texts in humanities disciplines. For example, Grafton and Most's observation that "Each profession [theology, law, and medicine] constructed a canon, mastery of which was both the price of admission to practice and the basis of participation in debate," is precisely aligned with the foregoing account of how the style of physical inquiry is conveyed through the study of Newton's mechanics. And, in the same way that the ubiquity of Newtonian pedagogy is an index of discipline-wide esteem, "[t]he fact that canons exist at all suggests a high level of consensus about both the value of texts and the nature of their content" (Grafton and Most 2016, 7–8). As with canonical approaches to scientific inquiry, scholarly canons develop and persist on the basis of disciplinary consensus.

But the fact that canonical texts in the humanities are *not* valued primarily for their truth content is so obvious as to scarcely bear mention. Hobbes' *Leviathan* is a canonical text in the political philosophical tradition of Western civilization. Every year, it is read by (or, at least, *assigned to*) thousands of students in introductory courses on political theory and political philosophy held in universities that reside in some form of representative democracy. But no one working in the Western philosophical tradition today accepts Hobbes' argument that we are rationally and morally compelled to submit to the rule of a sovereign king. *Leviathan* is not beautiful in its presentation. It is not exciting. It is not a romp. So why do we knowingly subject students to a somewhat tedious, nearly four hundred-year-old book whose central thesis and moral foundations are agreed to be unsound? Because *Leviathan* is widely recognized as the foundational text in the social contract tradition, the framework within which modern theories of democratic government are articulated. What we see in *Leviathan* is the inauguration of a language of scholarly thought, a general form of currency through which to trade and refine ideas central to Western political thought. Reading *Leviathan* is a way of inducting students into that tradition, giving them a feel for the general intellectual style through which problems of political theory are articulated and solved – "the price of admission to practice and the basis of participation in debate." As the progenitor of a lineage of thought, concepts at the heart of modern political thought are present in *Leviathan* in a general but recognizable form. Over the course of a semester, students will see these concepts subject to certain distortions and refinements as are required by their application to cultural moments very unlike those with which

Hobbes grappled; Harvard Square in the 1960s raises a fundamentally different set of sociopolitical questions than those of Trafalgar Square in the 1660s. And yet, we want students to recognize in John Rawls' *A Theory of Justice* both the tenor and themata through which political thought has been expressed since *Leviathan*. For related reasons, we now expect political theorists to situate their ideas with respect to Rawls' pathbreaking work. It too is a canonical text.

What we have in both the natural sciences and the humanities, then, is an approach to inquiry and to the training of future scholars that is focused on and constrained by the development of scholarly consensus. In each domain, consensus is used by members of a discipline as the clearest possible index of what ought to guide research in the future. The more entrenched it becomes, the more it comes to function as something like a language of scholarly thought and communication – less a body of conscious, substantive commitments as to the truth of certain propositions than it is a framework and spirit through which to reflect on, express, and investigate questions of disciplinary import. In each domain, the body of elements that have achieved consensus may indeed include propositions that are regarded as true. But the fact that those propositions are true need not be what explains why they have become part of the disciplinary canon. Most true propositions will not be so lucky – and many false propositions will be.

Connecting the character of scholarly output in the natural sciences with that of the humanities is important because it invites us to consider them as somewhat disparate instances of a single phenomenon – *disciplinary knowledge* – rather than parallel universes of intellectual pursuit. Disciplinary knowledge is comprised of norms of practice around which consensus has been achieved, and through which research questions and answers are defined and articulated. When scholarly output achieves this status in the natural sciences, we call it "scientific knowledge." In the remainder of this chapter, I want to examine the extent to which practices in contemporary humanities disciplines achieve an analogous status.

3.4 Consensus in the Humanities

I have already gestured toward the basic elements of my answer to the question of the extent to which practices in the humanities disciplines achieve a disciplinary status analogous to scientific knowledge: *scientific knowledge is to science as canonical texts are to the humanities*. Not in every respect, of course. But in the sense relevant for answering the question of whether the humanities create knowledge, I believe the thesis is sound. I now want to add more texture to the "humanities" side of the analogy, both as a way of elaborating the sense in which canonical texts function as a repository of knowledge, and as a way of providing assurances that the analogy with scientific knowledge is not merely an artifact of a sufficiently superficial level of description. My discussion of *Leviathan* above foreshadowed elements of the argument I will elaborate here – namely, that I want to begin by thinking of classic or canonical texts not so much as a collection of "must-reads" or as the foundations of civilization, still less as a collection of deep or fundamental truths. In place of that, I invoked the notion of a "language of scholarly thought" or a "general intellectual style," the acquisition of which is (1) facilitated by – even predicated on – the study of canonical texts and (2) necessary for the production of work that is recognizably scholarly. But those notions are pretty vague. What more can be said about them? And how can we use that further detail to understand the role of canonical texts as "the price of admission to practice and the basis of participation in debate"?

The primary means by which canonical texts impart the language of scholarly thought is through exemplification. Texts make their way into the discipline's canon on account of their unique capacity to exemplify that discipline's scholarly or intellectual values. Different texts within the canon can exemplify different values. This work is exemplary for its eloquence, that work is exemplary for its depth, and so on. These texts are the vehicles through which initiates are instructed in the substance of a discipline's scholarly values. If one wants to understand poetic eloquence, for instance, one reads Dante's *Divine Comedy* – in Italian, as many times as possible. To learn the art of blank verse in English, read *Paradise Lost* over and over again. Through sufficient and curated exposure to canonical texts, initiates begin to develop an intuitive grasp of the substance of the discipline's ideals, just as a child learning language gradually develops a competence for generating utterances that conform to the grammatical rules governing acceptable utterances in her linguistic community. These rules are never made explicit to the child, and a moment's reflection reveals that they need not be in order for her to reliably produce well-formed, even beautiful, utterances. Native English speakers could readily distinguish between grammatical and ungrammatical sentences long before the rules of English grammar were even articulated. The ancient Arabs already had a centuries-long tradition of exacting linguistic discrimination when the Persian al-Sibawayh wrote his *Book of Grammar* in eighth-century

Baghdad (Bod 2013, 76). Al-Sibawayh does not *legislate* the rules of Arabic grammar. He extracts them from sentences that native speakers regard as exemplary. Like the child learning a language and the scholar seeking to articulate that language's rules, the aspiring writer can, with surprising effectiveness, come to grasp the content of literary notions of eloquence or elegance through exposure to exemplary texts.

These examples provide evidence that knowledge of literary ideals can be acquired through exemplars. But there is also an argument to be made that many such norms can *only* be learned through exemplars. That much is clear at least in the case of al-Sibawayh. After all, he's the one articulating the rules. He is uncovering the rules as they are encoded in exemplary Arabic prose. The literary critic Michael Clune remarks on a related phenomenon drawn from the literature classroom:

> A student who asks, "What is so great about this poem?" or "Tell me the reasons for that move" is asking for a kind of knowledge that cannot be fully disclosed, or in some cases even partially disclosed, in advance of a sometimes lengthy educational process. (Clune 2021, 72)

The evidence in favor of this stronger thesis comes from a wide range of sources, many of which most of us have intimate familiarity. Anyone who has ever tried to learn a foreign language or an athletic skill can readily appreciate the futility of trying to develop something approaching competency simply by memorizing a list of rules. While such lists might provide some benefit, they are by no means a substitute for immersive exposure to exemplary instances. The reason for this is that much of the content of the norms governing competency in these domains amounts to what Michael Polanyi called *tacit knowledge* – knowledge that one has but cannot articulate. It is possible that much, perhaps most, of what comes to be known when one acquires something like a capacity for eloquence simply cannot be described. If a writer reliably produces works of great eloquence, she surely knows *something* about eloquence, even if she cannot describe how she does it – that is, even if her knowledge cannot be expressed in the form of propositions or rules.

There is no embarrassment in acknowledging that much of the knowledge that we take to be deeply significant is of this form, in part if not in whole; or, anyway, there *should* be no embarrassment. Indeed, Polanyi's original examples of tacit knowledge came from mathematics and the physical sciences, both of which are renowned for their propositional rigor. Normally it is considered a major intellectual achievement when someone articulates the content of implicit norms. More than three hundred years after the emergence of modern science, philosophers of science have yet to produce a set of principles for demarcating science from nonscience that commands wide assent. But there should be no debate as to whether Newton or Darwin or Einstein exemplify something about the distinctive character of modern science. We learn about that character by studying their work and their reasoning. The more examples we study, the finer our connoisseurship becomes. We hope to be able to use our refined sense of modern science to produce an articulation of some of its distinguishing features that resonates with anyone who has achieved the same discerning capacity that allows us to see the works of those luminaries as exemplary. But it would be a colossal mistake to infer that there is no content to the notion *modern science*, or that we do not know what makes something scientific in the modern sense, solely because we cannot (yet) articulate it.

The parallel between learning the norms governing eloquence and learning the norms governing modern science illustrates another point that is central to understanding the disciplinary function of canonical texts. Just as different canonical works exemplify different scholarly values, the relevant constellation of values will itself vary from one discipline to another. Perhaps *Leviathan* is exemplary in Western political thought because of its historical originality. Its claim to canonical status is best understood by observing where it falls in the historical tradition of political thought. *A Theory of Justice*, by contrast, exemplifies the creativity, clarity, rigor, and depth that came to define greatness in the twentieth-century English-speaking philosophical tradition. Neither stands out as an exemplar of eloquence – not by my lights, anyway. But then, eloquence was not prized as a specifically *scholarly* ideal in that latter tradition; no one confronted with the canonical texts of twentieth-century English-speaking analytic philosophy would ever come away with the illusion that one of the goals of scholarship is to produce beautiful prose. Similarly, it should be immediately obvious to readers that clarity was not something held in high esteem by the contemporaneous community of philosophers on the European continent. As everyone knows, different disciplines trade in different currencies. Transferring the coin of the realm from one disciplinary generation to the next requires a canon that exemplifies the intellectual values peculiar to that discipline.

In the same way that one's acquired norms for grammatical utterances are used to discriminate between well-formed and poorly formed sentences, the scholarly values exemplified by canonical texts are, or become, the criteria by which the quality of scholarly production is judged. Any member of a discipline aiming to produce high-quality work will use their grasp of these values to shape the form and content of their scholarship. Any member concerned with expressing the caliber of a given piece of scholarship will endeavor to illustrate the way in which it either embodies or violates the scholarly norms endemic to their discipline, exemplified by the canonical texts from which their own knowledge of those norms is derived. This discriminating function makes clear the sense in which the canon is more than a body of classics worthy of admiration. The community of scholars has imbued it with a normative significance that governs scholarly practice, often in specific ways. For that community, the canon functions as the "basis for participation in debate" precisely because it is the only plausible or effective means by which the currency of debate is acquired. Mastering the disciplinary canon is not simply a feat that budding scholars pull off in order to impress other people or advance their social standing, nor is it an arbitrary hoop through which they must jump to earn a degree. It is a prerequisite for inclusion in the scholarly community because it is known to *cause people to think the way scholars think*.

Thomas Kuhn's *The Structure of Scientific Revolutions* presents a novel and detailed account of the mechanisms through which scientists are enculturated into the community of scholars in the natural sciences. He famously employed the term "paradigm" in part to designate the cluster of values that mark off individual scientific disciplines. The term as used in *Structure* is afflicted with a certain degree of vagueness, about which Kuhn seemed slightly chagrined and which he attempted to alleviate in a very good essay some twelve years later called "Second Thoughts on Paradigms." There he affirmed that the dominant sense that he had intended "paradigm" to connote was that of an exemplar. The preceding discussion might have led us to expect as much, for natural scientists too need to train future generations in the language of scholarly thought. (Indeed, Kuhn came more and more to see the enculturation process in the natural sciences as the acquisition of a highly specialized language.) But our discussion of encounters with the canon might also have led us to predict the form that exemplars take in Kuhn's 1962 book, and there again we would not be disappointed. His opening remarks on paradigms in the natural sciences include none other than a list of classic texts: Newton's *Principia* and *Opticks*, Benjamin Franklin's *Electricity*, Lavoisier's *Chemistry*.

Of this list, he remarks: "these and many other works served for a time implicitly to define the legitimate problems and methods of a research field for succeeding generations of practitioners" (Kuhn 1962, 10). I think we have to assume that the phrase "for a time" here is not just a stylistic flourish. Kuhn seems rather to be emphasizing a notable feature of canonical works of natural science – namely, their relatively limited shelf-life as compared with canonical works in the humanities. In truth, Kuhn's list is in some ways highly unrepresentative, having been drawn from works that appeared before the twentieth century, around which time communication in the natural sciences began its inexorable march toward the now nearly exclusive use of journal publication. A list of natural science exemplars drawn from the late twentieth century, by contrast, would not include any books. Arguably, it would also not include any journal articles. As Kuhn explained in "Second Thoughts on Paradigms," the exemplars of the natural sciences – those vehicles which impart the substance and style of scholarly scientific output – were things like problem sets in textbooks, equations that admit of a variety of different kinds of applications, theories, and laws. Even before *Structure*, in 1961, he argued that the function of data tables in textbooks was to impart a sense of what "reasonable agreement" between predictions and measurements looks like in practice. In a postscript to *Structure* published along with the 1970 second edition, for instance, he refers to the "phage group," a recently emergent scientific community who had elevated bacteriophage to the status of exemplar (Kuhn 1970, 177; see Creager 2016).

These examples drawn from the natural sciences suggest that the natural scientific analog of a canonical text in the humanities tends to be much more "particulate" and much less tethered to a specific publication or specific form. The zombie students I invoked at the beginning of the chapter will not read Newton's *Principia*, and they will not learn Newton's laws in the form in which Newton expressed them. I think it is an open question whether Newton would have even recognized the modern formulation of Newtonian mechanics, even after we explained all the notation to him (although he *definitely* would have recognized that we're all using Leibniz's notation for calculus!). The classic works themselves mentioned by Kuhn served as exemplars just until practitioners found more refined, more effective tools for scholarly thought and communication. But, as we saw in the previous chapter, the new tools pick up where the old ones left off, resetting the "price of admission to practice" and redefining – sometimes radically so – the "basis for participation in debate." In both the humanities and the natural sciences, students (ideally) acquire the language of scholarly thought that is operative in their time. Some languages undergo more frequent and more radical changes than others. But that is true in reference to different humanities disciplines as well (*mutatis mutandis* for the natural sciences).

In several of Kuhn's examples – particularly those involving experience with data tables and problem sets – it is difficult to resist the conclusion that what students in the natural sciences are acquiring is an aesthetic sensibility or perceptual sensitivity, one that features at the center of the production of knowledge. Let's start with the way in which textbooks' data tables impart an ability to perceive when "reasonable agreement" between theory and observation has been achieved. Practitioners *need* an intuitive sense of reasonable agreement in order to pursue fruitful avenues of research; nature cannot by itself point them in the right direction. Experience with the data tables resultant from empirical measurements that bear on the predictions of accepted theories provides this intuitive sense. The discipline has incorporated this or that theory in part because of its reasonable agreement with observation. The data tables show us what reasonable agreement looks like. It is not a relation that can be boiled down to a set of rules in the form of, "If the agreement between theory and observation is within x%, adopt theory. Otherwise, abort!" It is the same sort of intuitive sense of eloquence that is derived from repeat exposure to works of great eloquence. Similar considerations apply in the case of problem sets. Why do science and math teachers inflict an unrelenting barrage of problem sets on their students – week after week, semester after semester, year after year? Why must our zombified physics students endure one tedious hypothetical scenario after another involving a pulley and a block of wood weighing 2 kg? (I know zombies aren't supposed to have phenomenal consciousness. But I feel like, if there's one thing a zombie could experience, it would be tedium. All that staring ….) Because it is the only means by which they can acquire the knowledge of how to organize and produce solutions to the kinds of problems that characterize research in physics. It makes sense that the "canonical texts" in the natural sciences are text*books*, rather than works of novel scholarly achievement (see, e.g., Olesko 2005). These texts are canonized not because of their ability to model exemplary physical research; that is the province of exemplary physical research. Their value, like that of laboratory exercises, lies rather in their capacity to bestow upon students the rudiments of the language of scholarly thought out of which they will one day compose their own exemplary scholarly utterances.

This brings us to the last and arguably most important kind of knowledge that is acquired through repeat exposure to canonical texts: an aptitude for *generating* work of scholarly significance. As the student develops a sensitivity to the violation of and obedience to scholarly norms in a given discipline, she begins to lay the foundation of the ability to produce her own novel scholarship. Owing to her now-intimate acquaintance with the tradition of exemplary scholarship in her discipline, she is able to use her knowledge of the norms of scholarship to produce work that obeys and reflects those norms. In the most desirable circumstance, she will extend her discipline's understanding of the variety of ways in which its norms can be exemplified. Clune (2021, 74) observes that, in the context of literary studies,

> When radical results are produced, they usually derive from a conservative approach to method. In literary studies, the patient application of that network of tacit practices and knowledges known by the famously vague term *close reading* ... has been the primary means of creating valuable and original insights.

By "conservative approach," he means an approach that is squarely in line with – indeed, developed necessarily through engagement with – the norm-exemplifying canonical scholarship. Although Clune asserts that there is something un-Kuhnian about this dynamic, it is in fact about as Kuhnian as it is possible to be. It is precisely through their unceasing attempts to extend familiar models to new terrain – in other words, their conservative approach – that natural scientists eventually "break" those models and wind up in dire need of radical new alternatives. In the next section, I look at the causal role the canon plays in the precipitation of such moments of "crisis" (Kuhn's term).

3.5 Canon, Coherence, and Crisis

One of the most important insights that appears in *The Structure of Scientific Revolutions* is the idea that revolutionary transitions in scientific understanding are made possible only by the way in which scientific training and research imposes constraints on how practitioners conceptualize the features of nature that they study. Like so many of the observations made in that book, the notion that radical upheavals of scientific thought – upheavals that, mind you, unveil entire worlds of scientific discovery – could be dependent on the *close-mindedness* of the very scientists doing the revolutionary research was – *is* – deeply counterintuitive. Especially at the time Kuhn was writing, this assertion was for some people deeply unsettling (Reisch 2016, 2019). The United States was still recovering from the shock of *Sputnik* when *Structure* was published in 1962. The successful launch of a satellite by the Soviet Union was taken to be a demonstration of Soviet scientific superiority, which in 1957 translated into civilizational superiority *tout court*. This achievement pitted two deeply entrenched Cold War mythologies against one another. On the one hand, the idea that communism and communist sympathies were the result of a "captive mind" imprisoned by "brainwashing" was taken for granted in many circles within American culture (Reisch 2016, 9). Equally influential, though, was the notion that modern scientific inquiry derived its astonishing power from its total commitment to freedom of thought and the pursuit of bold ideas, making it a particularly good fit for Western liberal democracy and an assurance that the way of the West was the path to success. Kuhn presented a powerful case against this latter catechism, effectively explaining why we'd been beaten by the Soviets: captive minds produce better science. Better science means better civilization. Checkmate. (Speaking of which, it did not help that Russians had held the World Chess Championship title since before WWII.)

So, what was Kuhn's argument? It goes essentially like this. The whole point of scientific training is to get practitioners to see the world in a particular way. Kuhn meant that quite literally, and much of *Structure* is dedicated to providing compelling evidence as to the plausibility of that thesis. We want practitioners to see the east-to-west motion of the stars across the sky as a byproduct of the fact that *we're* spinning in the opposite direction – not as a reflection of the stars' inestimably speedy race around Earth. We want practitioners to see an object moving horizontally at a constant velocity as something that is subject to *no* (net) forces – not, as Aristotle would have said, one that is subject to a constant force required to keep it in motion. We want them to intuitively expect a ball dropped from the mast of a moving ship to land directly beneath its point of origin – not some distance behind the origin, left in the wake of the ship that will continue to move. We want practitioners to see the world in a particular way in part because, as far as we can tell, that is how the world is. More importantly for the purposes of inquiry, though, we want them to see the world in such-and-such a way because that perspective has proven to be the most fruitful for the further development of our understanding of nature. Scientific training is designed to produce this effect on practitioners' perception of relevant parts of the world, with the eventual goal being for them to use that perspective to frame and pursue new questions that broadly presume the correctness of the world-picture with which they've been imbued.

Pretty straightforward. But how do we get practitioners to see things in the way we want them to? By using all the familiar brainwashing tactics, of course: repeat exposure to exemplary cases, rewarding characterizations of the phenomena that reflect a commitment to the orthodox worldview, punishing characterizations that deviate from the worldview – you know, standard "indoctrination" stuff (Reisch 2016, 26). The more informative, more explanatory, and less salacious version of that story is that research frameworks, whether they are based on model organisms, sets of physical laws, or families of chemical elements, tend to become widespread in science because they offer researchers a wealth of resources for the organization and growth of knowledge (Kuhn 1962, 9). In particular, they suggest strategies for characterizing phenomena, and thus structuring research problems in a way that makes them solvable. Understood in this way, the reward for characterizing a certain phenomenon in the mode of the orthodox view is that one produces a characterization that connects the phenomenon to what is already familiar, comprehensible, and relatively easy to work with. Physicists do not enjoy increased social prestige by insisting on characterizing an explosion as a "time-reversed, perfectly inelastic collision." For the rest of us, that's just a weird, annoying thing to do. But it makes it a lot easier for the physicist to calculate the forces involved in an explosion, and calculation is a big part of problem-solving in physics. The availability of problem-structuring strategies like this one promises rewards for those who employ them, because employing those strategies tends to result in solved problems (Haufe 2024). For related reasons, the researcher who avoids using tried and true methods threatens his prospects of solving problems; he punishes himself. The self-reinforcing nature of this process, iterated across several generations of an ever-expanding range of subdisciplines results in an entire disciplinary culture that is saturated with approaches to phenomena modeled off of the progenitor. That saturation, Kuhn argued, shapes the very content of practitioners' perceptual experiences.

The idea that immersion in a disciplinary culture transforms one's perceptual experience was profoundly significant for Kuhn. In his estimation, it is the only way to acquire a perceptual faculty sensitive enough to detect unexpected deviations from a system's normal behavior (what he called *anomalies*):

> Without the special apparatus that is constructed mainly for anticipated functions, the results that lead ultimately to novelty could not occur. And even when the apparatus exists, novelty ordinarily emerges only for the man who, knowing with precision what he should expect, is able to recognize that something has gone wrong. Anomaly appears only against the background provided by the paradigm. The more precise and far-reaching that paradigm is, the more sensitive an indicator it provides of anomaly and hence of an occasion for paradigm change. (Kuhn 1962, 65)

It is the investigative pursuit of anomalies – putative violations of the norms governing a system – that ultimately leads to deep revisions to how practitioners understand and ultimately experience the behavior and composition of nature. Kuhn believed that the way in which immersive scientific training transformed perceptual experience was the only truly reliable mechanism for the detection of anomalies, because perception is sensitive to a much broader range of information than propositional cognition. Here we return to Polanyi's emphasis on things we know but can't articulate, which Kuhn rightly appreciated (Kuhn 1962, 44). It is such a simple and obvious point; it is difficult to comprehend how it could ever have been controversial.

Certainly it is not controversial that new forms of experience are unlocked through expertly curated long-term immersive exposure to exemplary works of art, literature, and other domains of humanistic endeavor. Experts see things in a painting that novices don't, taste things that novices don't, hear features of music or language that novices don't, even feel feelings that are out of range for the uninitiated. That this constitutes a kind of knowledge is reflected in the fact that expert agreement on questions of eloquence and similarly aesthetic criteria is incredibly common. But its status as knowledge does not depend on whether it is tapping into some objective, mind-independent reality. If a flood had accidentally deposited a bunch of twigs arranged to look exactly like the words to *Paradise Lost*, would it have been eloquent? The least acceptable answer to that question is an affirmative one, and it makes clear precisely the sense in which knowledge of that sort cannot exist in the absence of a background of fact-fixing community norms like those governing the aesthetic judgment of well-trained scholars. Recalling our earlier discussion, the possibility of knowledge in the disciplinary sense rests on whether there are community-wide norms that govern members' judgments and pursuit of scholarly endeavors. In Clune's words, "Expert judgment, as opposed to private judgment, cannot be isolated from interpretive skills and disciplinary knowledges" (Clune 2021, 85).

In closing this chapter, I want to look at how the themes of consensus, judgment, and the language of scholarly thought exemplified by canonical texts factor into the production of knowledge in the humanities in ways that are analogous to their role in the natural sciences. The analogy with language acquisition once again proves to be a helpful entry point. In his history of humanism, Makdisi (1990, 93–94) reports that humanists aspiring to a unique stratum of mastery of the Arabic language would spend "a great many years" living in the desert with bedouin Arab tribes.

But not just any bedouin tribes. Arabic scholars recognized something like an approved list of tribes, known for the particular purity of their speech, owning to the fact that they had historically been isolated from non-Arabic speaking peoples. These bedouin tribes had no *formal* knowledge of the descriptive rules governing acceptable utterances. Rather, what they had, and what could be acquired from them alone, was an acute and reflexive sensitivity to proper Arabic speech. The consensus among scholars of Arabic (particularly Arabic poetry) was that years embedded with these tribes was the only means by which anyone – including native Arabic speakers – could develop the intuitive grasp of classical Arabic necessary to generate speech eloquent enough to satisfy the scholarly community's standards. Ernst Curtius expresses kindred sentiments in his classic study, *European Literature and the Latin Middle Ages*:

> European literature is coextensive in time with European culture, therefore embraces a period of some twenty-six centuries (reckoning from Homer to Goethe). Anyone who knows only six or seven of these from his own observation and has to rely on manuals and reference books for the others is like a traveler who knows Italy only from the Alps to the Arno and gets the rest from Baedeker.[7] Anyone who knows only the Middle Ages and the Modern Period does not even understand these two. For in his small field of observation he encounters phenomena such as 'epic,' 'Classicism,' 'Baroque',… and many others, whose history and significance are to be understood only from the earlier periods of European literature. To see European literature as a whole is possible only after one has acquired citizenship in every period from Homer to Goethe. This cannot be got from a textbook, even if such a textbook existed. One acquires the rights of citizenship in the country of European literature only when one has spent many years in each of its provinces and has frequently moved about from one to another. (Curtius 1953, 12)

This practice is instantly recognizable as a version of the process Kuhn relates from the natural sciences. My primary concern here, though, is to get us to see it as a species of the same genus that includes expertly curated and immersive exposure to canonical texts in humanities disciplines. Premodern Arab humanists had their canonical texts as well: the Qur'an and a small collection of pre-Islamic Arabic poetry (Makdisi 1990, esp. Part IV, Chapter 1). Like the pure-speaking bedouins, these texts occupied the familiar disciplinary status of norm-exemplifier and training instrument. Together, these repositories of linguistic and aesthetic norms constituted both the "price of admission to practice and the basis for participation

---

[7] A famous nineteenth-century German publisher of travel guides.

in debate." Although different disciplinary canons serve as repositories for different sets of scholarly norms, it holds nevertheless that sustained, tutored engagement with the canon is essential for transforming a practitioner's perception in a way that allows disciplinarily significant properties to enter his awareness. Even the most hostile critics of the canon in literary studies accept this premise, their concern being that exposure to the traditional canon of Western literature imparts readers (victims?) with the *wrong* set of norms (Guillory 1993, esp. 19–28). The idea that canons transmit values is taken for granted; this is the foundation on which the "canon debate" rests. My point is simply to connect this widely accepted foundational notion to the natural scientific process described by Kuhn, and to the practice of language norm-acquisition through exposure to exemplary speech. Each of these is an instance of the phenomenon whereby a scholar is endowed with certain unique, discipline-specific perceptual capacities that make productive inquiry possible at the scholarly level.

A central part of the Kuhnian story for how a canon enables transitions of truly fundamental intellectual significance focuses specifically on the consequences of acute scholarly perception. At a very general level, Kuhn's idea was that sustained, immersive experience with a relatively narrow range of related phenomena is essential to cultivate a perceptual capacity that is sensitive and discriminating enough to detect intellectually significant deviations from a system's standard behavior. As the historian of science Larry Holmes pointed out, lots of unexpected stuff happens in the context of a scientific investigation. It takes a disciplined improviser to separate the insignificant unexpected stuff from the unexpected stuff with the potential to lead to new insights (Holmes 2004, esp. Chapter 9). The form of "discipline" he has in mind, as did Kuhn, was a commitment – be it tacit or intentional – to fit anomalous phenomena into existing, well-established conceptual categories. There are two sources of motivation for this commitment to disciplined classificatory practices. The first is deceptively practical: never do with more what you could do with less. Why "deceptively" so? Because, in the service of inquiry, there are important intellectual reasons why we would want to limit the number of categories into which we think things can fall – namely, that the fewer categories we have, the more deeply acquainted we become with each category, making it more familiar, intuitive, and thus easier to structure an investigation around. How familiar is any of us with the aesthetic category *inblime*? Not at all familiar, that's how much. I just made it up. Can you imagine using that category to organize your research? Exactly. That's why it helps to stick to categories like *lively* and *eloquent* – categories we know how to wield with relative precision and that allow us to communicate with other scholars.

The second reason – which went unmentioned, perhaps unnoticed, by Kuhn – is more purely intellectual: we actually learn more about the essence of the category itself by seeing how many things we are comfortable using it to classify. How can we learn things about our own categories, you might ask? Don't we decide the criteria according to which things are or are not included in those categories? Sure, sometimes (unless they are hard-wired into our psychology). But the properties that we mark off as criterial for inclusion in a given category will not be the only properties those objects have. We were classifying things as mammals way before we knew what distinctive kinds of genes mammals had, for example; we learned something about the category *mammal* when we looked at the genomes of members of that group. This same kind of discovery occurs across the sciences, including mathematics. The illustrious mathematician, physicist, and philosopher Henri Poincaré put great emphasis on the idea that we learn new things about the essence of our mathematical definitions when we try to extend them to domains for which they were not initially designed. Such exercises help us to learn "the soul of the fact" (Poincaré 1910, 78). He was expressing something that had long been observed by mathematicians. His countryman, the geometer Michel Chasles, argued that we learned a lot about the notions of *point*, *line*, and *plane* when we began extending them to non-Euclidean scenarios at the turn of the nineteenth century (Chemla 2016).

But this learning process only works if (1) we have a sufficiently refined sense of how the category behaves, and (2) we are strongly resistant to the idea of expanding the set of categories we use to structure scholarly inquiry and experience. As long as we are disciplined in this way, we guarantee that we (a) learn as much as there is to be profitably learned about the limits of our current categories, and (b) only invent new categories when we encounter phenomena we simply cannot tolerate classifying with existing resources. We don't want to use *inblime* unless we absolutely have to. The staunch conceptual/perceptual conservatism that defines this process ensures that, when we *do* christen a new category, it will be because its members are fundamentally unlike anything else we know of. Things that are inblime are so incomprehensibly different from everything we've ever encountered; they really deserve their own category. Nor is the growth of knowledge and the role of exemplars therein limited to the natural sciences and mathematics. It is the process that grounds Clune's observation above that "radical results [in literary studies]...usually derive from a conservative approach to method."

We have been able to subsume both the training of natural scientists in a tradition of consensus practice and the training of humanists in a tradition of canonical sources under a general framework of disciplinary knowledge, whereby the values and norms that define, guide, and promote scholarly inquiry in a community are acquired chiefly through carefully managed sustained engagement with exemplars of scholarly achievement. Through this mechanism, scholarly consensus in a discipline is perpetuated across several generations, whose members contribute to an ever-broadening and ever-deepening reservoir of disciplinary knowledge that can be used to constrain inquiry within parameters that are recognizably reasonable to the community of scholars. That tradition of constrained inquiry, in turn, eventuates in the creative exhaustion of existing conceptual resources and the consequent need for scholarly innovation.

Clarity, eloquence, and depth are characteristic values that scholarly works in humanities disciplines are expected to satisfy. Those values take specific forms in specific disciplines, and a significant part of training in these disciplines involves – or *did* involve – developing a feel for the community norms governing what sort of work reflects them. Much of the knowledge that these disciplines produce and impart is constituted by a deep, intuitive sense of what these values look like in concrete form, a sense of what it is like for scholarly output to exemplify them. It is not the propositional knowledge that comes from sufficiently precise descriptions of phenomena. But then, neither is the majority of scientific knowledge of that form. It is the tacit knowledge acquired through encounters with instances of exemplification.

3.6 Contra Consensus?

I want to briefly consider two objections to the view of humanistic knowledge I've developed in this chapter. The first comes from the able mind of John Guillory, who rejects the "consensus" model for understanding the formation and preservation of literary canons. His primary complaints seem to be that the notion of consensus is overly "electoral," and that it misleadingly depicts the formation of a canon as "only the sum of individual decisions" of practitioners. In reality, he claims, such a process could never be sufficient to perpetuate a canon, which also requires "institutions" (specifically university classrooms) to serve as a platform and a site of enforcement (Guillory 1993, 27–28).

> The work of preservation has other, more complex social contexts than the immediate responses of readers, even communities of readers, to texts; as we shall see, these institutional contexts shape and constrain judgment according to *institutional* agendas, and in such a way that the selection of texts never represents merely the consensus of a community of readers.

These overt protestations notwithstanding, I interpret Guillory's views as broadly in line with the account of the perpetuation of scientific knowledge I've given above. The main difference seems to be that, where Guillory sees a qualitative difference between situations in which scholarly agreement is backed up by institutional enforcement and situations in which it is not, I see a difference of degree. That is, I think that institutions – classrooms, say – are particularly effective means by which scholarly consensus is preserved and transmitted to the next generation of practitioners; they are not the only means. We know this because we know of lots of instances in which consensus in maintained and transmitted despite the clear absence of institutions in the substantive sense that Guillory intends. Until the mid-nineteenth century, for example, modern scientific knowledge was developed overwhelmingly outside the confines of institutions. Communities were held together – much as they are today – through publication and informal networks of correspondence. What caused and maintained widespread agreement among community members was the simple fact that the ideas around which they converged were disproportionately effective in facilitating their intellectual aims. Institutions are very powerful mechanisms for concentrating scholarly attention and resources. But, at least in the natural sciences, they cannot normally drive or warp scholarly priorities in a way that fails to satisfy broader scholarly aims. Broadly speaking, natural scientists endeavor to solve problems. No institutional agenda that failed to facilitate problem-solving in a form recognizable to practitioners could hope to substantively influence the direction of research in a community. Or, to put it another way, that the community's research might be substantively influenced by institutional agendas says more about the disciplinary community than it does about the institution.

Have I interpreted Guillory's notion of "institution" too narrowly? I don't think anything I've said above suggests a specific conception of what makes something an institution. The basic thrust, one that Guillory's argument requires, is that there is something external to the disciplinary community that sets or at least substantively influences its values, its priorities, and its direction. I won't say that there are no such entities. What I will say is this: that kind of persistent influence from external sources is fundamentally at odds with the maintenance and growth of disciplinary knowledge (for detailed arguments, see Haufe 2022, esp. Chapters 2 and 3). Kuhn himself observes the extent to which communities of natural scientists strive to isolate their research agendas from the demands of the broader social milieu. But the tendency to resist intellectual pressures from outside the disciplinary agenda is much older and more widespread than modern science. It can be readily observed in the perpetual splitting of disciplines into distinct disciplines, subgroups, and new specializations. (Relatedly, and just as telling, is the rarity of instances in which two disciplines genuinely hybridize.) El Shamsy (2013), for example, relates that the jurists and theologians among Muslim intellectuals had begun to diverge as scholarly communities by the second Islamic century/ninth century CE; each of these communities would shortly come to constitute distinct humanities disciplines (Makdisi 1990). Disciplines inevitably fissure precisely because they develop subcommunities with dueling sets of values. Each subcommunity cannot envision a world in which it can productively pursue its scholarly objectives and remain beholden to a certain set of scholarly norms (namely, the set by which the other subcommunity is gradually becoming distinguished) that has become increasingly ill-fitting as inquiry has progressed. Scholarly communities routinely break apart due to the sanctity of internally developed norms. And yet they're supposed to be highly responsive to external influences? I don't think so.

Guillory, in dismissing Stanley Fish's (1980) concept of "interpretive communities" distinguished by specific sets of interpretive norms that fix the facts concerning the truth and meaning of literary interpretations, submits what he apparently thinks is a *reductio* when observing that there is no limit to how many such communities there could be. But that's just true. The natural scientific "interpretive communities" that Kuhn sought to elucidate might include only a very small number of individuals (see, e.g., Kuhn 1962, end of Chapter 5). What begin as "interpretive communities" within a discipline often will eventually grow into disciplines in their own right (see Haufe 2022, Chapter 5).

The second objection comes from the philosopher William Lycan. With respect to philosophy, Lycan observes that there are no matters of disciplinary consensus. On this basis, he denies that any of the examples discussed in fellow philosopher Gary Gutting's (2009) book, *What Philosophers Know*, actually constitutes knowledge. What I like about this is its tacit approval of the thesis that absence of consensus implies absence of knowledge. What I do not like about it is the way in which Lycan interprets the notion of consensus. Lycan professes to embrace what he calls the "Principle of Humility," which with all due modesty states that we cannot claim to know the truth of a philosophical proposition as long as at least one smart philosopher does not accept that proposition. Since no philosophical theses have met with universal acclaim, apparently there is no philosophical knowledge. It is worth noting that, if this is what consensus means, then it would follow that there is no scientific knowledge either. Maybe Lycan would bite that bullet; sometimes one man's *tollens* is another man's *ponens*. But I think that there are more mutually satisfying options available.

At the beginning of this chapter, I exposed two myths that dog the idea of scientific consensus. One myth was that a scientific community needs to be in a state of unanimity with regard to the truth of some proposition in order to qualify as having achieved consensus on that proposition. I believe that something like this conception of consensus underlies Lycan's Principle of Humility. Although the Principle of Humility has a strong intuitive appeal for me, on balance I believe that it is not fit for use in the context of disciplinary epistemology. Something like it is warranted in contexts where competent individuals disagree over the truth value of specific propositions. But the formation of disciplinary consensus, as I have tried to explain, is not entirely or even primarily a matter of agreement as to a proposition's truth.

As an alternate means for gauging the presence of consensus in philosophy, let's experiment with the version of canon-consensus we've developed in this chapter. That will require that we engage in some egregious violations of the Principle of Humility. The sting that comes with violating it, however, is only felt against a backdrop that treats all questions of knowledge as belonging to the same species, a species whose native environment is the adjudication of the truth of well-formed propositional claims. There are compelling reasons for thinking that scientific knowledge develops under very different conditions and for very different reasons. I also believe that scientific knowledge is not unique in this regard. Over the last two chapters, I have tried to construct an alternative conception of epistemology that is specific to the peculiarities of scholarly inquiry pursued in a disciplinary context, whether that discipline is rooted in the natural sciences or the humanities. If we momentarily divest our epistemological intuitions of their authority as we explore the nature of disciplinary knowledge, new and important epistemological vistas unveil themselves.

On my account, what makes something an object of consensus is that members of the scholarly community generally agree that the object in question exemplifies norms that ought to be used as a guide for framing scholarly inquiry. We saw the way in which Newtonian mechanics does this – not by presenting physicists with the Sacred Parchment whose tenets they must commit to their bosom upon pain of professional sanction, but by proving itself as a superb way of giving them what *they* want: an approach to structuring research problems in physics that allowed them to calculate force and that can be modified to deal with novel challenges. And not strictly on account of the historically unprecedented fruitfulness of Newton's laws of nature in particular. More than this, in fact, researchers were (and still are) drawn to the "Newtonian style" of problem-solving, whereby one constructs a simple, mathematically analyzable representation of some natural phenomenon (Cohen 1983).

It is evident to anyone acquainted with contemporary political philosophy that this is precisely how Rawls' *A Theory of Justice* functions in that discipline. According to the account I've articulated in this chapter, its canonical status implies that the book is an object of scholarly consensus. I also pointed out, though, that this canonical status does not imply that scholars generally agree on the truth of its claims, no more than they agree with Hobbes that we should all submit to the rule of an autocrat. Rather, what they generally agree on is that *A Theory of Justice* exemplifies in some way or other norms that ought to be used as a guide for framing problems of political philosophy. Yes, there are a handful of card-carrying "Rawlsians," but their numbers are small in comparison by the legions of scholars who take a "Rawlsian approach" to this or that problem. It is common for people who explicitly reject Rawls' substantive claims to nevertheless employ such an approach – say, by focusing on the design of institutions as the central challenge of political theory, or by using the Veil of Ignorance as a tool for reflecting on fundamental moral commitments. Jerry Cohen, for instance, wrote more than one entire book criticizing Rawls' conceptions of justice and equality (Cohen 2000, 2008). Yet, his approach to the philosophical consideration of these problems is instantly recognizable as a Rawlsian one, suitably modified to accommodate Cohen's distinctive intellectual style.

It is hard to say exactly what makes an approach to political philosophy "Rawlsian" – or, say, an approach to philosophy of science "Kuhnian," which is another case study in Gutting's book about *What Philosophers Know*, and which is undoubtedly a canonical work in the philosophy of science. I have drawn heavily on Kuhn in this chapter, despite the fact that there are fundamental components of Kuhn's image of science that I do not find plausible and to which I do not appeal – components that Kuhn believed to be among the most important elements in his model of science.

It seems to me, though, that, in spite of that, my approach to the problem of disciplinary knowledge is still thoroughly Kuhnian. To admit as much is not to confess philosophical or historical sympathies. Rather, it is an expression of the adoption of a particular means of structuring and answering philosophical questions about knowledge in intellectual communities, of which the natural sciences are merely one kind. There are aspects of this approach that are easily identified by members of the discipline of history and philosophy of science, among whom Kuhn's *Structure* was highly influential but not exactly persuasive.[8] This discipline is perhaps most clearly distinguished by its tradition of bringing the history of science to bear on philosophical questions about the nature of scientific knowledge. Most members of that community feel that both Kuhn's understanding of historical episodes as well as his philosophical interpretation of those episodes were wide of the mark. That has not stopped them from converging on the scholarly norm of investing the history of science with epistemological relevance. Importantly, the prioritization of this fairly innocuous norm has led to the emergence of a scholarly discipline that is independent of the discipline of philosophy of science and of history of science. This is exactly what we would expect if Fish's notion of norm-driven "interpretive communities" was accurate. The idea that Fish's model implies the existence or potential for an enormous variety of tiny norm-determining communities is not a defect of that model. Such a tendency is clearly discernible across intellectual history.

Where does all this leave us with respect to Lycan's Principle of Humility and its implications for consensus in philosophy or other humanities disciplines? It is an empirical fact that consensus in the natural sciences does not obey the Principle of Humility. According to my argument, this fact is explained by the nature of the demands on disciplinary knowledge, rather than something specific to the natural sciences; disciplinary communities do not require universal agreement in order to fulfill the disciplinary function that consensus is supposed to fulfill. I then argued that humanities disciplines have historically drawn on a similar body of shared scholarly norms in order to frame and propagate inquiry, just as the natural sciences have. Together, these arguments suggest that the Principle of Humility is not an operative or appropriate constraint on disciplinary knowledge, although it may be appropriate for other species of knowledge. This conclusion is bolstered by the instances of disciplinary

---

[8] See Lakatos and Musgrave 1970 for a series of wide-ranging criticisms of Kuhn, which thereafter became something of a hobby in the philosophy of science.

consensus in philosophy that I mentioned above, which Gutting (2009) has described as examples of "what philosophers know" and which function in philosophy as objects of scientific consensus function in the natural sciences. Furthermore, all of the instances of disciplinary consensus canvased in the chapter serve as repositories of scholarly norm exemplification, which (so I argued) is the goal served by a discipline's canonical works. I therefore conclude that, *pace* Lycan, there is consensus in philosophy, and it looks a lot like consensus in the natural sciences.

3.7 Conclusion

Inquiry needs to be guided by constraints in order to lead to knowledge. In the natural sciences, some of these constraints come from scientific consensus, which exerts normative pressure on how inquiry ought to proceed. We are accustomed to thinking that the normative power of scientific consensus derives from its ability to indicate the truth of some empirical claim about nature. According to this picture, scientific inquiry aims at truth and requires it for making progress (perhaps by definition, perhaps for causal reasons). Scientific consensus is valuable because it sifts the truths from the falsehoods, providing members of scientific communities with the parameters within which productive inquiry can operate.

Against the enormous seductive power of this picture, I have presented an account of the disciplinary function of scientific consensus that, while compatible with the legendary truth-signaling ability of consensus, can do without it. There is a very simple reason for this devil-may-care attitude toward truth: we routinely grant normative constraining powers on the basis of considerations that have nothing to do with truth. To take one of many compelling examples, there is a strong preference in a wide range of natural sciences and in mathematics for theories and models that are easily visualizable.[9] There are lots of interesting observations that one could make about this preference, but the idea that visualizability is a guide to truth is not among them. Yet, there are clear and easily relatable reasons why we would expect scholars to exhibit such a preference when attempting to understand nature in a deep and systematic way. Analogous explanations can be given for the other "theoretical virtues" (or "epistemic virtues"). Once we sever the supposed connection between consensus and truth, we

---

[9] In chemistry, see Rocke (2010). In mathematics, see Tappenden (2005). In evolutionary biology, see Provine (1971, 140; 1989, 309). In paleontology, see Huss 2009. In elementary particle physics, see Bacciagaluppi and Valentini (2009, 476–519), and so on.

avail ourselves of a much more permissive, more unifying, and ultimately more explanatory conception of consensus, one with the power to illuminate the general process by which knowledge grows.

Consensus is often wrong – at least, we come to view it as wrong. But it rarely fails to be productive. It promotes the language of scholarly thought in a discipline, allowing practitioners to refine their ability to communicate, debate, and achieve greater understanding. By narrowing the aperture of scholarly concern, it enables deeper, more refined stages of inquiry, promoting the pursuit of advanced versions of questions whose importance the community has validated, rather than barking off after yet another passing fad. This process of persistent refinement, well known to natural scientists, inevitably leads to encounters with phenomena that defy description – literally. These encounters *necessitate* the development of new categories as a way of capturing experience. As I show in later chapters, some form of this process has long been recognizable to art historians and scholars of the literary arts.

The growth of knowledge involves both more and less than the accumulation of propositions to which practitioners readily grant their assent. It is the building of a *culture* of inquiry, in which – like all other cultures – most things that are known are *felt* or *understood* rather than consciously believed. This alternative conception of knowledge does not comport well with the dominant epistemology of the last several centuries. That epistemology was built upon and continues to be maintained by a model of knowledge that takes things like propositional attitudes based on perception as exemplary. However, the focus of epistemic concern in disciplinary contexts is the *facilitation of further inquiry*, not the durability of propositional attitudes *per se*. Only at the bleeding edge of practice does the truth value of very narrowly specified propositions become an object of particular interest, it being the currency of active scholarly debate. Here knowledge becomes increasingly indistinguishable from warranted presupposition, which itself grades imperceptibly into warranted assertion, tolerable conjecture, and, finally, disputed claim. No doubt there are even finer-grained distinctions than this, each of which captures a stage in the developmental process through which ideas become knowledge.

We have reached a critical juncture in our exploration of knowledge in the humanities. Some general conditions for the production of knowledge have been described, along with equally general descriptions of instantiations of these conditions in both the natural sciences and the humanities. I now want to look more carefully at the nature of humanistic knowledge and the process by which it is acquired. I begin this investigation in Chapter 4 by examining knowledge of language in more detail. Using language as a model of the kind of nonpropositional knowledge that humanistic research generates, I develop a more refined conception of evidence in the humanities. Perhaps unsurprisingly, it will turn out that the probative capacity of certain forms of evidence derives in part from its relation to the kind of disciplinary consensus examined in detail in the present chapter – another thing that knowledge in the humanities shares with scientific knowledge. To achieve this result, we will have to once again resort to debunking some of the persistent myths surrounding scientific knowledge.

CHAPTER 4

Knowing What Matters

> When you can measure what you are speaking about, and express it in numbers, you know something about it; but when you cannot measure it, when you cannot express it in numbers, your knowledge is of a meagre and unsatisfactory kind: it may be the beginning of knowledge, but you have scarcely, in your thoughts, advanced to the stage of *science*, whatever the matter may be.
>
> William Thompson (Lord Kelvin), *Popular Lectures and Addresses vol. 1* (1889)

Frankly, I don't understand why these lectures were so popular. A certain kind of person – the kind of person for which I imagine Lord Kelvin would have had little patience – instinctively wants to respond, "Uh-huh. And is that principle something you can express in numbers? No? Then I guess you've got a problem." As tempting as it is to write off this comment as an extreme and self-refuting manifestation of scientism, I want to encourage us to resist that urge in the hopes that we might actually learn something quite deep. Rather than interpreting Kelvin as enunciating some general conditions on knowledge, let us generously imagine that he is in fact expressing a widely recognized principle governing the practice of physics in the late nineteenth century. No one engaged in research in any of the well-developed branches of physics at that time would have found anything in Kelvin's comments worthy of objection. Moreover, it resonates with a general conception of science which was then popular, and which raised no small amount of trouble for the fledgling "science" of evolutionary biology (Kelvin himself was not a fan).[1] So these are not just the incoherent ramblings of a grumpy old codger. It is the coherent expression of prevailing (if rarely articulated) disciplinary and cultural norms.

---

[1] Strevens 2020, Chapter 3.

What is it about measurements that Kelvin thought made them essential to knowledge in physics? What role do measurements play in physics? The classical answer to this question, itself canonized as part of the Scientific Method, holds that the point of measurement is to test or "check" a theory, to see if its quantitative predictions are borne out by the world. The implication, sometimes made explicit, is that a lack of agreement between a theory's predictions and our measurements means we must abandon the theory. But as anyone who has ever done an undergraduate lab exercise knows, this conception of the relationship between theory and measurement, despite its wide popularity and intuitive appeal, is not how things actually work in scientific investigation, nor in its anemic pedagogical imitation. Students do not race up to the lab director, breathlessly shouting, "Professor! You're never going to believe this. Galileo's theory of acceleration in free fall is wrong!" Similarly, and for reasons that are easy to appreciate, the professional scientist whose measurements deviate from their expected values does not suddenly abandon her theory. In either context, the first question is normally, "What went wrong?" That is, given that the theory is *correct*, what explains why our measurements did not conform to it? I hasten to point out that, if this sounds scandalous ("That's what they're doing?!"), we owe much of our pearl-clutching instincts to the Scientific Method's ahistorical caricature of scientific research. Upon reflection, it should seem natural to see the relationship between theory and measurement as an iterated feedback or balancing process, in which we learn about the theory itself as well as how to do effective measurements. Good quantitative theories take considerable effort and ingenuity to develop. A practicable approach to obtaining relevant measurements can often be even more demanding (more on this below), not to mention expensive. Abandoning the theory when our predictions don't pan out would not be sensible. This more sophisticated understanding of the theory–measurement relationship, however, does not negate the fact that measurements do play a central role in both the continued use of a theory, as well as in its inevitable rejection. But the precise nature of their probative role is rather unlike what we've come to expect from the misleadingly distorted versions of scientific research to which we've been habitually exposed.

Kuhn (1961) says something interesting about this. He says that the primary function of measurement is to gauge whether there is "reasonable agreement" between the theory and the physical world. What? Too squishy to be considered "scientific"? Let's think about it for a moment. Exact agreement is out of the question; it's not even clear that "exact agreement" is a coherent notion. Quantitative theories can often be calculated to arbitrary degrees of precision. What *would* make agreement "exact" in these cases? Clearly then, the most we can hope for is precision to a certain number of decimal places. How many? The correct answer to this is, in part, "As many as our current instruments will allow." But even that answer is idealistic, because the inherent vagaries of experimentation warrant a certain amount of magnanimity when judging whether measurements support a theory or not. Because those inherent vagaries, like the precision of instrumentation, vary across discipline and across time in a given discipline, the views of practitioners in different times and of different fields will diverge when it comes to how tolerant we ought to be when predictions and measurements are not exactly aligned. Much like the question, "What is art?," the issue of what level of agreement is "reasonable" is to be resolved by each community in its own time.

Instead of being "unscientific," then, the idea that scientists seek nothing more (or less) than "reasonable agreement" with theory is essentially unavoidable. Now, this does not prevent us from stipulating, for instance, a threshold level of statistical significance that data ought to reach before being candidates for publication – an opportunity not afforded to researchers before the twentieth century (and yet, so much knowledge!). But it must be borne in mind that this threshold is given to us neither by nature nor by reason. It is an arbitrary stipulation, subject to the prevailing fancy of the community of scientists. Indeed, as I write, practitioners in the social sciences are debating whether to raise the stringency of their significance threshold from 0.05 to 0.01 (error rate of 1/20 vs. 1/100). A quantitative threshold can never be anything more than an attempt by the scientific community to find an apt numerical characterization of the phenomenon of "reasonable agreement," because the notion of reasonableness is an irreducibly value-laden one. It does not supervene on a set of value-free conditions. As Clune remarked in the previous chapter, asking for the conditions that constitute a property like reasonable agreement "is asking for a kind of knowledge that cannot be fully disclosed, or in some cases even partially disclosed, in advance of a sometimes lengthy educational process."

Nor does disclosure imply articulation. We saw several examples in the last chapter of certain concepts in the humanities that cannot be learned by memorizing a list of rules or definitions – indeed, cannot even be expressed in simpler terms, although they might routinely be associated with certain conditions. Eloquence, for instance, might be routinely associated with a high idea-to-word ratio. There I claimed that the content of the concept *eloquence* is disclosed, not through explicit instruction regarding what to look out for, but through immersive exposure to exemplars of eloquence. In a similar fashion, Kuhn suggests the way in which the scientist acquires her discipline's conception of *reasonable agreement* is through routine exposure to the data tables which appear in textbooks. These tables are characteristically comprised of two columns, one showing the mathematically derived predictions of a scientific theory for the value of some dependent variable, the other showing the measured values of that variable. Kuhn has to be right about this. What the hell else could they be doing there? Certainly not to convince the student that the theory is correct. Lacking a professionally developed sense of what reasonable agreement looks like, she's really not in a position to make that assessment. But through repeated exposure to such tables, she starts to develop an understanding of what it means for a measurement to reasonably agree with theory. That is, she comes to know what matters for reasonable agreement.

Natural science cannot do without the concept of reasonable agreement, and yet it is irresolvably woolly in the way that only literary or philosophical concepts are reputed to be. Does this mean that science is actually not as rigorous as we thought it was? I don't think that's the right reaction. Instead, let us humbly conclude that we were just wrong about what rigor looks like in the first place. It does not entail the absence of value judgments guided by subjective human experience. This harebrained fantasy has, I think, seriously weakened our ability to understand both the contribution of science and of the humanities. The fact that there is no mind-independent sense in which the quality of reasonable agreement can be justly interpreted does not mean that there is no fact of the matter as to what constitutes reasonable agreement. Rigorous scientific inquiry involves not *suspending* one's value judgments, but refining them such that they conform to the disciplinary norms that fix the facts about when agreement between theory and measurement is reasonable.

In this chapter, I provide a more detailed model of what these states look like and how to conceive of them as a form of knowledge – knowledge of what matters. In the next chapter, I develop a picture of how central and ubiquitous this kind of knowledge is to scholarly inquiry, providing a range of examples of how it is used in both the natural sciences and the humanities. The humanities are, or at least, can be, very good at producing this kind of knowledge. But they generally do not get credit for it, because it looks so unlike the caricature of scientific knowledge in which we have so much of our civilizational self-image invested. As I have tried to show, the reality of scientific knowledge is far more wide-ranging than that shallow conception can allow. Once we accept the manifest breadth of epistemic resources that scientists bring to bear on the study of nature, the fact that the humanities are engaged in the production of knowledge will be clear.

The proximate goal of this chapter is to elaborate on the brief comments made earlier about the role of exemplification in the capacity of canonical texts to contribute to the language of scholarly thought – that is, to the knowledge base that both anchors and propels inquiry in a given discipline. Those earlier comments were somewhat vague, because describing the substance on which they rest would have diverted attention away from our efforts to articulate more fully the nature of disciplinary knowledge and the role of consensus therein. The detail I did allow focused on the way in which sufficient exposure to exemplars affects the perceptual experience of practitioners, and on the influence of those effects on the form and direction of subsequent inquiry. As fascinating as I'm sure that all was, it was also a bit hand-wavy. Exemplars are doing a lot of work in my answer to the question of whether the humanities create knowledge, but I have not given a thorough enough understanding of their mechanics in order to see whether they can deliver on those weighty demands. This chapter attempts to build up the edifice of exemplification such that we can be confident in the importance of its contribution as well as the generality of its scope across the disciplines. With that edifice in place, we will be better positioned to appreciate the essential role that exemplars play in the production of knowledge.

The previous chapter also contained a risqué subtext, which I would now like to fully expose before things go any further. My argument there implied that humanities disciplines can produce knowledge so long as they achieve scholarly consensus. We can point to numerous historical instances in which a scholarly community converged on the notion that certain texts were special for the way in which they exemplified the intellectual or scholarly values central to inquiry in a certain discipline. Having argued that this is the form that consensus tends to take in humanities disciplines, it follows straightforwardly that the humanities at least *can* produce knowledge. But it also suggests that knowledge might not be possible in the absence of scholarly consensus. To the extent that contemporary humanities disciplines lack such a consensus, they do not produce knowledge. This is why it was worth confronting Guillory's and Lycan's anti-consensus arguments with such force. Where Guillory sees the misguidedness of the notion of scholarly consensus, and where Lycan sees the extreme improbability of consensus, our community-centered epistemology sees an absence of knowledge. Clearly, then, there is a lot hanging on the matter of whether the humanities achieve consensus.

As an antidote, I provided some general reasons for thinking that it was normal for humanities disciplines to come to consensus, and I provided a couple of illustrations of how consensus is reflected in the high degree of uniformity of practice inspired by certain scholarly achievements in the humanities. But there was little more than my personal assurance backing up the claim – absolutely central to my argument – that this uniformity of practice constituted a kind of knowledge. I hope I was clear enough about the kind of knowledge it is *not* – namely, propositional knowledge that can be easily articulated in words or symbols. Given the considerable controversy over what the humanities contribute to the minds of those who study them, though, it would appear that a significant amount of substance is required to clarify the sense in which the mysterious capacities to which I alluded constitute a species of knowledge. Thus, one thing we're going to want out of the next two chapters is a more fine-grained, well-grounded articulation of the specific cognitive content that is acquired through experience with disciplinary exemplars, which I argued were the primary vehicles for imparting the "language of scholarly thought." The hope is that this cognitive content will be recognizable as a species of knowledge – knowledge of what matters – and will hold up in the face of an appropriate level of scrutiny. I provide this finer-grained articulation in the present chapter. Scrutiny begins in Chapter 5, where I examine the parallels between the humanities and the natural sciences with respect to how important this content is for productive scholarly inquiry.

The fulcrum about which each of these chapters turns is the concept of *salience*. Salience is the property of being *particularly* noticeable, of standing out against a backdrop of lesser features. My argument in this chapter begins by developing the connection between salience and the demand for explanation. I move on from there to defend the claim that exemplars exemplify certain properties by making them salient, and that different classes of exemplars are defined by the sets of properties that they make salient. Scholarly training is, I argue, largely a matter of developing the ability to be sensitive to the salience of certain properties. Salience is the crude oil that, suitably refined, underlies the intellectual curiosity that fuels rational inquiry. But it is equally the guardrail that discriminates in favor of some lines of inquiry and against others. One's sense of salience is one's sense of what matters. When that sense aligns with disciplinary norms, it becomes knowledge – knowledge of what matters. A scholarly community with the potential to generate knowledge must, therefore, partake of a shared sense of salience, for it is only through the exercise of this shared sense that community members can develop the kind of agreement I have been calling disciplinary knowledge.

4.1 Unreasonable Agreement?

In 1983, science journalists William Broad and Nicholas Wade published *Betrayers of the Truth: Fraud and Deceit in the Halls of Science*. In it, they accused scientists from the second-century astronomer Ptolemy to the early twentieth-century physicist Robert Millikan of scientific fraud. They parlayed these and similar accusations into a general indictment of the rationality of science, which they based on the claim that, "In the acquisition of knowledge, scientists are not guided by logic and objectivity alone, but also by such nonrational factors as rhetoric, propaganda, and personal prejudice." That someone would make such a salacious claim about scientific inquiry in general is not particularly noteworthy. That sort of thing was becoming increasingly fashionable around that time, aided in no small part by the compelling case that Kuhn had made for resisting the "conventional portrait," which, they claim, "bears little resemblance" to the way scientific inquiry actually works (Broad and Wade, 8–9). In the view of Broad and Wade, the way scientific inquiry actually works is through the perpetration of fraud and deceit, exemplified by the fact that "scientists are not guided by logic and objectivity alone."

Now, I have appealed liberally to Kuhn's model of scientific knowledge thus far because of how it elegantly undermines the "conventional portrait." Unlike Broad and Wade, though, I have not taken the specific ways in which that portrait fails as an indication of the generally fraudulent and deceitful behavior of natural scientists. For all their iconoclasm about the true nature of scientific practice, Broad and Wade were still clearly committed to an even more entrenched conventional portrait about the nature of knowledge itself. Because the facts about real scientific investigations did not comport with their prior commitments about how scientific inquiry has to work, there could be only one conclusion: deviations from that conventional epistemological portrait are evidence of a breach of sacred scholarly covenants.

This is an absolutely classic reaction to the kind of phenomena reported in historical studies of science, over which Kuhn generalizes in *The Structure of Scientific Revolutions.*[2] Having taught this book many times, the most common reaction I receive from undergraduates is, "Why is Kuhn so critical of science?" What is so interesting about this reaction is that Kuhn *does not criticize* natural science at all; he merely describes it. But his description is so spectacularly at odds with the conventional epistemological portrait concerning what makes science epistemically special that students cannot find any meaning behind the text besides the idea that it is an expose of how truly awful science actually is. Similarly, Broad and Wade can see nothing in the illness of fit between their conception of scientific knowledge and the historical facts about how science has worked except that scientists must be misbehaving.

As seemingly unavoidable as this reaction is, there is an alternative approach, one that begins with the presupposition that natural sciences do generate knowledge much of the time, and which then goes on to try to understand how this is actually done. When we do this, however, we end up deriving a picture of knowledge that is much less like the epic distortion wielded by Broad, Wade, and my students (blameless though they may be), and much more like the kind of scholarly activity that lies at the center of humanistic inquiry. The two domains are more alike than they are different. The fact that this is seen as a cause for convicting the sciences of fraud, rather than congratulating the humanities on the production of knowledge, says a lot about how tight the conventional portrait's hold over us is, and how much there is still to be done in dethroning it. Toward that end, I am going to review one of the fraud cases prosecuted by Broad and Wade, showing how it exemplifies knowledge of what matters, rather than malfeasance. Conveniently, this case looks at knowledge of what matters specifically in the context of trying to achieve reasonable agreement between theory and measurement.

4.1.1 *Millikan's Measurements*

Robert A. Millikan won the 1923 Nobel Prize in physics, in part for his measurements of the charge of the electron done about a decade earlier. If you've ever heard the phrase, "oil-drop experiment," those measurements are what it refers to. The basics of the experiment are kind of important here, because they alone can give us some acquaintance

---

[2] Kuhn leaned most heavily on an excellent series of studies, *Harvard Case Studies in Experimental Science*, commissioned by Harvard President James Conant to be used as teaching texts for part of Harvard's general education requirement. Written in the late 1940s, these studies are still remarkably fresh and provide a glimpse into the phenomena that inspired Kuhn's pathbreaking work.

with why Millikan proceeds in the way that he does, why there was (is) some controversy over his studies, and how the whole issue turns on knowledge of what matters in the context of this particular experimental set-up.

The first thing Millikan did was to produce an electromagnetic field of a particular strength, which can be known exactly by controlling the amount of electricity flowing in and then using some well-established physical laws to calculate it. Using one of those old-timey perfume sprayers, he then aerosolized some oil into a little chamber above the field. As the droplets fall (due to gravity), they experience some drag due to air resistance. That effect can also be calculated, using what is called Stokes' Law. Once you subtract the effect of air resistance, you know how fast a drop would be falling if gravity were the only force involved. Millikan set up a microscope so that he could watch a single drop of oil fall and measure the time that it took.

In Millikan's set-up, there is a space below this chamber that contains two electrified metal plates (5,300 volts). These plates are set a certain distance apart, and the strength of the field can be calculated based on their voltage (V) and distance (d) from one another (V/d). The upper plate had a little hole in it, through which a single drop would sometimes fall. Once the drop was in between the plates, Millikan would turn on the electricity, causing the negatively charged drop to accelerate upward toward the positively charged metal plate. He would then measure the time that it took the drop to travel a given distance upward. Knowing the strength of the field, and having calculated the upward acceleration due to electromagnetic force, he could calculate the charge of the electron. Because a charged particle's acceleration is determined by the strength of its charge and the strength of the field it's in, Millikan could derive what the charge would *have to be* in order to accelerate the relevant amount in a field of that strength.

Before we look at the details of Broad and Wade's fraud accusations, there is some relevant historical context as well as some experimental niceties that deserve attention and emphasis. First, the historical context: why is he doing this? Two things had becoming increasingly clear to physicists at the end of the nineteenth century. The first was the existence of the electron, the discovery of which is normally credited to J.J. Thomson upon the publication of a series of papers in 1897–1899. Together, these papers seemed to provide convincing evidence that there was a particle that was responsible for electric charge. As Thomson put it at the end of his 1899 paper, indeed, it seems not improbable that this is the fundamental quantity in terms of which all electrical properties can be expressed. For, as we have seen, its mass and its charge are invariable, independent both of the processes by which the electrification is produced and of the gas from which the ions are set free. It thus possesses the characteristics of being a fundamental conception of electricity; and it seems desirable to adopt some view of electrical action which brings this conception into prominence (Thomson 1899, 565).[3]

The perception of this idea's plausibility among physicists, and of the theory of atoms themselves, would only grow with time.

The second bit of historical context relates to the quantum theory, which had also appeared during this period; Max Planck's 1900 paper, "On the Theory of the Energy Distribution Law of the Normal Spectrum" is taken to be the opening salvo.[4] This theory posited that energy exists in discrete units – *quanta* – and that the physical distribution of energy in a system could be modeled as a statistical distribution of these discrete units. The stability of the electron's mass and charge and its demonstrated role in electrical phenomena were exactly the kinds of things that we would expect to see if energy was bundled into little packets. In fact, in that 1900 paper, Planck provides a calculation for what we should expect for the charge of the electron, "the elementary quantum of electricity": 4.69×10^{-10} e.s.u.[5] (That number will be important later.) Each of these ideas became increasingly widespread and entrenched over the next decade, as a large group of physicists – giants like Einstein and Rutherford, for example – developed independent lines of investigation that all seemed to point in the direction of Thomson and Planck, and the community of physicists opposing the discrete theories of matter and energy shrank to a mostly ignorable periphery.

By the time Millikan began his inquiries into the charge of the electron in 1909, the view considered most plausible among physicists was that the electron was the particle responsible for electric charge, and that the amount of electricity in a charged body was just its number of electrons. Thus, the total charge of a body would be its number of electrons, multiplied by the charge of a single electron. That is, charge comes in *integral multiples* of the charge of a single electron, which does not change. Remember also that prior claims had been made concerning what the value of that charge actually was. Thomson himself had reported a value of 6.5×10^{-10} e.s.u.

---

[3] Quoted in Smith 1997, 27–28.
[4] Bain and Norton 2001, 454; Baggot 2011, 11–15.
[5] Planck 1900; reprinted in ter Haar 1967, 82–90. Quote is from p89 of this volume.

Knowing What Matters 81

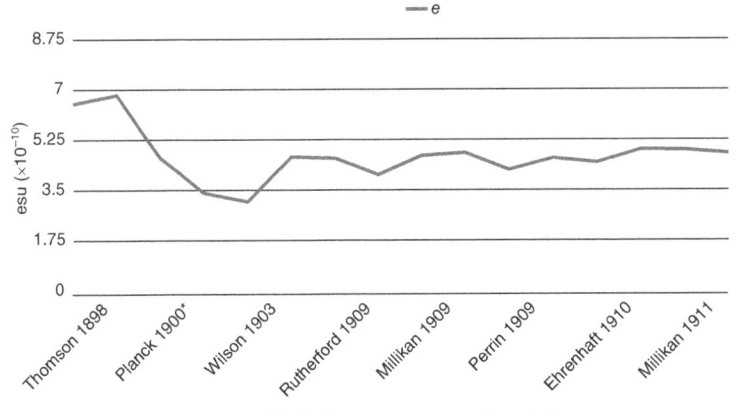

Figure 4.1 Published measurements of *e*, 1898–1911

back in 1898, followed by an updated measurement in 1899 of 6.8 × 10^{-10} e.s.u. In characteristic fashion, a decade of measurements performed by a large number of investigators began to exhibit an increasingly restricted range of observed values, facilitated by the refinement and updating of measurement techniques and the discovery of sources of systematic error. Millikan's final value of 4.774 × 10^{-10} e.s.u., reported in 1913 and retained after he had won the Nobel Prize ten years later, was dead on within the neighborhood of plausible values (Figure 4.1).

This is the background knowledge with which Millikan undertook his oil-drop experiments of 1910–1913. Although practitioners would not have regarded any of these matters as having achieved consensus, there would have been every expectation on the part of a rapidly growing majority that the electron's charge would eventually settle very close to the values that Millikan and others were reporting; Millikan's 1913 measurement was calculated to be accurate to within ±0.009 × 10^{-10} e.s.u. So plausible was this neighborhood of values, in fact, that Neils Bohr expressly assumed the value 4.7 × 10^{-10}, reported by Millikan in 1909, in developing his mathematical theory of the atom.[6] Similarly, members of the community would by and large have expected the mounting evidence in favor of discrete packaging of energy – and of the electron as an instance thereof – to continue to strengthen (which it did). Thus, it would have been natural and appropriate for Millikan to use this neighborhood hovering around 4.6–4.8 × 10^{-10} as a set of guardrails that could tell him whether his experiment was working properly; anyone in his position would have done this.

---

[6] Heilbron and Kuhn 1969, 206, n. 66.

Likewise, it would have been natural and appropriate to employ as an interpretive framework the idea that whatever charge he was measuring was some integer multiple of the charge of a single electron. Again, this would have been viewed as totally above board by the community.[7] These, in essence, were Millikan's guiding presuppositions, both of which would have been viewed as completely unproblematic by a growing majority of physicists – though, like everything else at the cutting edge of research, still tentative. As physicist and historian Gerald Holton put it, any alternative approach "would force one to turn one's back on a basic fact of nature – the integral character of e – which clearly beckoned" (Holton 1978, 210).

We now need to look at the actual running of the experiment itself, in order to gain a deeper understanding of the fraud accusations, as well as of the role of "knowledge of what matters" in Millikan's investigation. The first thing to note is the use of Stokes' Law to calculate the effect of air resistance on the acceleration of an oil drop as it descended through the chamber. Stokes' Law tells you that effect for a spherical particle of known radius through a fluid of known density. The first problem Millikan encountered was that the oil drops he was observing were so small that they tended to interact with the surrounding air as if it were made of other, solid particles, rather than as if they were moving through a homogeneous substance like swimming in a pool. Under these conditions, Stokes' Law would not give the correct estimate for the resistance experienced by a drop, which in turn compromised calculations for its effective downward acceleration. Since this latter quantity was essential for calculating the electron's charge (see above), there would have to be some way of correcting Stokes' Law such that it gave a reasonable estimate under these unusual conditions. Millikan included this corrected version of the Law along with experimental validation of its accuracy in his 1913 paper.

Hopefully the bewildering dimensionality of this experiment is starting to sink in. But remember that we haven't actually gotten to the running of the experiment itself, which is where most of the controversy lies. The above considerations, essentially the preamble of relevant physical theory, are a cakewalk compared to the delicacy of the actual measurements. The multitude of challenges that one would run into in the course of this experiment are well represented by commentary made in Millikan's

---

[7] Holton 1978; Niaz 2005. The exception, Felix Ehrenraft, was one of the few remaining holdouts who still subscribed to an anti-atomist philosophy. His dispute with Millikan has fueled the enduring fascination with this case.

lab notebooks. Some drops, for example, are too heavy, encountering relatively little air resistance and so falling too quickly to accurately measure their descent, thus complicating the amount of charge required to experience a specific upward acceleration in an electrical field of that strength. The rise and fall velocities of the drops themselves were measured by observing them through a microscope and timing their travel with an early twentieth-century stopwatch. Recall also that the drop's radius and spherical shape were required for the use of Stokes' Law, and reasonable estimates needed to be calculated or assumed – that is, they simply could not be measured. Holton (1978, 210) summarizes the obstacles, which are *characteristic of all experimental work*:

> Admittedly the integral character did not come through in every one of these runs, but that was to be expected. In real life, observations of this sort are beset by a number of difficulties, some more obscure than others; but one feels sure that eventually they can be explained and removed or dealt with by plausibility arguments. Millikan's notebooks record many different observations and hypotheses explaining "failed" runs: the battery voltages have dropped, manometer is air-locked, convection often interferes, the distance measurement may have to be recalibrated, the temperature of the room must be kept more constant, stopwatch errors occur, the atomizer is out of order.

Now, there is a mythology about scientific knowledge that it consists only of propositions that can be falsified through experiment. It should be readily apparent, however, that how that would actually work in the context of real experimental investigation is very far from clear. For these and other, equally if not more compelling reasons, historians and philosophers of science overwhelmingly reject both the relevance and coherence of the notion of falsifiability as a way of understanding the development and character of scientific knowledge.

Any given run of the experiment – each particular oil drop – faces an unwieldy arsenal of concerns when interpreting the results. For instance, if on a given run Millikan's calculations show the value of the charge to be 2.5×10^{-10} e.s.u., – way outside the neighborhood of plausible values as reported by others over more than a decade – what should he do? What *any* experimenter *would* do in these circumstances would be to assume that something had gone awry during that particular run of the experiment. Maybe there was a minute temperature change, maybe the stopwatch had some dust in the gears – who knows? A certain damagingly simplified view of science would demand that Millikan and the rest of the physics community rethink the consensus developing around the likely value of electron charge. But this is precisely why knowledge of what matters matters matters so much. As David Goodstein (2001, 57), one of a number of physicists who have examined Millikan's notebooks, observes, "What scientist familiar with the vagaries of cutting-edge experimental work would fault Millikan ..."?

> I don't think that any scientist, having studied Millikan's techniques and procedures for conducting this most demanding and difficult experiment, would fault him in any way for picking out what he considered to be his most dependable measurements in order to arrive at the most accurate possible result. (Goodstein 2000, 35)

It is easy for experimental scientists, traumatized by the self-inflicted torment of empirical inquiry, to see reflected in Millikan's procedure the exercise of his knowledge of what matters in the context of a particular run of the experiment. He is bringing the sensibility developed through his enormous experience, awareness of relevant research elsewhere, and routine exercise of raw talent, to intuitively gauge the reliability of this individual oil drop's drop for bearing on the question he is trying to answer. Realistically, any drop suggesting a value of 2.5×10^{-10} would probably not have been a difficult call; it would have been chucked out immediately: "a failed run — *or, effectively, no run at all*" in Holton's words (1978, 209; his emphasis). Broad and Wade are able to find fault with Millikan because they are not "familiar with the vagaries of cutting-edge experimental work." In point of fact, none of the *physicists* who examined Millikan's notebooks and compared them to his published work found any fault with his approach. Given their intimate knowledge of what matters in the context of experimental work, Millikan's discrimination against some drops and in favor of others made perfect sense.

4.2 Salience and the Demand for Explanation

The next step in our journey is to abstract away from the particulars of Millikan's oil-drop experiments to formulate a general characterization of knowledge of what matters. I will then use this characterization to illuminate the nature of humanistic knowledge in finer detail. Both the sciences and the humanities train practitioners to exercise refined judgments. The ability to exercise refined judgments rests on knowledge of what is worth paying attention to – knowledge of what matters. What is the nature of this knowledge, and how is it acquired? In this section, I argue that the notion of salience lies at the core of knowledge of what matters. Salience is the capacity of a property to stand out or grab our attention against a backdrop of uninteresting or unnoticeable humdrum. The ability to treat and to detect particular properties as salient constitutes a form of knowledge, one in which the humanities specialize. Without it, disciplinary inquiry in general would be less than futile. It would cease to exist.

In the case of Robert Millikan, we saw how, contrary to the "conventional portrait" of scientific knowledge, the ability to obtain meaningful results from his experiment required him to possess and exercise a kind of connoisseurship that allowed him to reliably differentiate between a failed run of the experiment – "effectively not a run" – and a run that had produced information that he could use to formulate a better understanding of nature. In what did his connoisseurship consist? Partly, it resided in his knowledge of developments that had occurred in his branch of physics in the last 10–15 years. To the extent that these developments exhibited some uniformity or directionality (which, as we've seen, they did), they formed the increasingly solid, uniform background from which a reasonably sized deviation would require explanation. Olenick et al. put it this way:

> He [Millikan] had a pretty clear idea of what the result ought to be— scientists almost always think they do when they set out to measure something ... it's actually a powerful bias to get the result he wants, because you can be sure that when he got a result he liked, he didn't search as hard to see what went right. But experiments must be done in that way. Without that kind of judgment, the journals would be full of mistakes, and we'd never get anywhere. (Olenick et al. 2008, 244; quoted in Niaz 2005, 698)

By "when he got a result he liked, he didn't search as hard to see what went right," they mean that when a result comported with background disciplinary knowledge, it did not stand out as in need of explanation. It was in the neighborhood of expectation, not a deviation that needed to be made sense of.

But, as we have seen, not every drop behaved in this way. When a drop fell too quickly, or exhibited some other unexpected properties, it stood out as requiring *some* kind of account. That account could even be something as general as "something wrong." Holton curates an amusing and instructive selection of comments in Millikan's notebooks (brackets represent date of recording):

> Very low Something wrong [11/18/1911]. Very low Something wrong [11/20/11]. This is almost exactly right & the best one I ever had!!! [12/20/11]. Possibly a double drop [1/26/12]. This seems to show clearly that the field is not exactly uniform, being stronger at the ends than in the middle [1/27/12]. Good one for very small one [2/3/12]. Exactly right [2/3/12]. Something the matter.... [2/ 13/12]. Agreement poor. Will not work out [2/17/12]. Publish

this Beautiful one.... [2/24/12]. BEAUTY one of the very best [2/27/12]. Perhaps Publish [2/27/12]. Excellent [3/1/12]. This drop flickered as tho unsymmetrical [3/2/12]. (quoted in Holton 1978, 212)

The main thing to notice here is that deviations from expectation – expectations derived from loads of experience and acquaintance with professional literature – issue a demand for explanation: "Something wrong"; "Something the matter"; "This drop flickered as tho unsymmetrical." By contrast, we generally don't see him saying "this went well, for some reason," or "bizarrely accurate" – except in the case where he says, "Good one for very small one," suggesting that drops of that size don't normally go that well. In all cases, a question arises only in the context where some event stands out. This capacity to stand out as worthy of attention or explanation is what I'll call salience.

Whence come the background expectations against which certain things stand out as salient? I have already remarked on the source of Millikan's background expectations – the evolving state of disciplinary knowledge and his experience with precision experimentation. His case in fact points the way toward a more general understanding of how the sense of salience develops in disciplinary contexts. This process appears to have two components, which the Millikan example suggests are not easily separated. The first is a set of expectations for what certain aspects of one's domain of research are normally or probably like, such as are derived from disciplinary training combined with an ongoing acquaintance with developments in one's field. These are the sorts of expectations that gave Millikan a sense of when something was "very low something wrong." There is no precise threshold that defines such a state. There is only the professionally developed sense of the range of "reasonable agreement," outside of which certain qualities stand out as salient. The second component is the set of background expectations formed on the basis of one's own professional experience. In addition to his expectations of certain values of charge, Millikan's sense that there was "something wrong" would have been honed partly through his prior experience with experiments in general and with that experimental set-up in particular. How, for instance, does he form the judgment "Good one for very small one"? After watching many, many drops through his microscope, he has acquired a sense of how large a drop tends to be when the experiment works as needed – that is, when it avoids a failed run. He is not measuring the size of these drops. "Very small" just means "looks very small compared to the typical useful drop." He is eyeballing it, the same way he is eyeballing "reasonable agreement." If we accept the testimony of the physicists who investigated Millikan's case, rather than the testimony of our cultural burlesque of scientific knowledge, the exercise of this kind of judgment is completely unavoidable in science. Now, if I was doing the oil-drop experiment, that would be cause for concern. I have no background in science, or in experimentation of any kind. The closest I ever got to an experiment was putting some plastic on a hot burner of an electric stove (I was like twenty when I did this). I would not be a good candidate for eyeballing oil drops, because I lack the requisite experience and disciplinary knowledge that give rise to background expectations against which certain phenomena can appear salient.

Two episodes in the history of science provide glimpses of how this sense of salience is acquired over time, each of which highlights the particular role of one of the components of the process (disciplinary knowledge and experience). The telescope was first used by Galileo for astronomical purposes in 1609. Uranus, officially declared a planet in 1781, was the first planet discovered using a telescope. (The six planets known up until then had been known since antiquity, being observable with the naked eye.) After nearly two hundred years of telescopic observation, only one measly planet. Following that, however, astronomers using conventional telescopes went on to discover some twenty more planets in the first half of the nineteenth century. Apparently, the discovery of a new planet opened up the possibility that there were more planets out there, which, in turn, caused astronomers' background expectations to shift in a way that made previously unnoticed phenomena salient – a "paradigm-induced change in scientific perception," as Kuhn described it (Kuhn 1962, 116). By way of amplification, Kuhn also refers to the fact that early modern astronomers, committed to the Aristotelian notion of the immutable celestial sphere, recorded the first sighting of a new star in 1576 – less than fifty years after the publication of Copernicus's book. By contrast, Chinese astronomers,

> whose cosmological beliefs did not preclude celestial change, had recorded the appearance of many new stars in the heavens at a much earlier date. Also, even without the aid of a telescope, the Chinese had systematically recorded the appearance of sunspots centuries before these were seen by Galileo and his contemporaries. Nor were sunspots and a new star the only examples of celestial change to emerge in the heavens of Western astronomy immediately after Copernicus. Using traditional instruments, some as simple as a piece of thread, late sixteenth-century astronomers repeatedly discovered that comets wandered at will through the space previously reserved for the immutable planets and stars. (Kuhn 1962, 116–117)

What Kuhn wants us to see in this vignette is the effect of theoretical expectations on astronomers' sense of salience.[8] As those expectations changed, astronomers' sensitivity to particular stimuli underwent a related shift.

The other example, an illustration of the changes in salience effected by hands-on experience, bears a coincidental relation to Millikan. Carl Anderson, Millikan's student at Cal Tech, won the Nobel Prize for physics in 1936 for his discovery of the positron. The research that led to this discovery involved taking photographs of particles making tracks in a bubble chamber. When Anderson first looked at these photographs, he had no idea what the tracks were. But after five years of looking at scores of such photographs, he was able to differentiate between different kinds of particles based on the appearance of their tracks, as well as (like his mentor) intuitively distinguish between an informative photograph and a noisy, useless one – "a failed run." Using the photographs he judged to be informative, Anderson was able to convincingly argue that they constituted confirmed observations of the positron (Galison 1987). Kuhn (1962, 111) comments on this phenomenon as well:

> Looking at a bubble-chamber photograph, the student sees confused and broken lines, the physicist a record of familiar subnuclear events. Only after a number of such transformations of vision does the student become an inhabitant of the scientist's world, seeing what the scientist sees and responding as the scientist does.

In both cases, we see clear illustrations of the propensity of specialized experience and disciplinary communication to induce changes in the sorts of properties that stand out to practitioners. Each of them contributes something distinctive to practitioners' demand that certain phenomena are worthy of explanation and attention. In the case of astronomy, specific changes in the distribution of scientific opinion led to changes in what was understood to be a theoretically plausible interpretation of experience. These changes, in turn, resulted in a newly acquired awareness of properties that bore directly on the revised understanding of theoretical plausibility. In the case of the positron, years of experience with the same set-up looking at the same phenomena gave Anderson a sharpened sense of perception, allowing him to see features and distinctions in his photographs that would have been unnoticeable to the uninitiated. In both instances, the probative power of the technology – cloud chamber or

---

[8] Actually, he wants us to see something much stronger: "The very ease and rapidity with which astronomers saw new things when looking at old objects with old instruments may make us wish to say that, after Copernicus, astronomers lived in a different world" (Kuhn 1962, 117).

telescope – depended on practitioners acquiring a sense of the salience of certain properties, which the new technology would then allow them to explore.

Each mode of sense acquisition corresponds to a well-known variety of scientific progress: (1) the opening up of a new domain of inquiry, followed by (2) the gradual refinement in the quality of our judgment in that domain. I now wish to draw attention to the way in which a shared sense of salience lies at the heart of disciplinary knowledge and drives its development. The argument for this thesis is fairly straightforward, and has to an extent already been made. I used the examples of Millikan, astronomy, and the positron to illustrate the manner in which features that stand out as salient to a researcher call out for some kind of explanation. This phenomenon can also be found in mathematics, where the salience of a theorem's symmetry or unity prompts mathematicians to seek *other* proofs of that same theorem, proofs that they take to be more explanatory.[9] This suggests that, when researchers share a sense of salience in a given domain, they will share a sense of what in that domain stands out as worthy of explanation. Think about the last time you had some kind of imaging done – X-ray, ultrasound, MRI, whatever. There are features of those images that will stand out to a radiologist but not to you. She might see something concerning, something that lies outside the normal range of manifestation for that part of the body. Or something that should not be there altogether, like a lawn dart.[10] These features of the image cry out to her for explanation. But of course you'll want a second opinion. Having "done your own research," you've since learned that perfectly normal anatomical conditions can sometimes be mistaken for lawn darts in an X-ray. Unfortunately, Radiologist #2 also instantly recognizes the classic metal dart-like manifestation of the lawn dart.

What sort of reasoning lies behind the search for a second opinion? It must go something like this: "Certain features of the X-ray stand out as salient to Radiologist #1; she believes they warrant further attention and explanation. Radiologist #2 is also trained to examine X-rays. If something on the X-ray demands explanation, it will also stand out as salient to Radiologist #2." We recognize that there are certain features of images that

---

[9] Lange 2014, 2015. Ording 2019 introduces the non-specialist to this practice through a tour of 99 proofs of the same theorem.

[10] Lawn darts was an outdoor game in which you fling a sharp heavy object into the air and allow it to land dart-first some distance away, enormously popular when I was growing up until a bunch of people predictably impaled themselves. Lawn darts shouldn't just not be in your body; they should not exist.

radiology as a discipline has deemed to be particularly worthy of scrutiny. We also recognize that radiologists are specifically trained to notice these features, that the whole point of becoming a radiologist is to be able to notice these attention-demanding features. The radiologist is immediately aware of these features because, in contrast to people without her training, they stand out as salient for *her*. This sense of salience is her knowledge of what matters. Because radiologists share this sense of salience, they tend to form overlapping opinions as to which features of an image require further attention and explanation. They share a knowledge of what matters.

This shared knowledge of what matters, embodied in a cultivated sense of the salience of certain features, is what separates experts from the rest of us. It is how experts are able to effectively communicate with one another on the esoteric matters that fall within their purview. In one of the most profound insights in twentieth-century nonfiction, Kuhn observes:

> No period between remote antiquity and the end of the seventeenth century exhibited a single generally accepted view about the nature of light. Instead there were a number of competing schools and sub-schools, most of them espousing one variant or another of Epicurean, Aristotelian, or Platonic theory ... Each of the corresponding schools derived strength from its relation to some particular metaphysic, and each emphasized, as paradigmatic observations, the particular cluster of optical phenomena that its own theory could do most to explain. Other observations were dealt with by *ad hoc* elaborations, or they remained as outstanding problems for further research.
>
> At various times all these schools made significant contributions to the body of concepts, phenomena, and techniques from which Newton drew the first nearly uniformly accepted paradigm for physical optics. Any definition of the scientist that excludes at least the more creative members of these various schools will exclude their modern successors as well. Those men were scientists. Yet anyone examining a survey of physical optics before Newton may well conclude that, though the field's practitioners were scientists, the net result of their activity was something less than science. Being able to take no common body of belief for granted, each writer on physical optics felt forced to build his field anew from its foundations. In doing so, his choice of supporting observation and experiment was relatively free, for there was no standard set of methods or of phenomena that every optical writer felt forced to employ and explain. Under these circumstances, the dialogue of the resulting books was often directed as much to the members of other schools as it was to nature. (Kuhn 1962, 12–13)

A shared sense of what matters is the common foundation upon which deeper and more refined levels of understanding are achieved. In short, it is what makes disciplinary knowledge possible. And it is by no means confined to the natural sciences.

4.3 Knowledge of What Matters in the Humanities

At the center of a number of accounts of aesthetic education is the development of a capacity to notice features of a work of art or literature that enable the ascent to higher planes of reflection and appreciation. The development of this capacity occurs through tutored experience in which a master (critic) draws a student's attention to certain features that are of particular significance in understanding a given creative work. Macdonald (1954, 127), for example, argues that the duty of the art or literary critic is to guide us to "what is not obvious to casual or uninstructed inspection." In similar fashion, Hampshire (1954, 165) argues that, "The greatest service of the critic" is to bring to our attention "particular features of the particular object which *make* it ugly or beautiful" because it is "difficult to see and hear all that there is to see and hear."[11] In line with these observations, Sibley (1959, 442) remarks that

> We may simply mention or point out non-aesthetic features: "Notice these flecks of color, that dark mass there, those lines." By merely drawing attention to those easily discernible features which make the painting luminous or warm or dynamic, we often succeed in bringing someone to see these aesthetic qualities … In mentioning features which may be discerned by anyone with normal eyes, ears, and intelligence, *we are singling out what may serve as a kind of key to grasping or seeing something else* (and the key may not be the same for each person). [Emphasis added]

Beyond this, "[r]epetition and reiteration often play an important role," and the critic will "make use of contrasts, comparisons, and reminiscences" as he points to certain features, all as a way of raising the profile of those features for the student in an attempt to make them stand out against the background of the rest of the work. By repeatedly drawing attention to the same features, or same kinds of features, the critic endows them with a significance that they would not have had otherwise. And by bringing in contrasts and comparisons that connect with "the known sensitivity, susceptibilities, and experience" of the student, the critic adds greater definition to the features in question, allowing them to be more clearly perceived relative to features of lesser significance. These latter aspects of the work fade further and further into the background as the student becomes more attuned to the features that matter.

Drawing on this well-established tradition, Clune (2021) argues that the capacity to discern such features is the substance of expertise in art and

---

[11] Macdonald 1954 and Hampshire 1954 are both quoted in Sibley 1959. Sibley is quoted in Clune 2021.

literary criticism. Here is how he describes the phenomenon in reference to the capacity to read a literary work in historical perspective:

> By internalizing, for instance, the history of twentieth-century America, certain features of a text show up for the expert as possessing a salience in terms of that history. The reader becomes aware of this knowledge through the identification of the feature. Thus, *knowledge creates a background against which certain aspects of a work appear in distinctive ways.* They would not appear this way for people ignorant of the history. But neither would they appear this way to people who know the history but have not learned how to internalize it as a means of transforming and extending their perception of a literary work. (Clune 2021, 85; emphasis added)

Background knowledge of American history is to the expert on American literature what background knowledge of previous measurements of the electron's charge was to Millikan. In the latter case, that knowledge was what allowed him to see measurements in a certain neighborhood as unremarkable, and measurements outside that neighborhood as requiring some kind of explanation. In the literature expert's case, some aspects of the text possess a relatively low resonance, reflecting as they do the prevailing literary norms of their time. Other aspects, however, profit from this subdued background presence by gaining salience through their departure from it. The two states – background and salience – are inextricably linked. Without most features receding into the background, neither the scientist, nor the critic, nor the literary historian has any bearings for distinguishing the importance of some features from the unimportance of others. The expert uses her sense of salience as the principal guide to that which is worthy of explanation. The possession of a capacity to see important features as salient against a mostly ignorable background is what defines someone as an expert.

As in the natural sciences, norms that govern what matters in a discipline emerge when – and *only* when – humanists possess a *shared* sense of salience, when each individual's capacity for foregrounding certain features as particularly worthy of explanation functions in more or less the same way. In either context, a shared sense of what demands attention is required in order for scholars to engage in the esoteric forms of communication that distinguish groups of scholars as disciplinary communities, and that, more importantly, allow them to develop more refined states of understanding. Just like Kuhn's pre-paradigm scientists, the absence of a shared sense of salience among critics "produces a morass" (Kuhn 1962, 16). Without it, the aesthetic investigations of individual scholars will tend to diverge to whatever degree their interests do, as the features demanding an explanation in one scholar's view constitute part of another's background. Because there is no commonly held conception of the distinction between a fact and a *mere* fact, no specific range of scholarly attention seems particularly warranted. "No wonder, then" he writes, "that in the early stages of the development of any science different men confronting the same range of phenomena, but not usually all the same particular phenomena, describe and interpret them in different ways" (Kuhn 1962, 17).

But with general scholarly agreement regarding what demands explanation and what can be profitably ignored, scholars can work toward a *better* understanding of the meaning or significance of a work. Echoing Hume in "Of the Standard of Taste," Clune (2021, 96) writes, "the standard of value is the consensus of qualified critics." Communicating with each other through the language of scholarly thought, scholars can debate more precisely about what it is that makes *this* line of the poem so beautiful, or what makes *that* part of a biographical sketch so enchanting or endearing. In Clune's words,

> Consensus in literary studies refers less to a singular decision than to a spectrum. On one end lies broad or even tacit acceptance of some truth or judgment. At the other extreme lies the half-formulated preference of an individual professor. Between these extremes lies a field vital with tensions, dynamic with disagreements, and connected by a shared sense of what is required to make a judgment and interpretation public and present to the expert community. A judgment that achieves this public status, that places itself before the eyes of other experts for argument and evaluation, participates in the collective process of expert judgment. (Clune 2021, 95)

When that which stands out to one stands out to all, the community frees itself from very general disputes about what matters, about value, and about valid judgment. Naturally, this does not shut down all scholarly debate; that is neither possible nor desirable. What it does is provide the scholarly community with shared criteria for judgment, criteria against which the community can, through debate made coherent by the ability to make reference to some commonly held normative standards, measure the caliber of individual scholarly efforts as community-wide inquiry moves toward the elaboration of disciplinary knowledge.

Of course, it is possible for scholars to talk past one another, but those mostly futile discussions are often reflective of a lack convergence among scholars regarding what requires explanation, what constitutes a valid argument, and so forth. While this may sound like a familiar description of some of the more vexed humanities disciplines today, it is certainly not "just part of what it is to engage in humanistic inquiry." Nor is it a condition to which only humanities disciplines are susceptible. Such circumstances are familiar to anyone acquainted with transitional periods in the history of the natural sciences, of mathematics, and of formal logic. The entire seventeenth century stands as a monument to this phenomenon in the natural sciences. What's that? Modern science had not quite solidified yet? Fair enough, but let us observe two points in response. First, the foment of modern science itself is precisely the sort of transition that needs to be borne in mind, being as it was partly a transition in conceptions of what constitutes a valid interpretation of natural phenomena.[12] Second, the natural sciences in modern times are by no means immune to such scenarios as debates over what qualifies as a valid argument, or which phenomena are in particular need of explanation. Indeed, it is often the most "rigorous" sciences that experience these events most acutely. But don't take my word for it. Next time you get a chance, try eavesdropping on an argument between dark matter theorists and partisans of the Modified Newtonian Dynamics (MOND). Or between conservation biologists and invertebrate paleontologists over whether we are currently experiencing a mass extinction event. These are debates which no empirical advance seems to be able to settle. The absence of consensus does not merely amount to a diversity of plausible opinions, but to the absence of facts altogether concerning what constitutes a valid scholarly interpretation.

Hume's community-centered account of the standard of value in aesthetic interpretation is of a piece with his approach to the more general problem of how inductive inferences can be justified. This approach – or, at least, Nelson Goodman's (1954) reading of it – holds that inductive inferences are justified when they conform to the accepted norms of inductive practice. Could matters possibly be otherwise? Surely no moderately reflective person would be tempted to respond, "No. Inductive inferences are justified when their p-value reaches 0.05." Even if we grant the dubious notion that this is what justifies an inductive inference in our time, are we actually supposed to believe that no inductive inferences were justified before we started calculating p-values? The 0.05 significance level is an accepted norm of inductive practice. It has not always been. Nor will it always be. Perhaps the sciences will move *en masse* toward a more restrictive threshold. Or perhaps they'll loosen the reins a bit, as we did during the Scientific Revolution when it became generally accepted that

---

[12] In a nearly inexhaustible literature attesting to this historical fact, Joy 2006 stands out as exemplary (in my opinion).

demonstrative certainty was far too demanding a standard for knowledge (see, e.g., Harrison 2007, chapter 3).

Like the norms governing acceptable inductive practice, those governing what matters in a discipline are subject to change. This kind of change characteristically involves changes in what sorts of features demand explanation, be they features of nature, features of a work of art or literature, or – as I argue below – features of concepts themselves. In science, Kuhn argued, these changes are accompanied by a "shift in vision," such as occurred after the discovery of Uranus, in which aspects of nature previously rendered as invisible background take on a high degree of salience. Likewise, Clune (2021) diagnoses the current state of literary studies as undergoing a related shift – specifically, a shift in what scholars take to be the aesthetic criteria by which a work ought to be judged. When disciplines are in the process of such a shift, we *expect* certain debates to be irresolvable. As I argued in Chapter 3, disciplinary consensus fixes the facts concerning which norms are operative at a given time; in the absence of consensus, there are no facts of the matter regarding what matters. But outside of such periods, we tend to see humanities disciplines debating productively, developing nascent ideas, refining those that have been historically stable, and gradually shifting the balance of scholarly thought toward some views and away from others. Indeed, Bod (2013) documents precisely this tendency as he surveys the history of a wide variety of humanities disciplines. This developmental pattern is the characteristic one exhibited by natural sciences during periods in which widely shared norms and priorities cause practitioners to behave as a coherent group – not out of a desire to cooperate, but simply due to the overlapping concerns of individuals (the same kind of thing that causes rush hour).

My goal in this section has been to characterize an important species of disciplinary knowledge – "knowledge of what matters" – through the idea of a capacity to see certain features of a phenomenon as salient. Understanding the essential importance of knowledge of what matters across all disciplines has required us to look more closely than is customary at the details of practice across both the natural sciences and the humanities. The natural sciences could not conceivably function without substantial overlap among practitioners in the sorts of features of nature, of investigation, or of inference that stand out as salient. In my account, it is this shared sense of salience among practitioners and the way in which that overlap facilitates further inquiry that qualifies it as a species of knowledge. While this shared sense of salience has long been a widely appreciated dimension of humanistic inquiry, its status as knowledge has, I believe, been occluded by a woefully inadequate epistemology of science that has proven to be as seductive as it is resilient.

4.4 Exemplification and the Emergence of Salience

I want to conclude this chapter by arguing for a particular set of claims regarding how a scholarly sense of salience is acquired. I then want to draw out some of the implications of that set of claims for broader issues surrounding disciplinary knowledge. A key part of my argument is that the scholarly sense of salience – the knowledge of what matters in a discipline – is derived from exemplars. Accordingly, in this final section I give an account of how a sense of salience is acquired through exposure to exemplars. In line with the preceding discussion, a central component of this account will rest on how exposure to exemplars explains the role of salience in motivating the demand for explanation, that high-octane brand of intellectual curiosity that drives the development of inquiry in all disciplines.

In the last chapter, I argued that canonical texts get canonized on account of their unique capacity to impart an understanding of a discipline's intellectual values. Here I provide more detail on how this actually works, adding more support for my bold assertion that the substance of these values can only be learned through exemplification. If that bold assertion turns out to be correct, the conclusion that disciplinary knowledge requires exemplars will be unavoidable.

4.4.1 How to Exemplify

Does this book exemplify what can be done in an attic? That's where most of it was written. Yet, somehow that fact seems incidental to both it and attics. Surely it does not exemplify what can be done with a stub pen. Even though it *could* have been done with a stub pen, it was *in fact* done on a computer.[13]

Why doesn't this book exemplify what can be done in an attic, given that it was done in an attic? I think there are two plausible answers to this question, each of which gives us insight into the nature of exemplification. One answer is that the book fails to draw sufficient attention to its possession of the sorts of qualities that really give us a sense of what it is like to do

---

[13] I borrow the "stub pen" example from Goodman 1968.

something in an attic. Maybe the prose isn't quite the way it needs to be, or perhaps it covers the wrong themes. Could it be that the organization of the book simply lacks that "done in an attic" sort of feel? Those proposals have a strange ring to them, which the other of the two plausible answers helps to explain. That other plausible answer holds that the reason this book fails to exemplify what can be done in an attic is because the concept *done in an attic* is not something that holds any meaning for us. Plainly, there *is* nothing that being done in an attic is like. The book lacks a "done in an attic" feel because there is no such feel in the first place. It can't exemplify a quality that doesn't exist. To say that the book's prose isn't quite the way it needs to be in order to exemplify being done in an attic has a strange ring to it because there isn't any way the prose *could* be that *would* allow it to exemplify being done in an attic. There's just nothing like doing it in an attic. To put it another way, there is no distinguishing set of features to which the term "done in an attic" refers (beyond the trivial ones of being done in an attic).

Even when there is a distinguishing set of features – an "essence," if you will – mere possession of them will not always be sufficient to allow an object to exemplify those features. According to the movie *Zoolander*, wetness is the essence of moisture. But (I daresay), a wet diaper does not exemplify moisture simply because it is wet. Being a man is arguably part of my essence. At least in normal contexts, though, I do not *exemplify* what it is to be a man. I mean, I'm OK and everything. But do I have what it takes to be the standard-bearer for men as a class? I don't think so. That heady honor is reserved for Mr. Tom Selleck. Unambiguously belonging to a class – you know, the way I unambiguously belong in the class *man* – does not thereby grant an object the status of exemplar. This principle is easy enough to appreciate in the case of Haufe v. Selleck. It makes all the more sense in the context of highly artificial properties like "done in an attic," where it becomes difficult to form a conception of what it would even take to qualify – or *fail* to qualify – as an exemplar. Raccoon fighting is definitely the kind of thing that can be done in an attic. But so is raccoon peacemaking.

There is a third, relatively straightforward kind of failure. For all its many virtues, moisture does not seem to be something this book is capable of exemplifying. It's not even a *little* wet (it better not be!). Similarly, there seems to be a class of objects that could never be candidates for exemplifying *green* – viz., the class of objects that are not green. No nongreen object, no matter how flashy or memorable, could ever hope to exemplify green. Such an unfortunate object could, of course, bring the idea of green to the front of one's mind; I imagine all of this green/not green conversation has you pretty fixated on greenness. But neither that conversation nor our steamy conversation about moisture *exemplifies* the properties on which it is focusing. Merely referring to those properties is not enough.

These exemplification-fails have brought into sharp relief the two dominant criteria that seem to govern exemplification: possession and reference (Goodman 1968). This most recent failure was a result of a lack of *possession*: an exemplar *possesses* the property it exemplifies. There's a very good reason that all nongreen objects fail to exemplify *green*: they're constitutionally incapable of exemplifying green. Likewise, there's a set of remote possible worlds in which this book exemplifies moisture, but they all involve degrees of saturation that are too shocking to contemplate. Prior to failures of possession, we witnessed some stunning failures of *reference*. I do not exemplify the property of being a man, although I do possess that property. My problem is that I'm just not *enough* of a man for my presence to bring the category "man" to the front of one's mind. There's something about my unenviable degree of masculinity that prevents me (the object) from functioning as a *symbol* of masculinity – that is, from functioning as an indication that there is an entire class of objects like me, composed only of things in possession of the same manly essence. Only a sufficiently virile man – a man like Selleck with a weapons-grade mustache made from the baleen of a humpback whale – is man enough to inspire reflection on the elements of manliness itself, on what it means to be a member of this distinguished guild. He's more than just a man; he's a symbol that stands as a monument to the very existence of man itself.

The way to render more precise the relevant difference between me and Selleck is in terms of salience. Whatever qualities make a man, both Selleck and I have them. But the way in which he has them seems to accentuate their salience to a degree that is simply out of my reach. I have a mustache, but it's not weapons-grade. I'm taller than average, but I'm much closer to the mean than Selleck's statistically freakish 6'4". I'm a serious guy, but I'm also known for a certain *joie de vivre*, a certain knuckle-headery, that prevents me from exhibiting the strong, penetrating silence with which Selleck carries himself. We're both from Michigan, but he's from *Detroit*. I've ridden a horse; Selleck's got his own ranch. Each of the qualities that contributes to my overall masculinity score is a quality that Selleck has in noticeable abundance. His masculine qualities are salient in a way that mine simply aren't. This is why he's an exemplar of manliness, and I'm ... well, not that. His possession of manly qualities qualifies him for man-membership. But the *salience* of those qualities endows Selleck with powers of reference that transcend his individual manliness. That salience is responsible for converting Selleck, *the man*, into Selleck, *the symbol*. He's a spokesman for the National Rifle Association, for crying out loud. The closest I've ever gotten to a gun was the time I handled an Uzi belonging to a local dentist (I was 12). Exemplification is possession plus reference. Reference occurs when the qualities that matter for class membership are possessed with a salience that borders on unseemly.

4.4.2   Essence and Exemplification

We've listed a number of ways in which Selleck and I differ, differences that contribute to his iconic status. Each time we add an item to this list, we are given more insight into why Selleck exemplifies manliness, why I am deficient as a man, and what manliness itself consists of. The list could go on and on. Could it go on long enough for us to finally capture the essence of manliness? My guess is that no list of qualities that contribute to manliness could ever achieve general assent as exhaustive of what it means to be a man. That's not just because manliness is a contested notion. The range of plausible interpretations of manliness is wider than it's probably ever been, but even when or where it was oppressively narrow, I wager that no such list could have garnered consensus. Nor is it because the property of manliness has no essential qualities, in the way that the property of being done in an attic has no essential qualities. We are able to debate aspects of manliness precisely because that idea *does* have some meaning. By contrast, only philosophers or my teenage son could convince themselves that it is possible to have a meaningful debate on the topic of what it is like for something to be done in an attic.[14]

Rather, I'd like to argue that it is because there are *aspects of manliness that cannot be articulated*. There is some content to the concept of manliness; no one familiar with Haufe v. Selleck could deny that. This is content of which any competent English speaker has some understanding. But we understand more about manliness than we can say. Indeed, it is more than a little plausible to think that some of the people who understand it best are not among those who can best articulate it. At my grandfather's funeral, my father credited him (not Tom Selleck) with teaching him what it meant to be a man. I suspect that is at least partly true. But although

---

[14] In fact, after reading the claim about attic essences, my teenage son confessed to having felt the urge to argue about whether attics have essential qualities.

my grandfather was a very smart man, I have my doubts as to whether he ever explained manliness to his son. I also have my doubts as to whether he *could* have explained it. For one thing, he wasn't the sort of person who would have developed a fine-grained articulation of manliness. More importantly, though, he would have inevitably run into the problem I mentioned above – viz., that there is no such explanation to be had. But, of course, he wouldn't have needed a fine-grained articulation in order for my father to have learned the concept from him. In fact, the whole point of that eulogy was for my father to express how he had learned about certain qualities of manliness through my grandfather's *exemplification* of them. My grandfather was not an icon of masculinity by traditional or contemporary standards. He did not have Selleck's stoicism. He once became highly emotional in the packed hotel restaurant where he and I were having breakfast together (also when I was 12. That was a weird year.).

From my father's experience, however, there were certain features of my grandfather's character that, in retrospect, corresponded to my father's interpretation of manliness. He acquired his understanding of those features through my grandfather's exemplification of them. Much later, my father was able to articulate some of that understanding. In search of ways to honor his father, he began to see aspects of my grandfather's character not just as bits of personality, but as instances of a class of features that contributed to his own conception of manliness. Some of these aspects, like patience, were highly salient features of my grandfather's personality. Others, like his liberation of concentration camps in Nazi Germany, he rarely discussed. From my father's perspective, those features were part of what made my grandfather exemplary as a man. It's not an accident that some of the more subdued or bizarre features of my grandfather's personality did not make it on my father's list of manly qualities. Neither the subdued nor the bizarre are good candidates for contributing to an object's capacity to exemplify, in that neither sort of feature tends to endow an object with the power to refer to a class that denotes it. Subdued features tend to lack salience (unless they're so subdued that their muteness is itself noteworthy), and bizarre features tend to fall outside those denoted by a class; that's part of what makes them bizarre. My grandfather wore plaid polyester pants. He wore them waist-high. This practice is not one we typically associate with manliness *per se* (although it definitely exemplifies *something*). It would have made no sense for my father to say, "In wearing waist-high plaid polyester pants, my dad taught me what it meant to be a man." No, only features of my grandfather's personality that were both salient and fell within the purview of manliness stood out as candidates for ways in which my grandfather exemplified manliness, because it is only such features that can endow an object with the capacity to function as a *symbol* of manliness.

It's important to appreciate that the quality of manliness is hardly distinctive in this regard. Yes: manliness is woolly, it's contested, it's unstable. All of that contributes to the lack of explicit consensus regarding what it is. But it does not *explain* that lack of consensus. Even for much more well-behaved predicates, a list of necessary and sufficient conditions will always be susceptible to challenges. That perennial susceptibility is often interpreted as evidence of a metaphysical mistake; if there are no necessary and sufficient conditions, the predicate must not denote anything real. But should we really conclude that, say, because of an absence of consensus on how to articulate the nature of a human being, that human beings aren't real? Why would we? Why pin our metaphysical hopes on whether we can articulate such conditions? We might instead conclude that there are aspects of the concept *human being* that can't be articulated. Human beings exemplify what it is to be a human being. We acquire our understanding of that concept through exposure to exemplary human beings (human beings like a certain Mr. Tom Selleck). We do our best to articulate the content of that concept. Some of those articulations gain wide and stable acceptance. The more precise and detailed they are, the more confidence we develop in them. And yet, just as surely, that detail and precision is what eventually allows us to see that a given articulation is flawed. As erudite scholarly debate works to refine our grasp of the meaning of *human being*, that same activity inevitably produces challenges to an increasingly fine-grained understanding. Admittedly, some of those challenges can be so acute as to shake our confidence in the reality of the category. But we also need to be honest about the fact that we know more than we can say, and we need to be open to the possibility that our failure to articulate the necessary and sufficient conditions for *human being* or *manliness* or anything else is a symptom of that inarticulable "tacit" knowledge, rather than some metaphysical disease.

Whether our focus is on nature, arts and literature, or history and philosophy, our attempts to articulate which qualities in particular an exemplar exemplifies unavoidably amplify the salience of those qualities, increasing the demand for their attention and explanation. We described above how J. J. Thomson's investigations with cathode rays led to his discovery of a "corpuscle," which he pointedly observed as having the highly salient quality of a stable mass-to-charge ratio. For physicists in Thomson's community, a stable mass-to-charge ratio would have been salient because of the way in which it strongly suggests the presence of a fundamental particle: every increase in the quantity of matter produces a precisely commensurate increase in quantity of charge. It's about as close to a smoking gun as one could get in 1897. The singling out of this mass-to-charge ratio as particularly significant rapidly led to independent investigations of the alleged particle's mass as well as its charge. Millikan, as we saw, was a prolific contributor to the latter set of investigations. These investigations continue right up to the present day; a consensus report on the charge of the electron was released as recently as 2018 (Newell et al. 2018).

As our ability to articulate the electron's essential properties reaches untold degrees of precision, the salience of those properties seems only to increase, intensifying the demand for explanation. Our measurements of those properties, and of analogous properties for other fundamental particles, are the most precise measurements ever made. *And* they are in reasonable agreement with the values predicted by physical theory. But some people, like the late Nobel laureate Steven Weinberg, are just impossible to please. In an event at Case Western Reserve University in 2018 "celebrating" the 50th anniversary of the Standard Model of particle physics, Weinberg complained that the Standard Model must be incomplete because it does not *explain why* the properties of the fundamental particles have the values they do. To me, this is kind of an odd complaint to make. There have to be some facts that are just brute facts. Facts about fundamental constituents of matter seem like good candidates for brute facts, don't they? I mean, at least as far as concerns the material universe. Specifically, what I'm incapable of grasping, and what Weinberg felt acutely, is how the complete lack of ambiguity surrounding certain features of the fundamental particles beckons the physicist – *taunts* him – to understand why those features are the way that they are. The finer-grained our articulations of those features become, the more salient they become. The more salient they become, the louder they cry out for explanation. It's not a cry that I can hear, because it is broadcast at a frequency to which only theoretical particle physicists and a few other masochists are attuned. But I recognize the symptoms; you don't need to be able to hear a dog whistle to know when it's being blown.

This familiar pattern is not unique to the natural sciences. We can see it manifest, for instance, in the reception of Rawls' *A Theory of Justice*. Recall that this is one of Gutting's instances of "what philosophers know." The wellspring that drives much of Rawls's argument is the Veil of Ignorance, a thought experiment in which we are to imagine the deliberations of parties who are designing institutions for a society to which they belong but in which they do not yet know their circumstances. They are as if behind a veil, a veil of ignorance. (So, yes, it's aptly named.) When the design of institutions is set, the veil is lifted, and the parties get to find out if they are rich or poor, clever or dim, healthy or sick, etc. Rawls argued that the deliberations of these ignorant parties would be dominated by a principle of rational choice known as *maximin*, meaning that they would – as something like a bet-hedging strategy – make sure that the worst-case scenario in the society was still pretty good (they will "maximize the minimum" state of well-being).

Twenty-three years later, I can still remember the exact moment I was introduced to this thought experiment. I remember where I was sitting in the classroom. I remember the specific inflection in the voice of my professor, Frank Thompson, when he said, "… if you didn't know who you were." Having taught this lesson for more than a decade, I know that my experience was not unusual. There's something about the Veil of Ignorance that just really grabs students in the way that it rationally compels us to embrace a principle of equality. In particular, it is a very powerful way of highlighting differences in well-being that are, as Rawls says, "arbitrary from a moral perspective" (Rawls 1971, 74). Given that innate talent is a matter of luck, it would be morally arbitrary to reward people based on talent. It would make no more sense to say that those lucky talented people deserve better lives than it would be to say that people who lose the genetic lottery deserve the suffering they will inevitably endure. Given that being born to rich parents is a matter of luck, it would be morally arbitrary to reward the children of the wealthy with disproportionate access to the kinds of opportunities that matter for well-being. And so on. The parties behind the Veil of Ignorance, fully aware that the class into which they will be born is not within their control, will elect to minimize the differences between classes, as a way of ensuring that they will not be too badly off if they are born at the bottom. Those parties, fully aware that they cannot control whether they will be born with blue or brown eyes, will prohibit any system that discriminates against eyes of a certain color. Such differences in rewards and punishments would be morally arbitrary, because rewarding and punishing people for things that are outside of their control is the height of moral arbitrariness.

I commented earlier on how Rawls' framework forms the disciplinary background within which political philosophers generally work. Understanding a little more about how that status developed allows us to appreciate the connection between salience and the demand for explanation in the humanities. The essence of Rawls' general approach, and the Veil of Ignorance in particular, was to accentuate the salience of our intuitive discomfort with morally arbitrary inequalities by constructing a framework in which the *arbitrariness* of inequalities naturally stands out among moral considerations associated with justice. Indeed, the moral arbitrariness of certain forms of inequality is brought into such stark relief through Rawls' framework that it essentially inaugurated a conception of the just society as one that minimizes morally arbitrary differences in well-being. Much of the subsequent literature presupposes this conception of justice, and then proceeds to debate more focused questions about what sorts of inequalities qualify as morally arbitrary. Because the Veil of Ignorance is so effective at making palpable the moral arbitrariness of rewards based on things like innate ability and parentage, subsequent theorists felt the urgent demand of trying to better understand the precise conditions that would qualify an inequality as arbitrary from a moral point of view. Probably as a result of their efforts to arrive at a more precise articulation of the conditions of moral arbitrariness, political philosophy eventually reached something like a Weinbergian state: less than a year apart, both Jerry Cohen (2008) and Amartya Sen (2009) complained that the Rawlsian approach fails to *explain why* morally arbitrary inequalities are unjust (as opposed to merely accentuating the salience of the fact that they are unjust).

Another milestone in philosophical knowledge that Gutting examines is the work (really, a single 3-page paper) by Edmund Gettier (Gettier 1963). Gettier's not as widely known outside philosophy as Rawls, but the developmental arch of disciplinary scholarship subsequent to Gettier's achievement in epistemology, as well as the mechanism he used to motivate that achievement, resemble that of Rawls in ways that are highly instructive. Gettier constructed something like a recipe or a template for demonstrating the deficiency of the widely embraced conception of knowledge as "justified true belief." Here is the kind of thing Gettier inspired: Suppose you are driving in a part of the country populated *almost* entirely with fake barns; say they're barn façades or something. At the precise moment you're driving past the only real barn in fake barn country, you look out the window at it and form the belief that it is a barn. Question: do you *know* that it is a barn? Well, let's check. Is your belief true? Yup. Is it justified? That depends on whether you've *ever* been justified in forming the belief that some actual barn is a barn. It looks like a barn. It quacks like a barn. It's got everything that any other real barn has.

If you were justified in believing that any of *those* real barns was a barn, you're justified in believing this one is. So it looks like you have a justified true belief. And yet most people hesitate to attribute knowledge to someone in the fake barn country, even when she is basing her judgment off of a real barn. There is some ingredient of luck, chance, accident … something that just does not jibe well with our intuitions about knowledge. Whatever this ingredient is, Gettier's recipe is a powerful expectorant for eliciting our sense that it is missing, and that its absence is salient because of how central that ingredient is for whether someone is in possession of knowledge. Consequently, a great deal of philosophical epistemology right down to the present day has been fixated on devising one or another "Gettier-proof coating" – that is, some account of knowledge that provides the missing ingredient to which Gettier's recipe so powerfully draws our attention (Stalnaker 2012, 754).

As with Rawls, Gettier's approach begins with a basic intuitive understanding of what matters (in this case, what matters for knowledge), and provides a simple, adaptable framework (like the Veil of Ignorance) for experimenting with different attempts to articulate what those ingredients are. All of these attempts adopt as a foundational premise the notion that the specific feature whose salience the framework is designed to accentuate – moral *arbitrariness*, or *accidentally* justified true beliefs – is in some way central to the concept under investigation. Like the Veil of Ignorance, Gettier cases function as exemplars by generating scenarios in which the salience of a certain feature cannot reasonably be ignored. The features are so unabashedly salient in these contexts that the cases supply more than instances of a certain phenomenon; they function as symbols for the classes to which they belong. However, because our understanding of concepts like justice and knowledge derives from reflection on exemplars, each effort to articulate our intuitive knowledge of what matters in these contexts necessarily leaves out essential content. Simultaneously, those efforts invite critical scrutiny which becomes increasingly adept at exposing the gaps between our intuitive knowledge, on the one hand, and our propositional articulation of it, on the other. I do not believe that these gaps can ever be permanently closed. All we can do is develop more satisfactory articulations of our knowledge of what matters, articulations that ultimately confront challenges through which we come to better understand the contours of those gaps, and which ultimately come to be seen as necessary but unsatisfactory way stations on an endless quest to come to grips with the content of human experience.

4.5 Conclusion

Lord Kelvin's famous dictum is part of our epistemological lore. The heart of that lore is a dogma which holds that we can only properly be said to *know* something if we can articulate it. While Kelvin's extreme view that we can only know something if we can articulate it *mathematically* is not tenable, it is merely the least tenable species of an entire genus of views which implausibly deny the possibility of nonpropositional forms of knowledge.

We learn about what matters from exemplars. But we learn more from exemplars than we can be taught, and we know more about them than we can say. The challenge of articulating that knowledge is what drives scholarly inquiry forward. Our epistemological mythology confuses those efforts to express that knowledge propositionally with the knowledge itself. Propositional representations of our knowledge are the currency of scholarly debate; there is no alternative. These representations attempt to distill clusters of salient features that we perceive an exemplar as exemplifying, features that seem to us to matter most for our understanding of the relevant phenomenon. The more precisely we can render these features, the more they stand out and demand our attention. As we endeavor to produce ever finer-grained articulations, we inadvertently exclude other features, features which themselves might eventually emerge as salient and which might thus call for fundamental revisions in how we represent what we know. In the next chapter, I explain in detail how this process of revision is led by knowledge of what matters.

CHAPTER 5

In Defense of How Things Seem

5.1 Taking Stock

Over the course of the last three chapters, I have been building up a model of knowledge – disciplinary knowledge – that is designed to accommodate central phenomena associated with the development of disciplinary inquiry. I began in Chapter 2 by chipping away at some common prejudices that might stand in the way of recognizing this species of knowledge, as well as those that might stand in the way of recognizing the form that it takes in various disciplines, from the hardcore natural sciences to the hardcore humanities. I want us to see this species of knowledge as a specific phenomenon that takes on different manifestations depending on the environment in which it is operative, but one which nevertheless maintains a substantive underlying unity across the disciplines. This unity across disciplines explains why the characteristic features and patterns associated with disciplinary knowledge are identifiable across the natural sciences and the humanities.

In Chapter 3, I began to chisel out the basic contours of these characteristic features and patterns. At the center of my account, there were the closely connected notions of *canonization* and *consensus*. Besides targeting some more prejudices, I attempted to show the manner in which certain general conceptions or styles of inquiry form something like a culture in a fairly traditional sense, and that these cultures exert pressure on members of disciplines to adhere to specific norms concerning what practitioners ought to investigate and how they ought to do so. These norms, I maintain, are derived from exemplars, models of practice that have achieved a normative status and that have come to serve as community-wide frameworks for guiding the articulation of research problems and their solutions.

In Chapter 4, I endeavored to provide a more detailed and substantive understanding of the content of disciplinary knowledge by pointing to the way in which practitioners must employ some conception of importance – "what matters" – when doing research. The norms governing what matters are not abstract facts about values that reside in Plato's heaven. They are the norms upon which the practitioners in a research community have converged as they attempt to guide their own research in conformity with the exemplary status of some of the discipline's prior achievements. To know what matters in a given discipline is to grasp this set of community norms. A practitioner's grasp of a norm amounts to a sense of the salience of certain properties – properties of nature, or of creative human output – properties that stand out as salient to her either because of a prior perceptual bias, or, more typically, because disciplinary training has focused specifically on cultivating a reflex for attention to certain kinds of details and for treating other details as unimportant. This sense of salience is acquired through exposure to and training on exemplars, which have achieved their hallowed status by virtue of their unique capacity to accentuate the salience of properties that are relevant to developing an understanding of the subject matter that falls within the discipline's purview. The "cost" of learning from exemplars is that it is not possible to articulate all that we have learned. According to my computer's dictionary, I have used scare quotes around "cost" in order to "elicit attention or doubts." That sounds about right. In fact, I do not think it is a cost, because, as I have said, I think we have good reasons to believe that inquiry is fundamentally driven forward by the unachievable goal of trying to fill the gaps between what we know and what we can say. We attempt to produce articulations of our knowledge, articulations that give salient properties their due and that constitute expressions of our understanding of why those properties matter. Some articulations come to enjoy widespread use within a research community and thus become part of the framework that guides inquiry …right up to the point where we are forced to choose between one or more of those articulations, on the one hand, and phenomena that have recently emerged as salient but which no accepted articulation of our knowledge can (yet) accommodate. There is no escape from the realization that much of what we know cannot be expressed in propositions, perhaps not even in nonpropositional utterances or inscriptions. Perhaps there is some knowledge that is genuinely inexpressible.

We are now prepared to confront the final idol – the big one. If much of what we know, and of what we know as scholars, cannot be expressed in propositions, does that not mean that it is forever consigned to the murky and muddled regions of the mind? After all, ain't inarticulate speech nothing but a bunch of fuzzy thinkin'? If something cannot be articulated, it is at best a "meager sort" of knowledge, a lumpy ooze of half-formed ideas.

In Defense of How Things Seem 109

I have been hearing versions of this prejudice for the better part of my life. For most of that time, it made a lot of sense to me, even when it was being used against me as an indication of why I probably wasn't cut out for philosophy. Thinking about it now, though, I wonder how we ever convinced ourselves of this, or why. Or how much Bertrand Russell is to blame.[1]

But if some of our knowledge cannot be articulated, how does it make itself manifest? It will not surprise anyone who has followed the argument of this book up to now that there are things that we can do with knowledge besides talk about it.[2] Millikan, as we saw, used his knowledge of experimentation and of professional discourse to guide his exemplary investigations of the charge of the electron. Neither was something he made explicit; I doubt that he (or anyone) could have. Broad and Wade deemed that lack of explication sufficient to accuse him of fraud. But no practitioner who looked at Millikan's work found any basis for these accusations, because their training endowed them with a knowledge Broad and Wade don't – *can't* – have. Those practitioners understood the expert knowledge that drove and justified Millikan's procedures, which they deemed consistent with accepted norms of scientific practice. Millikan and subsequent researchers all made effective use of this knowledge, despite not being able to articulate its content. That kind of knowledge manifests itself not in the form of beliefs, but rather in the scholar's sense of *how things seem*.

How things *seem*? Can I be serious? Oh, you bet, mister. I'm as serious as a heart attack. I'm so serious that I am staking the entire case for the plausibility of this book on this single claim: knowledge of what matters manifests itself in the form of how things seem. If how things seem to experts does not qualify as a form of knowledge, then the humanities do not produce knowledge. They do not produce understanding. They produce nothing but words.

As in previous chapters, I begin this part of the investigation by looking closely at an exemplar of scientific achievement – in this case, some discoveries from everyone's favorite early modern weirdo, Johannes Kepler. I intend to extract from this episode an unassailable principle about the ubiquitous and essential role of expert intuition in the production of scientific knowledge. In predictable fashion, I then show how this species of intuition functions as a primary source of data for a variety of domains of humanistic inquiry. Given that the

---

[1] Surely less than 100%. Russell (1911) defends a kind of knowledge that he called "knowledge by acquaintance," which is "direct" and unmediated by propositions.
[2] See the excellent defense of this thesis in Farkas 2018.

charge of the humanities is to articulate the content of human experience, I argue, we should accept no other source of data as primary.

The inflection point for this discussion will be an examination of investigative procedure in linguistics, which is part humanistic and part scientific. Here we find that speakers' intuitions about grammatically, for example, about whether a sentence seems grammatical or not, are more than useful data. They straddle the border between being the most informative window we have into the content of existing rules governing the grammar of a speaker's language, on the one hand, and being genuinely constitutive of those rules, on the other. Regardless of where one stands on this question, speakers' linguistic intuitions are indispensable to theories of grammar, because they provide insight into the content of speakers' experience of language processing. This intense, overwhelming focus on the content of human experience is a common element across a wide range of humanities disciplines. But there is significantly more going on here than merely sharing a focus on human experience. In fact, speakers' intuitions about grammatically play a very specific sort of evidentiary role in linguistics – and analogous intuitions play this same very specific role in disciplines across the humanities. There are, I shall argue, good reasons for this pronounced overlap, all of which descend from really basic principles of causal inference that are also embraced across the natural sciences. More than anything, the reason why these commonalities of practice are important is because no one disputes the probative value of speakers' intuitions for developing accurate articulations of grammatical norms (well, not *no one*; I will discuss some instructive recent dissent). Given that, as I argue, analogous intuitions play precisely analogous roles in other humanities disciplines, we should grant probative status to those intuitions as well.

But not *just* for other humanities disciplines. I conclude this chapter by renewing the plea to recognize scientific expertise as a form of non-propositional knowledge. The scientific community's view on this has always been one of ambivalence. On the one hand, it recognizes, appreciates, and promotes the essential and reliable status of expert intuition in the development of scientific knowledge. On the other hand, it often seems to want to reserve the moniker "knowledge" for statements about nature that have achieved consensus after experimental verification. It is time to bring this epistemological conservatism to a close. Mistakes were made, and a lot of people got hurt in the process. Scientific inquiry would not be so successful if it were guided by whims, lucky guesses, and serendipity. Yet it is not plausible to think that the only thing that matters to the production of scientific knowledge is experimentally verified statements that have achieved consensus. There is something in between, something which is identifiable and which reliably causes scientific progress but which cannot be articulated. Rather than relying heavily on it in practice but being coy about it in public, natural scientists need to be adamant about the indispensability and the reliability of tacit knowledge. The worst that could happen is that we give up a seriously deficient and outdated conception of knowledge and replace it with something that is capable of accommodating the experience of scientific inquiry.

5.2 Circular Reasoning

Johannes Kepler was not an exemplary scientist. One of his biographers, Arthur Koestler, described him as a "sleepwalker" who, mostly by accident, stumbled upon the discoveries which laid the foundation for Newton's scientific revolution. The historian of science I. Bernard Cohen labeled him a "tortured mystic" whose "weird contraption" consisting of nested Platonic polyhedra inscribed in smaller and smaller spheres was "more dear to him than the three laws which bear his name" (Cohen 1985, Chapter 6). The fact that there are only five regular polyhedra gave him, in historian Owen Gingerich's soaring words, a "rather cuckoo idea" for why there would necessarily have to be six planets (Gingerich 1994, 20). In the *Mysterium Cosmigraphicum*, Kepler openly acknowledges the relative legitimacy of the sun's claim to "visible God." His reflections on the medieval metaphor of the "music of the spheres" led to the realization – stunning for him – that the ratio of maximum and minimum angular velocities for neighbor planets approximates the relationship between harmonious musical notes.

This is just a small sample of the many strange observations, preoccupations, and investigations that characterize Kepler's research. And yet, in other ways, Kepler is one of the first instances in which we can see unambiguously the conceptual and methodological precepts that will come to define modern scientific inquiry. As such, it is in one way unremarkable that we also find reflected in his work several of the core philosophical puzzles which confront the production of scientific knowledge. The fact that these puzzles are so easily discernible even at this early stage speaks to their intimate connection to the practice of science itself. Even for someone as weird as Kepler, these puzzles are sure to emerge, because they are an inevitable byproduct of the struggle to understand nature. My particular interest in Kepler lies in a couple of instances of what can be called the "stopping problem" in scientific inquiry, instances which indeed underly

Kepler's fame as a transitional figure in the history of science. They are notable for the way in which they exemplify the constraints on scientific reasoning, and for how they highlight the ineliminable influence of human judgment at each stage in the production of scientific knowledge.

"The axiom of astronomy: celestial motion is circular and uniform or made of circular and uniform parts." These words were handwritten in Erasmus Reinhold's copy of Copernicus's *On the Revolutions*, discovered by astronomer and historian of science Owen Gingerich in 1973 in the Royal Observatory in Edinburgh (Gingerich 1994, 24). He would later find the same astronomical catechism inscribed in Paul Wittich's copy, then housed in the Vatican. Both Wittich and Reinhold belonged to the generation of astronomers that came after, and in the wake of, Copernicus's world-shifting book. And their faith in the axiom of astronomy is a poignant illustration of just how very traditional that book was. Neither Wittich nor Reinhold subscribed to heliocentrism. But they nevertheless saw Copernicus as squarely within the community of astronomers that extended back to Ptolemy. Heliocentric or not, his model embraced the axiom of uniform circularity.

The Ptolemaic orbital model was focused on circles. Big circles, little circles, circles upon circles, and circles upon *those* circles. When an ancient astronomer observed the heavens, he was expected to interpret their motions under the general presupposition that those motions were perfect. That perspective in and of itself does not dictate what form a perfect motion must take. For ancient astronomers, the perspective that celestial motion is perfect is crystalized by the notion of circularity: anything perfect is immutable; the only form of motion that is immutable is circular motion, being completely uniform and having no beginning and no ending.

Armed with the frame of circularity, ancient astronomers would then attempt to interpret the observed changes in a celestial body's position as marking different spots along a circular path. Often, initially successful attempts to characterize celestial motions as circular would fail, as with retrograde motion, when a body appears to travel backward.[3] In the event, observed changes in the position of a celestial body were interpreted as the result of *combinations* of circular motions, rather

---

[3] The explanation for why this happens in our system is verbally complicated, and not important enough to the argument to insert a diagram. It involves the way lines of sight interact with the observation of curved motion.

than, say, motions along some other kind of curve, or genuinely backward motion. Here, the drive to frame changes in position as *some* kind of manifestation of circular motion led astronomers to recharacterize celestial motion as motion around a circle whose center *also* traversed a circle around Earth. The reasoning went essentially like this: take the observations of a body's position over a period of time. See if you can find a circle around the Earth upon which they might fall. If no such circle exists, see if you can fit the positions onto a circle (an "epicycle") traveling around a center traveling around the Earth. If no such secondary circle exists, see if you can fit the positions onto a circle traveling around a center traveling around a circle traveling around a center traveling around the Earth. If that fails, well, you know what to do (hint: it involves circles…).

It was Kepler, not Copernicus, who broke with this tradition. What makes Kepler's astronomy distinctively modern is not his Copernican heliocentrism nor his later use of the telescope. Although both of these innovations constitute departures from well over a thousand years of astronomical tradition, it is his representation of orbital motion as elliptical that makes him stand out against the backdrop of Ptolemaic astronomy.

One question that has interested historians is, why didn't *Copernicus* reject the axiom of uniform circularity? After all, his heliocentrism shows that he was not overly attached to the Ptolemaic celestial system. I believe that the answer to this question is fairly straightforward. There is a reason why neither Wittich nor Reinhold wrote down any axioms other than the axiom of uniform circularity – such as, for example, an axiom to the effect that Earth was the stationary center of orbits. Quite plainly, there *were* no other axioms. Representations and calculations based on uniform circularity defined the game that astronomers elected to play when attempting to model celestial motions, much as the Parallel Postulate partly defines the Euclidean system that is used to represent the possible relationships between points, lines, and planes. Recalling our discussion from earlier chapters, the use of circular motion was part of the normative framework that constrained the way in which members of the community of astronomers went about their work. While astronomers had for centuries experimented with different systems of motion, it seems that it did not make sense to them to experiment with noncircular motion. Uniform circularity was, in fact, never a perfect fit with astronomical data. Each of the Ptolemaic devices – the equant, the epicycle, and so on – was developed and employed to accommodate this persistent problem.

Owen Gingerich, a highly accomplished astronomer and historian of astronomy, does not buy the idea that Copernicus was in the vice-grip of a conceptual attachment to circles (Gingerich 1994). For him, there is a much simpler, much more scientifically rational explanation for why Copernicus did not abandon circles in favor of ellipses – namely, that it wasn't until Tycho's superlative astronomical observations that we had data fine-grained enough to allow us to distinguish between circular orbits and elliptical orbits. "Without the accuracy of Tycho's measurements, Kepler could have modeled the orbit of Mars pretty well with an eccentric circular orbit and an equant" (Gingerich 1994, 27).[4] But with Tycho's data, anyone – well, any *astronomer* – would be able to see that no combination of circles upon circles could be made to work. It is a simple matter of scientific method: the theory of circular orbits predicts a certain path for a given celestial body – in this case, Mars. Tycho's unprecedentedly fine-grained observations relating to Mars prove that it is not moving in a circle. What more do you need?

So straightforward. So plausible. Right? I'll take it on Professor Gingerich's word (as should we all) that only Tycho's observational data allow us to distinguish a circular orbit from an elliptical one. The problem is that it actually explains nothing, because the poor quality of the data cuts both ways. In fact, it just amplifies the puzzle. After all, if our data were not fine-grained enough to distinguish between circles and ellipses, then there would have been nothing to prevent astronomers from using ellipses *before* Tycho. In other words, while the new data could, in principle, help to explain why Kepler stopped using circles, it cannot explain why *no one else did*. Kepler was not the first person in history to encounter difficulties modeling astronomical data as uniform circular motion; as I say, the fit with the data was never airtight. The entire edifice of premodern astronomy is built out of attempts to get around the complications one encounters when adhering to the axiom of uniform circularity. If elliptical orbits would have been just as good, why not try one? Why needlessly punish themselves with this circularity constraint? This practice was nearly 1,500 years old when Kepler picked up the problem. The Ptolemaic system that grew out of it was widely regarded as nauseatingly complex centuries before Kepler or Copernicus were even born – and not just by astronomers. Milton himself

---

[4] An equant was an imaginary point relative to which a planet exhibited a constant speed, thus obeying the "uniformity" constraint of uniform circular motion.

comments on the situation in *Paradise Lost*, imagining God's amusement at the absurd lengths to which they had been led:

> His secrets to be scann'd by them who ought
> Rather admire; or if they list to try
> Conjecture, he his Fabric of the Heav'ns
> Hath left to thir disputes, perhaps to move
> His laughter at thir quaint Opinions wide
> Hereafter, when they come to model Heav'n
> And calculate the Starrs, how they will wield
> The mightie frame, how build, unbuild, contrive
> To save appearances, how gird the Sphear
> With Centric and Eccentric scribl'd o're,
> Cycle and Epicycle, Orb in Orb...[5]

The impracticable consequences of the axiom of uniform circularity had been so long established that they had become common knowledge. Yet, astronomers continued to see fit to adhere to it.

The bizarre reluctance to sever their attachment to circles is compounded by the fact that circles and ellipses were known since ancient Greece to be part of a closely related family of curves (the conic sections), a tradition that untold generations of astronomers would have mastered as part of their training. They were not simply aware of ellipses, they were moreover aware of the essential connection between a circle and an ellipse. If obtaining a satisfying fit with observational data was the only thing that mattered to astronomers, there would have been every reason in the world to experiment with elliptical orbits. For astronomers before Kepler, there was clearly something *special* about the circle *per se* that had nothing to do with its ability to achieve an acceptable fit with observation. The idea that the data just weren't good enough is not plausible. It is worse than that. It is not logically cogent unless it is supplemented by adherence to the axiom of circularity. For example, I'm not attached to circles at all. I appreciate them. I value them. One could even say I revere them. Who wouldn't? But that's as far as I take it. If you gave me some planetary observations, and I couldn't make them conform to a circular pattern, guess what? I'm done with circles. Why not maybe try an ellipse? It's *so* close. To be perfectly frank, there's no real difference between these two shapes; a circle is just a special kind of ellipse. For reasons that seem to have little to do with accuracy, that was not the route chosen by astronomers before Kepler. If one combination of circles didn't work, there was always another.

---

[5] Quoted in Cohen 1985, 33.

5.3 Mind the Gap

The long legacy of uniform circularity in astronomy is a compelling illustration of an inference problem that we see across the history of modern science – namely, how do we know when it is time to throw in the towel and try a new approach? Unfortunately for Professor Gingerich's tidy tale, this is not something the data can, by themselves, compel us to do. If they did, the Ptolemaic theory would not have lasted for nearly 1,500 years. Uniform circularity was not a uniform success. When astronomers encountered a lack of fit between predictions and observations, they found a way to accommodate the discrepancy within the existing framework. Gingerich's account suggests that anyone in possession of Tycho's data would have taken the step that Kepler took, that it was not a bold step. But that would be quite like saying that anyone in possession of Darwin's data would have taken the step he took in rejecting the idea that species do not change over time – a tradition of an even more ancient vintage than that of uniform circularity. Lots of people had Darwin's data, and they found ways of fitting it within the research tradition of species immutability they had inherited. This is what made Darwin's *Origin* such a bold step.

The root of the problem is that there is no logically necessary next step that natural scientists are compelled to take when nature appears to violate their theoretically derived expectations. And more often than not, the steps they *do* take are flagrantly at odds with the most widely embraced model of how science works. This model holds that when evidence contradicts theory, the theory is wrong. What the Kepler episode shows is that the student of nature has a wide range of rationally defensible responses from which to choose as she attempts to reconcile the gap between theory and evidence. Sometimes she might modify the theory so as to accommodate the evidence. It is clear that Ptolemaic astronomers were very much OK with doing this, even if changes specifically having to do with uniform circular motion were off the table; to change that would be to stop doing astronomy. There is nothing special about the practice of Ptolemaic astronomy in this regard. Modifying one's theory is one of the defining features of scientific investigation. Alternatively, she might come to regard her earlier understanding of her own theory as not quite correct. Perhaps, as with the muon g-2 experiment mentioned in Chapter 3, she realizes that she miscalculated, and that the corrected calculations are in line with the evidence collected. She might even decide that the evidence wasn't all that relevant to the theory after all.

Despite 1,500 years of difficulties confounding efforts to use circular motion, Kepler restricted himself to it throughout his first major work in astronomy, the *Mysterium Cosmographicum*, published in 1596. In other ways, though, the book is an exercise in heterodoxy. He has broken with the axiom of *uniform* circularity, maintaining that planets speed up near the sun and slow down the further away they get. He also credits the sun as the source of planetary motion, whereas prior generations of astronomers were not in the habit of providing *any* physical interpretation of their planetary models (Gingerich 1994, 21). In this, he has essentially given up two of the three defining features of astronomical science (in addition to giving up geocentrism). Why not give up on circularity as well?

This is the part of the story that Gingerich nails. It is probably correct that grappling with Tycho's data shortly after publishing the *Mysterium Cosmographicum* is what ultimately lead him to chuck circles in favor of ellipses in 1609. The point I've been making is merely that no law of logic or reason required him to do so. He could have carried on like his Ptolemaic predecessors, like Copernicus, toiling away with yet more complex combinations of circular motions.

But something had clearly happened in the wake of Copernicus' book that had subtly destabilized the tacit consensus on how astronomy was to be done; Copernicus himself notes that the compound motion he develops is not perfectly circular (Gingerich 1994, 26). No doubt this is why Reinhold and Wittich saw it appropriate to articulate the axiom of uniform circularity, in line with Kuhn's observation that "Rules…become important and the characteristic unconcern about them should vanish whenever paradigms or models are felt to be insecure" (Kuhn 1962, 47). In the wake of the Copernican destabilization, the governing norms of uniform circularity and so forth begin to emerge from the indistinct epistemic background of astronomy, increasing in salience and, therefore, increasing their call for attention and explanation. Whereas prior to Copernicus these norms are presuppositions of the very practice of astronomy, suddenly even these foundational premises are up for grabs, so to speak. Just as his *On the Revolutions* had given astronomers the capacity to see things in the Heavens that had not previously been able to garner their attention, it also helped to endow elements of scientific practice with a degree of salience that made them targets of inquiry, rather than part of the fabric of inquiry itself, the framework through which inquiry is conducted. This episode also nicely illustrates the way in which a given piece of scientific knowledge will typically exhibit qualities of both a belief about nature and a tool of investigation. Indeed, this hybrid status seems to be part of what we mean by the term *axiom*.

Viewed in this way, we can understand how Tycho's measurements would have been causally relevant to the embrace of ellipses, without presuming that it was because those measurements contradicted models made from circles; astronomy was no stranger to that. Instead, what seems to have happened was that the axiom of circularity had become particularly salient and was finally poised to be interrogated. Once one decides to take that project up, the obvious next step for any competent mathematician would be to try an elliptical orbit. And using Tycho's data, the orbit of Mars can be modeled as a single (noncircular) ellipse. But – and this is central – earlier data could *also* have been modeled as elliptical orbits. In order for Tycho's data to be causally relevant to developments in astronomy, they had to come at a time when the axiom of uniform circularity had achieved a level of salience that made it a potential target for scholarly debate. This seems to only have occurred after Copernicus.

The reason I've spent so much time on this episode is because of the way in which it exemplifies our tendency to see things in scientific reasoning that are not really there, because we are so committed to the idea that those things *must* be there in order for the reasoning to be scientific. Gingerich sees logically compulsory behavior where there simply is none; Kepler did not *have* to, for logical reasons, embrace ellipses in light of Tycho's data. Those data contradict certain combinations of circular orbits. So what? Try some other ones. Likewise, Broad and Wade saw violations of scientific integrity where no practitioner does; Millikan did not count every run of his apparatus as a data point. So what? No experimentalist does. In both cases, the authors have perceived a potential breach of the citadel of scientific reasoning. Gingerich sought to clear the tradition of astronomy from a metaphysical attachment to circles. Broad and Wade sought to expose the seedy underbelly of scientific research, where "fraud and deceit" run rampant. The reality is more complicated than either of these campaigns is prepared to admit, because those additional complications did not comport well with certain deeply entrenched fantasies about scientific knowledge. The relevant fantasy in this case is that all and only empirical data must bear on scientific decision-making in order for those decisions to be rationally defensible in scientific contexts. Yet, no one before Kepler objected to the use of circular orbits in the face of incongruencies with planetary data. It is reasonable to assume that no one would have objected to his use of them, either. Like many generations of astronomers before him – generations which did not suffer from a dearth of deviations from circular orbits – he would have been seen as perfectly justified in staying the course and continuing in the tradition of uniform circularity updated to accommodate Tycho's data (it's probably worth pointing out that Tycho's own planetary model was composed of circles). But specific historical developments made it possible to call the axiom of uniform circularity into question at precisely that moment. These developments had nothing to do with planetary data. Rather, they were the effect of the way in which Copernicus induced a shift in astronomers' perspective on what was background and what stood against the background and in need of explanation.

Lots of highly consequential scientific choices are not decided by empirical data. In fact, let me go out on a limb: the vast, vast majority of choices made in the context of scientific inquiry are not decided by empirical data. This should not be surprising. From a purely logical point of view, empirical data cannot by themselves tell us what to believe, because there is an infinite set of theories that are consistent with any given dataset (Quine 1951). Well, then how are scientific decisions made? They are decided on the basis of "how things seem" to practitioners. In no way does this mean that natural scientists do not take empirical data very, very seriously. No one who has spent a significant amount of time with them, or paid close attention to the history of science, could fail to come away with the impression that their commitment to the integrity of their data, and to achieving "reasonable agreement" with it and the implications of theory, are both rather intense.[6] Instead, what the unavoidable use of intuitive judgment *should* suggest is that a highly cultivated sense of how things seem is essential for doing productive scientific work. Empirical data cannot by themselves tell practitioners what problems are important. They cannot by themselves tell practitioners when to continue pursuing a promising line of inquiry. They cannot by themselves tell practitioners when an experimental set up is working properly, giving the kind of information they are seeking. And they *definitely* cannot tell you when to stop using circles to construct planetary orbits.

Data must be supplemented by an expert sense of how things seem in order for science to go anywhere. Natural scientists do not customarily articulate the content of this sense of how things seem, because they are focused rather on articulating the structure of nature. That does not mean that it is not knowledge, or that it is "of a meager sort." We should not let a thoroughly discredited conception of scientific knowledge prejudice us against the epistemic bona fides of the way things seem to practitioners. Let us instead derive our conception of what scientific knowledge is by attempting to understand the social and cognitive factors that have

---

[6] See Pennock's (2019) discussions with scientists attesting to this sentiment.

caused scientific progress. Included among them is the practitioner's sense of how things seem. This sense is the manifestation of scientists' knowledge of the norms governing what matters in their discipline. It is acquired via the normal channels through which members of a culture typically acquire their knowledge of norms – immersive experience and an intense engagement with exemplars. And it is precisely analogous to the intuition that humanists use to guide their investigations of the content of human experience.

5.4 The Investigation of Linguistic Norms

There is a fear that how things seem cannot be integral to inference in the natural sciences. On the contrary, Kepler and countless other examples show that it is essential.[7] I now aim to show that this fear is without merit; either that, or much of modern linguistics is. In this discipline, how things seem is treated as far more than a passable if embarrassing stopgap where logic fails. In Chapter 3, I briefly discussed some features of how linguists study the grammatical norms governing a language. I now want to look more closely at this practice and its conceptual foundations, paying specific attention to the foundational and indispensable evidentiary role that speakers' intuition – their sense of how things seem – plays in research in linguistics. After describing these practices in what will probably seem like an annoying amount of detail, I explain why they make sense as a strategy for investigating speakers' knowledge of language. I then show how this strategy can be understood as an instance of a simple principle about evidence that is fundamental to all branches of empirical inquiry.

I go on from there to argue that this central feature of linguistic practice is a species of the same genus of inquiry that is common to all humanistic inquiry, a truism that was obvious to practicing humanists from very early on. I have no insight into why this practice is so widespread, but I won't let them stop me from speculating. Whatever the explanation is, it is a pronounced feature of general humanistic practice, so much so that one begins to suspect that there might be something special about it as a tool for investigating some of the norms that shape human experience.

Let's begin with the paradigm case: a language's rules of grammar. What are these rules? They are human conventions, knowledge of which is

---

[7] Strevens 2020 provides convincing and accessible illustrations in his Chapter 3, "The Essentiality of Subjectivity."

acquired as part of the language acquisition process. In ways that are still profoundly mysterious, our knowledge of these conventions is fundamental to the causal processes that govern both the production of utterances and their interpretation. A range of accounts exists regarding the form this knowledge takes, a range which includes disagreement over such basic issues as whether these rules are psychologically represented or not (see, e.g., Devitt 2006). There is, however, wide agreement across practitioners that speakers do possess this knowledge *in some form*, which makes sense given how stable the properties associated with it appear to be. If speakers' relationship to the grammatical rules of their language fails to qualify as knowledge given some particular view of knowledge, that is a problem for that view of knowledge. There is also general agreement among practitioners that we can study speakers' knowledge of grammatical rules by systematically probing their responses to sentences, in ways that I describe below. Relatedly, and perhaps most importantly, we know that knowledge of these rules is not associated with being able to articulate their content. That is, in fact, why it is possible to study this knowledge without asking questions directly about the rules themselves. For almost all people who have ever existed, knowledge of grammar has not been associated with the ability to describe the content of that knowledge. Even something as simple as, say, the idea that English is a subject-verb-object (SVO) language is a relatively recent development, and required the associated development of an elaborate taxonomy for organizing sentences into certain kinds of components.

The notion that English is SVO can be conceived of as a *theory*, a theory about some of the general properties of the psychological mechanisms that govern the production of sentences and their parsing, and the "subject/verb/object" taxonomy as perhaps an even more general theory concerning the kinds of categories that matter to the human language faculty. These theories are, *inter alia*, meant to explain some of the patterns that we find with respect to the form that native speakers' utterances tend to take, as well as in the conspicuous absence of certain kinds of linguistic phenomena of which the language faculty is clearly and demonstrably capable. We can, in other words, think of these theories as our best attempts to articulate some of the most salient features of human language. And it is probably important, in this regard, to reflect on the fact that these features have not always been salient. Chomsky's revolution in linguistics, for instance, was partly a revolution in the norms governing what constitutes a theoretically important feature of language, a feat accomplished by drawing attention to certain linguistic phenomena and emphasizing how peculiar they are when viewed against a certain intuitive background (such as that a toddler knows way more about her language than she has been taught, or the many highly predictable yet highly arbitrary features of language in general). Linguistic theories – whether maximally broad like Chomsky's Universal Grammar, middle-range like the theory that English speakers learn a SVO grammar when they learn English, or more specific theories regarding verb tenses and such – are tasked with explaining manifestations of a speaker's knowledge that are understood by the community of practitioners to be particularly revealing of what a speaker knows when she knows a language. As Chomsky's revolution shows, that understanding is subject to change.

One of the most interesting and salient properties of our knowledge of grammatical rules is the way in which they exert *normative* pressure, particularly on listeners. Native speakers have a well-documented and easily provoked bias against sentences that violate grammatical rules, and researchers use this bias to probe the contours of the language faculty (which, of course, they cannot "directly" observe). An encounter with an ungrammatical sentence tends to trigger an immediate and somewhat visceral reaction by listeners; Gross (2020) calls it an "error signal." Try it: utter the sentence, "Going the office to I." Not very nice, is it? Linguists differ as to what informational content this signal carries. Perhaps it carries the information specifically that the sentence has broken a rule, though not information as to the specific rule. This seems unlikely, because the error signal can also be triggered by sentences that are perfectly grammatical but difficult to parse. A more conservative view of the signal's content, then, would be that it tells the listener that there has been a parsing failure. This would occur whether the sentence was ungrammatical or grammatical but very weird, like the horrifying yet apparently grammatical, "The rat the cat the dog chased killed ate the malt" (Chomsky and Miller 1963).[8] As Gross and Culbertson (2011, 654) remark, "the relation between linguistic competence and the cognitive capacities recruited in meta-linguistic judgments remains obscure." Whatever the case, there is a sense of acute cognitive displeasure associated with the error signal, and it is standard research practice in linguistics to use that sense of displeasure to elicit a speaker's "acceptability judgment" regarding a sentence. A sentence like "I am going to the office" elicits a judgment of acceptability, whereas "Going to the office I" meets with strong disapproval. There is a wide range of variations on this gambit, involving tweaks like changes in the order of presentation

---

[8] Quoted in Häussler and Juzek 2020, 239.

of sentences, changes in sentence length, number of embedded clauses, even words and subject matter. But at the core of each of these is the researcher's desire to understand and articulate the conditions that make a difference to their normative appraisal of an utterance. These normative appraisals remain at the center of research practice in modern linguistics, as attempts to empirically validate their use continue to provide strong support (Sprouse and Schütze 2020, 45).

I want to pause for a moment to emphasize the way in which our sense of how things seem, taken as a source of high-quality data, is not to be trifled with. Indeed, it is particularly probative when certain kinds of norms are violated. An example I quite like is that of the norms regarding "personal distance" in a given culture. Most people have a strong sense of when an interlocutor is standing closer than is customary when speaking to someone, a feeling that was canonized in Judge Reinhold's hilarious portrayal of the "close talker" on *Seinfeld*. In fact, the phenomenon is so stable that an entire field of study has developed around it, christened with the very 1960ish moniker, "proxemics" (Hall 1966). At the same time, very few people who are not professional researchers could probably express what the appropriate speaking distance is in quantitative terms. I could not describe the magnitude of the prescribed distance in the Midwestern culture in which I was raised and in which I blissfully reside, but I have an acute sense of when it's been breached. One of my acquaintances is a close talker. A bizarre man in many ways, he habitually and unrepentantly violates people's personal space when talking to them. Having a conversation with him is discomfiting. Having spoken with mutual acquaintances about his habit, I know that my sentiments are widely shared. How close does he get? No idea; definitely too close. But I couldn't tell you whether it's like an inch over the line, or more like a foot. (Nice guy, though.) The important point is that there is a specific feeling that is triggered by violating these distance norms, and that members of a culture appear to agree on when those norms are violated.[9] Using estimates of what the preferred radius is, we can make predictions about when the feeling of distance violation will be triggered. There are many, many phenomena like this, in which some norm violation produces a sense of discomfort across

---

[9] The much discussed source is Sorokowska et al. 2017. This study shows subjects an image of two silhouettes at various distances from each other. But who knows what psychological phenomenon this is actually measuring? It also does not give us information about the range of estimates in a given control – only the mean. It would be really interesting to know how closely people's sense of personal space violations agree with one another in a given culture. I bet most reported distance violations would fall within a few inches of each other.

members of a given culture. Modern linguistics does a particularly good job of systematically and precisely mining this sense in order to develop theories of grammar that predict and explain phenomena associated with knowledge of a language.

Before going on to explain how and why acceptability judgments matter to linguistic theorizing, there is a further element of this practice that bears mentioning. One factor that appears to matter to the probative value of acceptability judgments is that they be mostly *unreflective*. That is, linguists typically want speakers' immediate appraisal of acceptability, unadorned with potentially intrusive and confounding reflection on whether the sentence "really is" grammatical/ungrammatical: "[t]he crucial difference between source intuitions and grammatical reasoning is their unreflective versus reflective nature" (Häussler and Juzek, 240–241). Implicit in this constraint are two important assumptions. The first is that it assumes that there is a distinction between knowing the rules that govern grammar in a language, on the one hand, and knowing how to articulate those rules. Moreover, the constraint of unreflectivity also implicitly recognizes the evidentiary authority of unreflective acceptability judgments and the concomitantly provisional and potentially corrupting status of attempts to transform aspects of those judgments into conscious thought. That is, what matters in most research contexts is speakers' bare sense of whether a sentence seems acceptable or not, and our ability to study this sense is understood to depend on shielding it from the potentially corrupting effects of speakers' subjecting that sense to some kind of scrutiny. Reflection is in this way treated by linguists as a source of systemic error.

The question that interests us here is the logical relation between acceptability judgments and linguistic theorizing: *why* are these judgments treated with such gravity by linguists? The basic idea is that the error signal that grounds judgments of unacceptability is *caused by* that part of the mind that hosts our knowledge of our language (Gross 2020, 22). One of the dominant features of that knowledge is its control over our propensity to parse sounds in our language. "Parsing," in the words of the great linguist Merrill Garrett, "is basically a reflex."[10] As soon as we hear speech, that parsing reflex kicks in. It is not something over which we appear to have any cognitive control; you *can't* treat speech in your language as

---

[10] Jerry Fodor attributes this comment to Garrett in the dedication to his 1983 classic, *The Modularity of Mind*.

mere noise even if you want to (Rey 2020, 37). When we encounter an utterance that cannot be parsed according to the specific rules that govern parsing in our language, an error signal is sent, and this signal tends to have "an associated phenomenology: a *felt* sense of badness, motivation, and norm violation of some particular strength" (Gross 2020, 21; emphasis in original). This sense is what speakers draw on in order to motivate their unacceptability judgments; in the ideal, unreflective case, it is *all* that they draw on. Because we understand unacceptability judgments to be expressions of that "felt sense of norm violation," we can use them to infer that a norm governing grammar has been violated: norm violation causes hearers to feel a sense of norm violation. Ergo (goes the logic), we can use the presence of this sense to infer that a linguistic norm has been violated. By systematically provoking the sense of norm violation, we begin to see certain patterns in the sorts of utterances that speakers deem unacceptable/acceptable. Our theories about grammar are our attempts to articulate general rules that can adequately describe those patterns (as well as patterns in other kinds of data that are causally related to our knowledge of grammar).[11]

We can see in this practice the instantiation of a very general principle about the use of evidence, for research practice in linguistics treats the "sense of how things seem" in the way all theories treat the evidence that purports to confirm them. For better or for worse, the world does not tell us how to investigate it. On the "worse" side of things, it can take a very, very long time to figure out how one might begin to answer a given question, assuming it's even a good question to ask in the first place. On the "better" side, inquiring minds are free to use any investigative means whose reasonability and propriety they can convincingly argue for. With a veritable cornucopia of means at our disposal, what are the sorts of considerations to which we might appeal in order to motivate the propriety of a method?

One way to gauge whether it makes any sense to apply a particular method, or to treat a certain type of observation as evidentially relevant to the question being investigated, is to ask what the support for a satisfactory answer to that question would look like. Suppose we're investigating the question of whether amphibians evolved from fish. What would we expect the world to be like if amphibians really did evolve from fish? Well, we'd expect there to have been ancestors of modern amphibians that have some

---

[11] See Sprouse and Schütze 2017 for a review of the types of data that are used to fuel theories of grammar.

characteristically fishy properties, which means there's a chance that there are some fossils that possess defining aspects of both lineages. We'd also expect those fossils to come from a specific time in Earth's history – right around the time reflected in the stratigraphic record in which amphibians first appear (~365 million years ago).

We expect these things because our understanding of evolution tells us that they are causal byproducts of the evolutionary process. We expect transitional forms because we understand the evolutionary process to be one that tends to proceed in small increments rather than huge morphological leaps, which would lead to the preservation of some fish-typical traits during the transition to full-fledged amphibians. And we expect the fossils to come from that time because that is the time at which amphibians are thought to have evolved from fish. The reasoning here is the same as in criminal investigations. We believe DNA evidence is solid evidence of someone's presence at a crime scene because some part of you needs to be at a place in order for your DNA to wind up there. Assuming TV's *Law and Order* is a reliable repository of facts related to criminal law, another source of evidence that plays an important role in criminal investigations is the defendant's mental state. If we think Jones committed the murder, one thing we'd expect to find is that Jones had (what he thought was) a good reason to kill the victim. We form this expectation on the basis of a causal theory relating certain kinds of beliefs to certain kinds of behavioral responses. We can use the fact that Jones might have believed he had a good reason to kill the victim as evidence for his guilt, because we accept the background theory which says that mental states are a cause of behaviors.

I take this to be a general constraint on how some phenomenon comes to qualify as evidence for a theory. When we form expectations about what the world should look like if the theory is correct, we do so because we believe that the theory has causal implications, and those causal implications inform our expectations about what we should find in the world. We would hesitate to claim that some fact about the world supports our theory if we did not think that the mechanism described by the theory was not in some way causally responsible for that fact. For example, it would make no sense to claim that Jones' DNA was evidence for his presence at the crime scene if we did not think that Jones' presence at the crime scene could have caused his DNA to end up there. The mechanism does not have to be the *only possible* cause of that fact to which we're appealing as evidence; it needs only to be *a* possible (direct or indirect) cause. (And obviously some facts are stronger evidence than others.) Thus, asking what we would expect the world to be like if our theory was correct is a good way of gauging the relevance of a certain kind of evidence because our expectations are informed by the theory's causal implications. When the world meets our theoretically derived expectations, we take that to be some indication that the theory's causal implications have indeed come to pass.

Linguistic practice reflects this principle about evidence in the way that it treats knowledge of language as the chief component of a psychological mechanism that causes certain feelings or intuitions. For example, suppose we thought that English had a SVO grammar. What would we expect to see? What would we expect the world to be like? Well, we would expect native speakers to speak in SVO utterances, and we would expect them to reject as ungrammatical utterances that lacked this structure. We expect these things because of our background commitment to a causal connection between the real rules of grammar for a language, on the one hand, and native speakers' intuitions about utterances, on the other hand. In particular, native English speakers' intuitive rejection of non-SVO utterances is something we'd expect to see because we believe that a native grasp of the rules governing a language causes certain kinds of reactions to purported instances of that language – for example, utterances or written sentences. When we find English speakers rejecting as unacceptable utterances like, "Scratched the cat the dog," we take that as evidence supporting our theory that English has an SVO structure, but only because we believe that native-speaker status causes certain phenomena, such as intuitive rejection of ungrammatical utterances. Given that rejection of non-SVO utterances is one of the causal implications of the English SVO theory, we should expect native English speakers to reject non-SVO utterances.

Thus, on this picture, we can see why native speakers' intuitive acceptability judgments might serve as an appropriate source of evidence for theories of grammar. Those theories have causal implications regarding speakers' sense of how things seem and associated forms of appraisal, and those implications encourage us to pay attention to native speakers' attitudes toward utterances in their language. We begin from the assumption that native English speakers possess knowledge of the norms governing English grammar. The idea is that possession of a language's rules of grammar has the effect of giving the possessor a certain capacity to parse utterances. We believe that this capacity, in turn, causes native speakers to react reflexively in certain ways to certain linguistic phenomena, particularly when utterances break the rules of grammar for their language.

Under certain conditions, linguists may decide to fundamentally revise their perception of the probative value of native speakers' acceptability judgments for supporting linguistic theories. For example, if they gave up the notion that possession of a language's rules of grammar resulted in a certain capacity to parse utterances, then they may decide not to appeal to native speakers' judgments as revelatory of grammatical rules. Similarly, were they to discard the assumption that the capacity to parse utterances can result in certain kinds of reflexive, intuitive judgments, they might no longer appeal to those judgments. In either case, it no longer makes sense to appeal to intuitive acceptability judgments as relevant data once the causal chain connecting possession of grammatical rules to intuitive acceptability judgments is broken.

There are other conditions under which linguists may decide to revise their esteem for native speakers' acceptability judgments, but which do not stem from a break in the causal chain connecting them to the questions we're attempting to answer. If, for example, linguists simply found an easier and more direct way of investigating a speaker's knowledge of grammar, then they would probably demote the probative value of acceptability judgments. Those judgments would still remain causally connected to grammar possession in the same way; it's just that we might find linguistic inferences based solely on those judgments to be relatively unconvincing when there is higher-quality evidence available.

As far as it goes, linguists' appeal to intuitive acceptability judgments does appear to be well-reasoned. There is a relatively simple causal theory connecting grammar possession to parsing, and connecting parsing to intuitive acceptability judgments. As long as we find that theory attractive, intuitive acceptability judgments seem like a fairly direct measure of one of the phenomena predicted by linguistic theory.

There is one further argument that we can make on behalf of the probative value of intuitive acceptability judgments for supporting linguistic theories, one which has to do with their inherent subjectivity. Why is it that subjective judgments are highly sought after in linguistics, but are generally avoided, or at best tolerated, in other sciences, even human sciences? The answer is, once again, that linguists subscribe to a causal theory that implies that native speakers will undergo a particular subjective experience, and that their status as native speakers – their linguistic competence – means that they will have reliable access to the contents of this subjective experience. The task of judging the acceptability of an utterance is not cognitively demanding – no more so than flinching, or kicking one's leg when struck just below the knee – and the linguist's working hypothesis is that the subject's self-report will be relatively unmediated by considered judgment. Here the perceived integrity of the data is dependent on the respondent's lack of reflection – that is, the more the respondent thinks about whether the utterance is grammatical, the less confident researchers are that they are detecting the effects of her competence as a native speaker. The adulterating effects of reflection are, it is thought, rooted in the presumed reflex-like nature of utterance parsing. Reflex behaviors work best when we don't think about them (next time you feel the urge to duck, try following an explicit set of instructions on how to duck). Respondents' reflecting on the grammaticality of a particular utterance increases the chances that the data we obtain from them will represent the judgments to which they are led by an explicit (albeit crude) theory of grammar applied to that utterance, rather than by the basic effects of their linguistic competence as native speakers. Native speakers' (crude) theoretical judgments as to whether an utterance is grammatical are not nothing, but they are far less probative than intuitive acceptability judgments. Indeed, they might actually be misleading.

5.5 Studying Rules by Breaking Them

Any natural scientist should be able to see foundational principles of scientific reasoning encoded in the way that linguists treat human subjective experience. Investigating the causal implications of a theory is just part of what scientists do. Of course, it makes sense to foreground human experience when your theory causally implies that people will have a certain kind of experience under certain, precisely specifiable conditions. Now, although I have spoken at length about the essential role that expert intuition plays in guiding natural scientific research, nowhere have I claimed that those intuitions are causally implied by theories in the natural sciences. But that's as it should be: theories in the natural sciences tend not to (be understood to) be focused on explaining the content of human experience, whereas theories in linguistics quite clearly are. Specifically, the latter are focused on explaining certain kinds of "acceptability" intuitions and the felt sense of norm violation with which they are associated.

I now want to suggest that the search for norm violations via the study of some form of "acceptability" intuitions is one of the defining features of scholarly humanistic inquiry. In our time, this kind of search has evolved into a highly systematic and carefully executed experimental research program in modern linguistics. But the essence of this practice – probing the specific contours of norms by attempting to provoke the feeling triggered by violating them – has always been central to the pursuit of humanistic knowledge. Humanists across a multitude of disciplines acquire knowledge of norms – what I've been calling "knowledge of what matters" – as part of a community of practitioners, particularly through their interactions with exemplars. Once acquired, they attempt to develop articulations of it, which they submit to the research community for scrutiny. The success of an attempted articulation – a theory – is determined by (1) how well it accommodates the salient features of exemplars and (2) whether phenomena that conform to it are able to *avoid provoking unacceptability judgments*.

There is no age in which humanistic inquiry is present but in which this two-pronged approach to getting at the essence of some aspect of human experience is absent. Socrates' iconic use of the *reductio ad absurdum* – a form of argument defined by its attempt to provoke unacceptability judgments – across the Platonic dialogues indicates that this approach had already achieved the status of mechanism for inquiry in ancient Greece. To take one well-known example, the Platonic dialogues are iconic in part for the distinctively Socratic way in which Socrates plumbs the depths of our understanding of notions of justice, of the good, of knowledge, and so forth. Socrates' method of inquiry is, as we know, to extract from his hapless interlocutor a specific articulation of one of these concepts. He then proceeds with his signature twin-flanked attack. On the one hand, he applies his victim's articulation to exemplary cases in order to make sure it gets them right (it doesn't). On the other hand, he concocts hypothetical cases modeled on that articulation to see whether they yield unacceptable consequences (they do). Stepping over the defeated corpse, he moves on to his next victim.

Likewise, George Makdisi's (1990) history of humanism painstakingly chronicles the development of the various humanistic disciplines and the deeply entrenched, indispensable role of exemplars therein.[12] Makdisi's highly original and peerless scholarship does not seem to have inspired much in the way of further attempts to elaborate on the many lines of inquiry he initiated in that book and its companion, *The Rise of Colleges*. Indeed, his work is virtually unknown within the humanities. One of the many fascinating observations he makes there concerns the Arabic name for the science of poetic meter, or prosody, founded by the Basrian philologist and lexicographer al-Khalil ibn Ahmad Farahdi (d. 178 AH/786 CE): *'arud*. Literally translated, this term meant, "the science of the rules whereby the perfect measure of Arabic verse are known *from those which are broken*" (Makdisi 1990, 130; emphasis added).

---

[12] The epigraph attributed to ibn 'Abbas comes from p 110 of this book.

The "breaking" of a rule of poetic meter amounted to nothing more than failing to conform to exemplary poetic practice. By studying a poem that provoked an unacceptability judgment from a competent poet, prosodists were able to develop very fine-grained descriptions of what the positive rules were. The poet's sense of acceptability in regards to meter was such a defining feature of the scholarly study of poetic meter that the word for poet in Arabic, *sha'ir*, literally meant "one who feels, knows, perceives, because more than any other person he has a perception for the composition of words and their orderly arrangement, knowing their minute particulars" (Makdisi 1990, 130). Both traditions, Greek philosophy and Arabic poetry, were already well-established scholarly communities during the periods from which these examples are taken, though neither had reached the level of theoretical sophistication that they would come to occupy in subsequent generations. Still, one can see even in these early stages a conscious and deliberate use of the two-pronged approach to the study of human experience: anchoring theories with exemplars and then refining them by prompting judgments of unacceptability.

I have already spoken at length about prong-1, looking at the details of how scholars use exemplars to derive an articulation of the features whereby they exemplify our understanding of particular norms. In the remainder of this chapter, I document the practice "whereby the rules are known from those which are broken" (prong-2) in other humanities disciplines a symptom of the fact that it is centrally important to humanistic inquiry. As we noted in Chapter 3 in the discussion of "crisis," it is also a common and crucial feature of scientific investigation.

5.5.1 Exceptions in Aesthetics

Earlier, I used Sibley's (1959) discussion of the content of aesthetic concepts to illustrate a point about the necessity of exemplars in the learning process whereby we acquire those concepts. A key feature of Sibley's argument there concerns his claim that

> Examples undoubtedly play a crucial role in giving us a grasp of these concepts; but we do not and cannot derive from these examples conditions and principles, however complex, which will guide us consistently and intelligibly in applying the terms to new cases. (Sibley 1959, 431)

If you'll recall, it is precisely this gap between what we *learn* from exemplars and what we *articulate* about that knowledge that, on my account, drives humanistic inquiry: there are no "conditions and principles" that "consistently and intelligibly" guide the application of these concepts because we know more about them than we can say. Any formulation is unavoidably partial.

Now, Sibley is actually arguing for a much stronger claim. When he says things like

> if we were to give special names much more liberally than either we or even the specialists do (and no doubt there are limits beyond which we could not go), or even if, instead of names, we were to use vast numbers of specimens and samples of particular shades, shapes, mottling, lines, and configurations, it would still be impossible, and for the same reasons, to supply any conditions. (434)

he is using such observations as evidence that our aesthetic concepts are "not condition- or rule-governed." It will come as no surprise that I agree with the claim that an exhaustive articulation of the content of these concepts is unachievable. But it's quite another thing to say that they are not rule-governed. In a similar vein, while it is probably appropriate to despair of ever having a complete account of native speakers' understanding of what makes a sentence "acceptable," no linguist seems to think that this shows that acceptability judgments are not rule-governed. They quite clearly are rule-governed. In effect, Sibley is subscribing to a version of the thesis that either there are rules that we can articulate, or there are no rules. This fallacious claim sounds plausible until we admit the existence of tacit knowledge.

I really don't think this undermines the value of Sibley's paper, though. His crucial insight was to connect the impossibility of specifying conditions for aesthetic concept application with the practice by which critics impart them to learners through exemplification. There is something else he says, though, that is really interesting and bears directly on the idea of studying rules by breaking them – viz., that we seem to be able to specify conditions or properties that definitely *do not* fall within an aesthetic concept's scope of legitimate application. In fact, he admits this is something of a partial exception to his thesis. I quote him at length:

> No doubt there are some respects in which aesthetic terms are governed by conditions or rules. For instance, it may be impossible that a thing should be garish if all its colors are pale pastels, or flamboyant if all its lines are straight. There may be, that is, descriptions using only non-aesthetic terms which are incompatible with descriptions employing certain aesthetic terms. If I am told that a painting in the next room consists solely of one or two bars of very pale blue and very pale grey set at right angles on a pale fawn ground, I can be sure that it cannot be fiery or garish or gaudy or flamboyant. A description of this sort may make certain aesthetic terms

inapplicable or inappropriate; and if from this description I inferred that the picture was, or even might be, fiery or gaudy or flamboyant, this might be taken as showing a failure to understand these words. I do not wish to deny therefore that taste concepts may be governed negatively by conditions. What I am emphasizing is that they quite lack governing conditions of a sort many other concepts possess. Though on seeing the picture we might say, and rightly, that it is delicate or serene or restful or sickly or insipid, no description in non-aesthetic words permits us to claim that these or any other aesthetic terms must undeniably apply to it. (426–427).

In a footnote, he indicates similar observations by Isenberg:

If we have been told that the colours of a certain painting are garish, it would be astonishing to find that they were all very pale and unsaturated; and to this extent the critical comment conveys information…This feature of critical usage has attracted much notice and some study…. (Isenberg 1959, 132)

This oft-noticed fact about the behavior of aesthetic concepts is characterized by Sibley as that they are "governed negatively by conditions"; Isenberg says it "conveys information." These are two sides of the same coin.

To say that an aesthetic concept is governed negatively by conditions is to say that its scope has identifiable boundaries, but that those boundaries can only be known insofar as we can see what is *outside* of them. Our sense of what is outside of them is acute, whereas our sense of what lies within them is vague. Stunningly vague, really, given how easily and precisely we can see the region beyond. Isenberg observes that we would be *astonished* to find a reputedly garish painting composed of a pale palette. How common is it to experience astonishment when confronted with something that very clearly *obeys* the norms that govern the application of a concept? I have a hard time imagining how that would even work. That's a puzzle. It should strike us as profoundly mysterious. That sense of astonishment conveys information. It is a species of the same genus of information that is conveyed by the "error signal" we receive when a sentence is grammatically out of joint. Perhaps it is a conspecific: "norm violated. Proceed with caution." Whatever its specific content, our perception of those norm violations helps us to gain an understanding of the limits of a concept's scope. As with poetic meter, as with grammar, we study the rules by breaking them.

5.5.2 *Provoking Disagreement in Philosophy*

In the previous chapter, I briefly but somehow exhaustively described the work of the famous twentieth century epistemologist Edmund

Gettier, who showed that whatever knowledge is, it is definitely *not* justified true belief (JTB). Since Gettier, philosophical epistemology has been very earnestly concerned with discovering the secret ingredient for a "Gettier-proof coating" to the JTB theory. When I introduced Gettier earlier, I mentioned how his hypothetical cases of knowledge were really good at giving you the feeling that there is something that the JTB theory of knowledge just does not capture. These cases – cases like "fake barn country" – seem to literally prove that whatever knowledge is, it is not *merely* justified true belief. How do they do this? By constructing a hypothetical scenario in which the JTB conditions are satisfied (belief: check; truth: check; justification: check), and then asking, "Is this knowledge?" When the answer that comes back is a resounding, "No," we infer that the JTB theory can't be correct, just as surely as we would infer that whomever told us that pale painting was garish did not know what the word "garish" meant. Gettier cases do not tell us what knowledge is; they don't even try to. They just tell us what it isn't.

Gettier did not invent this method. It's the same one Socrates uses. Philosophers have been wielding this irritating technique for thousands of years. We provisionally accept someone's articulation of a concept's content – "knowledge is justified true belief"; "is good" means "maximizes utility," and so on. Then we design a case where the truth conditions for that articulation are satisfied but where – "intuitively" – we balk at the notion of applying "good" or "knowledge" to that case. For, despite satisfying the conditions, it seems to fall outside the boundaries. The reason why intuitive judgments are treated as effective ways of arguing against philosophical theories is more or less the same as the linguists' argument for why intuitive judgments are probative for linguistic theories. Like linguistics, we start with the assumption that individuals possess a certain competence with respect to the application of their concepts, a competence which they enjoy in virtue of knowing the meanings of the words that express those concepts. Like being a native speaker, to possess a concept is thus to possess a competence with respect to the normative rules governing its use. Again, as in linguistics, a presumed consequence of conceptual competence is that it promotes certain kinds of responses – in this case, intuitive acceptability judgments regarding whether the conditions governing a concept's application have been satisfied.

Everyone knows (intuitively) that this "method of cases" cannot be used to prove a philosophical theory correct. Because there is no way to prove a philosophical theory correct – at least, not the kind of theories that list necessary and sufficient conditions. These theories gain strength not from fitting hypothetical cases, but from fitting *exemplary cases* – cases where we think that a concept is exemplified. The "fit" between philosophical theory and "data" – that is, our intuitive judgment that the exemplary case is, say, an instance of knowledge – is, we think, evidence that the theory is a good articulation of the concept's content; it would, if true, explain why we feel compelled to count the exemplary case as an exemplar. By looking at exemplary cases of knowledge, and noticing that their salient features always involve *justification, truth,* and *belief,* we begin to see maybe *why* we always seem to get that special "knowledgey" feeling whenever those exemplary cases are around. Then Gettier comes along and ruins everything by showing us that it is possible to satisfy those conditions and simultaneously trigger an unacceptability judgment – that is, a judgment that the intuitive norms for applying the concept have been violated in some way.

But, as Sibley and Isenberg show in the case of aesthetics, the cognitive significance of acceptability judgments and unacceptability judgments in philosophy is wildly asymmetrical; there is no positive equivalent of the phenomenologically intense "error signal" that is sent when norms are violated – some kind of "success signal." The only thing I can think of that might qualify is the feeling I get when I see a very elegant mathematical proof (NB: I can't follow anything more than five or six lines). I've heard other people express neighboring sentiments. There is a *definite* feel to this experience, like a deep fog or a heavy blanket being lifted off of me. In Pennock's (2019, 16) evocative terms, "the resolution to some puzzle is a feeling of utmost satisfaction." It is. It really is. Two other contexts: (1) I sometimes get a muted version of this feeling when confronted with a particularly apt metaphor; (2) also when a basketball team executes a very solid "alley-oop" (not just a normal dunk). It's so satisfying. But it's by no means obvious that this feeling carries informational content the way that the error signal does. What would it even be? If it is carrying information, it could very easily not be information having anything to do with norms or conditions. It also tends to be far less intense than the feeling associated with the error signal. In any event, besides these marginal and highly ambiguous cases, norm compliance generally goes phenomenologically unrewarded. As with so many other instances we've looked at – Millikan, pre-Kepler circular reasoning, grammaticality, etc. – the satisfaction of the norms for application of a concept basically goes unnoticed. If the norms are very deeply entrenched, their satisfaction might very well be unnoticeable. No one will ever hold the title of "Person who stands exactly the right distance away from someone when speaking to them."

A better person than I would be able to multiply examples from a much broader and more competent survey of humanistic inquiry. But I don't know how much more we'd actually learn by doing this. There is a pronounced uniformity with which the "study norms by breaking them" strategy is employed across subjects in the humanities. I find it surprising. There is no *prima facie* reason why prosody, grammar, aesthetics, and philosophical conceptual analysis should all take the same idiosyncratic approach to their respective subject matters. On the other hand, it makes a lot of sense that they would all employ *this specific approach*, given the way in which it conforms to a maximally general and commonsense framework for understanding the relationship between theory and evidence. That framework, which holds that we ought to seek evidence for a theory by looking for facts that are causally implied by the theory's truth, explains why each of these disciplines would seek out unacceptability judgments. These judgments are believed to be caused by our knowledge of the norms governing certain practices – poetic composition, sentence formation, word use, etc. It is known that breaking these norms is a much more effective way to access that knowledge than satisfying them, even if it is not known *why* this is so. Some of the perceptual systems that are deployed to detect norm violation, like the sentence parser, are *extremely* sensitive; very slight variations to a sentence can make a big difference to acceptability judgments. Others are less so. Our knowledge of the norms governing garishness, for example, appears to be less well-defined in certain ways. But even in a comparatively vague case like this, we can expect outbreaks of astonishment when the norms governing garishness are violated with sufficient audacity. In like fashion, Gettier cases are such blatant violations of the norms governing application of the concept *knowledge* that the guy is famous for having *proved* something in philosophy. It is not plausible to suggest that these reactions are unrelated to subjects' knowledge of meaning, of grammar, or of poetic meter. They might not be able to articulate it, but they are nevertheless able to *make productive use of it* by paying attention to their sense of how things seem.

CHAPTER 6

Reading What Lies Within

> For it seemed to me that they would not be as 'my' readers but the readers of their own selves, my book being merely a sort of magnifying glass like those which the optician at Combray used to offer his customers – it would be my book, but with its help I would furnish them with the means of reading what lay inside themselves.
> Marcel Proust, Remembrances of Things Past[1]

Throughout the Middle Ages and beyond, one can often see references in the Christian west to "two books" authored by God. One of them, the Scriptures, was an epistle to humanity outlining their moral duties and obligations – facts about how they ought to live, which could only be learned through divine revelation. Because it was written in plain language, this book could in principle be read by any literate person, although it was widely understood prior to the Reformation that only specially trained or designated individuals could correctly *interpret* what they read. The other of God's books was the great system of nature. To read this book required, above all, careful observation and reflection. Having been, in Galileo's words, "written in the language of mathematics," reading the book of nature would increasingly come to be seen as requiring training in the mathematical disciplines; it is more than snobbery motivating Copernicus to borrow as his epigraph the fabled inscription over the gate of Plato's Academy: "Let no one ignorant of geometry enter." Then as now, for an expert to read the book of nature was for him to organize a select group of particularly salient and important facts in a given domain such that those facts could be systematically described and understood. This comfortable image of scientific investigation, while accurate as far as it goes, occludes what is arguably of significantly greater value for the production of scientific

---

[1] v.III, 1089. Quoted in Nussbaum 2000, 468.

knowledge – what Proust might have called "the *means* of reading nature." Looking out from atop the cathedral of knowledge erected by Newton, natural scientists of the mid-eighteenth century could see nothing but promise in what lay ahead. It was one of those times, common across the history of science, in which entire communities brim with excitement over the potentialities unlocked by an epoch-defining scientific achievement. The astonishing power of Newtonian science had provided them not only with a convincing description of the unseen operations of nature but with something like a template for doing science itself, for constructing plausible analogies between the things Newton had satisfactorily explored and things he had left mostly untouched (Cohen 1956). More than anything, Newton's achievements – like those of Darwin, Copernicus, and a host of other historic contributors – provided practitioners with an endlessly satisfying *means* by which characterizations of nature could be generated.

References to another pair of books also feature prominently in the Middle Ages. Utterly pedestrian by comparison with the previous set, these two books contain nothing more or less than the complete inventory of an individual's deeds, dutifully recorded by an angelic scribe attending each shoulder; good deeds are written down by the angel on the right, bad deeds by the angel on the left. On the Day of Judgment, the books are weighed, one against another, as part of the assignment of one's fate in the afterlife. The weights of these logbooks are, of course, determined not by a simple inventory, but by the moral worth of the decisions that led to the actions they enumerate. The consequences of acting in haste, rather than through careful and informed deliberation; of acting narrowly in service of one's self-interest, rather than beneficently toward others, particularly the less fortunate; of succumbing to our anger – every entry reflects the result of a human choice, each associated with a specific moral gravity.

Descriptions of this ceremony can be quite detailed and interesting. One thing that stands out, particularly in Qur'anic discussions, is the dissipation of a fog of self-deception and willful ignorance that has impeded one's perception of moral truth. Here is one version, from Chapter 50 of the Qur'an, verses 22–23:

> [It will be said to the denier,] "You were totally heedless of this. Now We have lifted this veil of yours, so today your sight is sharp!"
> And one's accompanying-angel will say, "Here is the record ready with me."

Various traditions report the individual's state of mind at this stage as one of deep regret. There is no tomorrow. It's literally the Last Day. He is tormented by the record of his deeds, not only by what they describe

("We were among the evildoers"), but by his failure to see things in his life as they truly were. Would that he had had this degree of moral clarity and self-possession mere moments beforehand. He pleads to return to life for one more day, as the gaping maw of Hell hungrily declares its limitless capacity (Qur. 50:30).

It is hard not to sympathize with the condemned in this scenario. These Qur'anic narratives standardly refuse to elicit the sense of triumph we feel when a movie villain gets his comeuppance. Rather, the remorse and regret displayed by the individual when confronted with his record shift the focus of our attention to the pressing need to achieve a fine-grained moral perception of the events of our own lives while we still have them, and to acquire the means by which we might lift "this veil of ours" in time for it to matter. Little do we benefit from enhanced moral acuity and penetrating self-reflection in the afterlife. We ourselves must develop "the means to read what lies within" such that we might see our motivations, attachments, and impulses for what they are, enabling us to profitably shift the balance of our books while they're still being written. After all, Muhammad is reported to have said, "The [scribe] on the left hand raises his pen [i.e., delays writing] for six hours before he records the sinful deed of a Muslim. If he regrets it and seeks God's forgiveness, the deed is not recorded, otherwise it is recorded as one deed" (Al-Tabarani).[2]

In this chapter, I aim to motivate two important theses. The first is the idea that the humanities enable us obtain knowledge of ourselves by providing the means to read what lies within. Knowledge of ourselves is not scientific knowledge. It never will be. It is made up of the facts concerning what we implicitly take to be of value. Knowledge of ourselves is a special kind of "knowledge of what matters." It is knowledge of what matters *to us*. To "read what lies within" is as if to read the contents of our two books before they are complete, because to truly know ourselves is to be able to foresee what we are likely to choose and to do.

Should we value knowledge of what matters to us? How would we even begin to answer such a question? This points to my second important thesis: the humanities are the domain in which questions about what we *ought* to value are formulated, entertained, refined, re-entertained, and – occasionally – provisionally answered to some degree of satisfaction. The acquisition *per se* of knowledge of what matters to us is not meaningless, but

---

[2] *Al-Mu'jam al-Kabir* 7765.

it is relatively inert without a framework for reflecting on what we find. The humanities have a proven and unique capacity for fostering reflection on whether or not we should be satisfied with what we've discovered about the normative commitments to which we find ourselves reflexively or tacitly inclined. To put it one way, they promote the development of "second-order desires" – desires whose objects are desires themselves.

Questions about what you desire can often be answered straightforwardly – just think about what you want. Questions about what you *fundamentally* desire, less so, but still manageable – is that ear of corn what I *really* want, or do I just want an excuse for consuming an unconscionable amount of rich creamery butter? But questions about what we *should* desire require a different set of resources. Yes, I want to eat a stick of butter, but is that a good idea? *Should* I want to eat a stick of butter? In asking that question, I'm acknowledging the existence of something similar to an ordinary desire, some kind of consideration which is relevant to my desire but which has a normative component to it. The focus of that normative component is the important issue of whether my desire is *good*. Asking whether I *should* want to eat a stick of butter, given that I do, recognizes that there is a source of value that is independent of my first-order desires (the ones specifically directed toward butter). Moreover, it reflects the existence of a second-order desire – namely, the desire to bring my first-order desires in line with that independent source of value.

Humanities disciplines foster the exploration of that source of value and its congruence with our desires in various ways. Ultimately, I argue, these various forms of exploration succeed by enabling us to achieve a vantage point from which to view our personal commitments and desires with some degree of detachment. In doing so, they provide the means to avoid a pernicious kind of self-contamination that prevents an accurate reading of what lies within. It is a relative of the kind of contamination that concerns linguists when they're exploring native speakers' grammaticality commitments. Linguists prevent subjects' self-contamination by insisting that they *not* think too carefully about the acceptability of an utterance. The more we think about its acceptability, the more the effect of our "error signal" is dampened as our judgment makes room for other types of considerations. When that signal is dampened, it undercuts our attempt to break the rules of grammar – our primary means of studying them, of reading what lies within.

Humanities disciplines try to do something like the reverse of this. The assessment of our desires and our normative commitments begins as an incredibly noisy affair. When we first attempt to interrogate them, we do so in the context of a whole life full of complex personal relations, uncertainties, competing desires, and a host of other stressors which by themselves prevent the formation of a serviceable image of what lies within. Moreover, we approach this task without much in the way of training or practice. For example, the distinction between what we want and what is good is not an intuitive one for many of us; in the context of daily life, we are often selfishly motivated to deny that this distinction exists. We generally do not have ready-to-hand the sorts of tools that allow for systematic exploration of the full scope and magnitude of the normative commitments we see ourselves as embracing. I see myself as being committed to distributive justice. Do I then immediately see myself as being committed, as Rawls would argue, to the idea that inequalities in wealth and opportunity are morally justified only if they are necessary to benefit the worst off people in society? The demands of everyday life, with its exhausting complexity, rarely leave space for us to investigate the content of our professed commitments as deeply as that. Daily life does not reward nuance. It does not reward depth. Only in rare cases does it reward self-knowledge. Generally speaking, a life untouched by humanistic inquiry has neither the resources nor the motivation to separate the signal of moral acceptability from the noise. The humanities represent a quiver of mechanisms for subtracting different sources of noise, moving us toward a relatively contaminant-free environment such that we can more clearly discern our normative commitments and their implications. Humanistic inquiry in its various forms helps foster the relative detachment from our normative commitments that is essential for honestly judging their acceptability.

Lastly, and perhaps most importantly, the humanities have a demonstrated power for getting people interested in this kind of exploration, for luring us beyond the constraints of daily life, or personal preference, or cultural baseline, encouraging us to look at these constraints as a mere sample from among a vast range of possible alternatives. The humanities make knowledge of what matters to us matter to us. I have no idea what makes the humanities so good at this. But I have seen it happen too many times to too many students for it to be a coincidence.

The attempt to study rules of grammar by breaking them must begin with some reasonably clear, albeit tentative, articulation of what those rules might be: a theory. The idea that English has an SVO structure is a theory comprised of a set of well-defined categories (*subject, verb, object*) and their interrelations. A big part of what makes the SVO theory of English grammar usable in this way is the simple fact that it is a relatively fine-grained, disambiguated characterization of what that grammar might be like – something it shares with all productive scientific theories. Throughout this book, I have stressed how the natural sciences seek to produce characterizations of nature that can be used as "a sort of magnifying glass like those which the optician at Combray used to offer his customers" – a *means* by which we can obtain scientific knowledge of other parts of nature. But having a magnifying glass does not *per se* advance any project, be it humanistic or scientific. Every domain is viewed through some lens or other. What we want is a magnifying glass with some very specific capacities, capacities which render images with sufficient precision, and which allow us to either clearly recognize important features of our experience, or clearly recognize that important features of experience are not adequately represented. The ability of a characterization to function as a magnifying glass, so to speak, depends on whether the images viewed through it can be rendered with sufficient clarity and distinction. Does the characterization present us with the same blurry lines and blotchy images as does our unadorned vision, only bigger? Or does it, like the SVO theory, furnish us with some nice crisp edges that differentiate one kind of thing from another? Does the characterization permit the analysis of just one kind of thing, or does it encourage practitioners to extend its use as far as possible, promoting the design of clever strategies for loosening the reins of literal truth while remaining tethered in some acceptable fashion to the original characterizations whose success inspired us?

It is precisely this fate that Proust's protagonist wishes for his novel. Certainly, it is more than a mere description of events. He privileges some events over others. He presents those events in a specific format, one which allows him to accentuate the significance of certain features as others are consigned to the background. His story doesn't just report them; it hovers over them, granting us access to a kind of perspective that would be unachievable in the normal course of events. It *magnifies* them. Each of these aesthetic choices is ultimately made in the service of providing readers "a means of reading what lies within themselves." The story is told in such a way as to allow readers to connect it to their own lives. Like the scientist's apt characterizations, these connections can be more or less literal. Perhaps we too experienced love at first sight. Or perhaps, we experienced the premature loss of a father instead of a mother. Whatever the case, the story's effectiveness as a means of reading what lies within ourselves doesn't depend on the literality of those connections. It depends largely on whether the story can be made to appeal to us as a framework for developing an understanding of our inner selves.

6.1 The World-Making Power of Scientific Metaphor

> Reverend Lovejoy: That is a false analogy, young lady.
> Lisa Simpson: No, it's not. It's apt. APT!!!
> *The Simpsons*, "She of Little Faith."

How does knowledge of what matters lead to knowledge of what matters to us? In the remaining space, I propose a perspective on this question by following the process of knowledge production in the humanities through two final phases: (1) humanists' description of experience and (2) our use of those descriptions to acquire knowledge of ourselves. The fulcrum of my account is the notion of an *apt characterization*. In previous chapters, we looked at how humanists use exemplars to derive articulations of tacit knowledge. Those discussions focused predominantly on the content of seemingly ill-behaved concepts such as knowledge, eloquence, justice, and the like. What we saw in these scholarly efforts was a certain drive to produce characterizations of those concepts that manifest three essential qualities: (a) they should be accurate; (b) they should give salient properties the attention those properties deserve; and (c) they should facilitate further reflection in a structured way. Exemplars achieve their status as exemplars largely through their superior ability to serve as the wellspring of characterizations with these special properties.

This same kind of drive is evident in scientific practice. I have stressed at various points throughout this book how thinking about natural science as an enterprise devoted to discovering the truth about nature is perhaps not ideal. Part of the reason for this is the simple fact that there are a lot of truths about nature, and natural scientists just do not care about the vast majority of them. Of all the ways in which a bit of nature can be accurately described, natural scientists only care about a vanishingly small subset of those accurate descriptions. In particular, they care about the ones that give salient properties their due.[3] For example, while it is accurate to describe the sun as bigger than an ice cream cone, it is also scientifically worthless. "Size relative to an ice cream cone" is not an astronomically salient property – not at the moment, anyway. The kinds of accurate descriptions that really matter to astronomers are, for instance, ones that make hitherto unappreciated connections between different kinds of celestial phenomena, or between celestial phenomena and much smaller-scale physical

---

[3] See Kitcher 2001, Part I, for a systematic treatment of these issues.

phenomena (even smaller than ice cream). The classic example of this is the connection solidified by Newton between planetary orbits and the projectile motion of terrestrial objects. By Newton's time, the elliptical shape of orbits and the parabolic path of projectiles were among their most salient properties. Newton gave us a way to characterize both using the same bit of mathematics. But our ability to use the same equations to describe these two phenomena was not valued simply because we once again succeeded in our perpetual quest to accumulate more accuracies. Rather, it was because it provided us with a new framework for thinking about the motion of objects in general. As mentioned above, that framework would soon lend itself to thinking about natural phenomena quite distinct from the motion of objects.

A dominant vehicle by which these sorts of scientifically generative connections are achieved is the use of metaphor. The generations after Newton who hoped to extract yet further insights from Newton's work sought to extend its reach by treating their particular scientific interests (e.g., light or electricity) as *versions of* the phenomena Newton had tackled directly, just as physicists of today approach the analysis of an explosion as if it were a time-reversed, perfectly inelastic collision. Like other great scientific achievements, Newton's framework proved to be highly adaptable to new contexts through the use of these kinds of metaphors and analogies. The question of whether an explosion "actually is" a time-reversed collision, or whether electricity "actually is" a fluid, is secondary if it arises at all. The practitioner's primary concerns are, "What sorts of questions or potential insights follow if I conceive of an explosion as a collision, or electricity as a fluid? How is inquiry or analysis simplified? What promising leads or connections suggest themselves?". Accuracy alone cannot discriminate between better and worse ways of satisfying these demands. Not uncommonly, the primacy of accuracy is demoted when it presents significant obstacles to satisfying these demands. And in this last point, we are given some deeper insight into the kind of accuracy evoked by judgments of aptness. Recalling our earlier discussion of "reasonable agreement," the idea that a characterization is apt need not connote that it is perfectly accurate – what would that even mean? In the search for apt characterizations, the natural scientist will often be satisfied with descriptions that are *accurate enough*, while also providing a platform for further inquiry or understanding. Excruciatingly accurate descriptions – even mathematically precise ones – are often worthless.

Natural science as we know it would be impossible without the use of metaphor. Part of why this is so is the uninteresting reason that language itself subsists on metaphor; there is no such thing as an inherently literal statement. As Goodman (1968, 68) observes, literality is a by-product of habitual use of a certain metaphor: "with progressive loss of its virility as a figure of speech, a metaphor becomes not less but more like literal truth." So in one sense there is nothing special about the use of metaphor in the natural sciences. But metaphors do more than merely make language possible. They are generative of new perspectives, connections, and ideas in a way that literal statements are not. They force our attention in certain directions and on certain, often unappreciated properties, demanding that we view those properties from an unconventional vantage point. Darwin's famous metaphor of "natural selection" was deliberately designed to get readers to carefully consider the profound significance of certain affinities between the way breeders single out specific members of a flock for breeding based on their possession of favored characteristics, on the one hand, and the competitive advantage certain inheritable characteristics might afford an organism in "the struggle for existence." As I mentioned in Chapter 2, the specific facts about nature that make natural selection inevitable were known millennia before Darwin. Whoever doubted that members of a species differ slightly from each other? Or that they inherit traits from their parents? Or that some are better suited for the conditions of existence than others? But viewed through the lens of the well-understood art of breeding, these commonsense tidbits take on a stunningly new meaning. Thinking about reproduction in the wild *as if* Nature were a breeder unleashed the explanatory power of these platitudes.

Of course, most scientific metaphors do not achieve the epoch-defining status that Darwin's did. Their lot is considerably more modest, but it is no less necessary. Conceiving of electricity as a fluid in the manner of many eighteenth- and nineteenth-century scientists did not have the immediate effect of upending deeply entrenched views about humanity, morality, and purpose. Like most metaphors in science, its influence was felt almost exclusively among a specific class of practitioners, those who were in search of a well-formed, elaborate, yet adaptable framework that could be used to structure and advance inquiry. This pattern of appropriating well-developed ideas and adapting them for application to new scientific problems is just how science works. It is what explains, *inter alia*, the dogged commitment to certain scientific theories long after they have been known to not quite be technically correct. A scientific theory is more a technique or a way of doing things than it is a belief about nature. And metaphor is the primary device by which the reach of that technique can be extended. When we find that practitioners are prepared to frame an explosion as a collision – something which most normal people would regard as the exact *opposite* of an explosion – we are given a glimpse of the lengths to which they are willing to go in order to bring a phenomenon under an already well-anchored explanatory tent. Their ability to succeed is often in no small part dependent on finding an apt metaphor for framing the new phenomenon as a species of a previously well-established genus. Whether on the Earth-shattering scale of Darwin or the more pedestrian ripples of eighteenth century electricians, a metaphor's aptness seems to depend on whether it is accurate enough, on whether it accentuates the salience of significant features, and on whether it fosters some kind of new understanding, enhanced either in depth or in breadth.

One final aspect of the use of metaphor in science bears mention. Scientific metaphors do more than generate ideas and insights. When they are successful and long in use, they change the way in which practitioners see or categorize the world. Indeed, much of the generative power of metaphor resides precisely in its capacity to effect such changes. Witness that, whereas Darwin's early readers came to view the process described by Darwin as a kind of natural breeding, contemporary researchers generally see breeding as an instantiation of the fundamental Darwinian process. This inversion of perspective has been effected by the astonishing success of the Darwinian framework in expanding the scope of our understanding of the living world. The longer Darwin's metaphor remains in use, the more contexts to which it is successfully applied, the more it quietly recedes further into the background as a kind of default perspective, positioning itself as *the* thing in terms of which other things are to be understood. It is a nice illustration of Goodman's observation regarding the transition from metaphorical to literal truth.

The history of science records so many instances of this process, some aspects of which have been discussed in previous chapters. Rather than doing the thing where I go on to list several such instances, I'll cut to the chase: a central feature of the use of metaphor in science is that, when successful, it changes the way practitioners classify things. When they elect to treat object X as if it were a Y, after a time they often come to see object X as belonging to category Y. Really powerful metaphors like Darwin's are often viewed as revelatory in this regard; through the *Origin of Species*, we discovered that natural selection *just is* a form of breeding. The way they effect these changes is through their unique ability to direct the focus of our attention to certain features of a phenomenon, features that correspond more or less to the essential or distinguishing features of an existing category. In Darwin's case, he cleverly spends the first chapter of the

Origin treating the reader to all manner of trivia regarding the breeding of domestic flocks. When we finally get to the second chapter, "Variation Under Nature," we are already primed for thinking about groups of animals in terms of the differences between group members, the inheritance of those differences, and the potential effects of those differences on reproductive output; we scarcely need Darwin's delightful prose to lead us down the primrose path. The effect is as instantaneous as it is irresistible: in a few short paragraphs, we begin to see these two contexts, long held distinct by convention or philosophy, as fundamentally alike. We see the world in a new way. We now see the world not as composed of mutable domestic breeds *and* immutable species, but instead containing a process – the process of *selection* – which manifests itself in particular ways depending on the context.

Students of metaphor will observe that metaphor's capacity to shape conceptualization and perception is not limited to its function in scientific inquiry. It's simply part of metaphor's standard behavioral repertoire, playing out in a particularly specialized sort of linguistic community in ways that are both unpredictable yet highly determinate (Goodman 1968, 74). Outside of science, we see versions of these same effects. Metaphors in literature and in ordinary language are "framing devices" that are used to elicit a particular perspective on an often familiar object or event (Camp 2019). In the next section, I look at the role of metaphor in literature and philosophy in more detail. Following that, I draw on our earlier discussions of exemplars to develop a view of the humanist as what I'll call a "kind maker." I then show how the classifications articulated by humanists function as the means to read what lies within.

6.2 Metaphor and the Making of Experiential Kinds

The polymathic philosopher Richard Boyd makes the profound observation that metaphors in the sciences differ from literary metaphors in at least one very important respect. While particularly apt scientific metaphors quickly spread across a discipline, becoming common property of a disciplinary community (for precisely the reasons outlined in Chapter 3), literary metaphors exhibit a pronounced proprietary behavior (Boyd 1979). There is an obvious kernel of truth in Boyd's statement, but it appears to be highly context-dependent. To appreciate the kernel, just think about your favorite literary metaphor and reflect on how frequently it has come up in other literary contexts? Here's mine: the description of

Ethel Merman's voice as "the sound of the Queen Mary entering Walden Pond" (reportedly by J.D. Salinger). Despite the provable scientific fact that it is the best metaphor in history, it's not one you see every day, now, is it? Granted, one would have to be reading *a lot* of Ethel Merman-related literature, and I'm just not sure how much there is out there.[4] But even for more general, non-Merman features of human experience, Boyd's point seems to hold: literary metaphors are very much seen as the sole property of the work in which they appear. The idea of using someone else's metaphor strikes me as intuitively perverse. If I ever finish my highly unauthorized Ethel Merman biography, I definitely will not use Salinger's peerless characterization, other than maybe out of homage to him. And for those lucky enough to have lived some portion of their lives with an awareness of the metaphor, it would indeed be seen as a kind of homage or "shout-out."

If Boyd's observation is so sound, what makes it so precarious? History – that's what. As Ernst Curtius pointed out in his masterful survey of European literature from antiquity to the modern era, lots of very specific literary metaphors have been used by writers across two millennia, just as natural scientists continue to use many of the metaphors bequeathed to them by their seventeenth, eighteenth, and nineteenth century predecessors; some go back much further. The stability and proliferation of literary metaphors throughout most of literary history certainly not discourage the notion that writers, like their natural scientist counterparts, had found in these devices a satisfying and effective way of framing certain ideas. Indeed, it suggests that they were eager to participate in an established practice for which they saw themselves as further conduits. Why? Well, in science, there is a certain tendency to follow suit, but it is only partly driven by the expectation that doing so will have a direct impact on one's ability to solve problems. Much of the propensity to carry on a tradition of practice comes simply from the process of acculturating into a discipline for which those practices are a constituent part. Generally speaking, fledgling evolutionary biologists do not consciously decide that the best way to advance their research or their professional standing would be to frame their ideas about biological adaptedness in terms of breeding. They just become evolutionary biologists, and through that process they will inevitably come to frame – and think about – biological adaptedness in those terms. Part of their designation as practicing evolutionary biologists

---

[4] Yes, I Googled it; of course I did. There are roughly 729,000 hits. But the only one that matters is the Spotify link to a little crime against humanity entitled *The Ethel Merman Disco Album*. Released during the year of my birth (1979), after listening to just a few seconds of the first track I instantly understood why I've always been an optimist. Because how could things not get better from then on?

involves their embrace of the Darwinian process in some form and within some domain of applicability.

The historical pattern of the development and use of certain kinds of literary devices indicates something similar operating across most of the history of the humanities. As parties to a tradition, writers became conversant in the long established means by which certain sentiments were conveyed, through which certain experiences were conventionally understood, and upon which perhaps they meant to stand as a way of signaling their position within a disciplinary lineage. This all makes complete sense in light of Netz's (2020) observations concerning the differences in self-understanding between premodern literature (which functioned much more like modern scientific disciplines) and its modern counterpart (see Chapter 7 for discussion). The contemporary humanities are much more focused on an author's individuality, which would explain why Boyd's remark concerning the proprietary nature of literary metaphor is accurate as far as it goes. At some point, metaphors become proprietary along with the rest of literary output. But this marks a transition in the nature of the culture of the humanities, not a difference between the use of metaphors *per se* in science and in literature. Metaphors across the premodern period were treated as the common property of the community of writers; one also gets the sense that the use of a certain metaphor to frame a certain kind of experience was in some ways expected by readers. But again, as in the natural sciences, the use of a certain metaphor was not strictly liturgical. It persisted because of its consistent ability to resonate with writers and their audiences, because of its adaptability to the dominant themes of the age, and because it possessed a latent potentiality for further refinement and extension.

One of the several metaphors that receives extended attention in Curtius' study is that of the *world as stage*. By the time this frame emerges from Shakespeare's pen, it is already about 2,000 years old; Curtius marks Plato (*Laws*) as good a starting point as any. The reasons behind this metaphor's formidable endurance become clear as soon as one inspects its many instances across the history of the humanities. The notion of a stage is directly connected to all sorts of other phenomena – actors (us), an audience (also us), a director (God) – each of them pregnant with various associations from which further meanings can be extracted. Plato's version evokes a stage populated with puppets, manipulated by an all-powerful God for his own purposes. John of Salisbury, writing more than a thousand years hence, chooses as his focal connection the artifice of human behavior: "Learn from the actor that outward splendor is but empty show, and that after the end of the play the personages keep their real countenances" (*Policraticus*).⁵

> In addition, he combined its separate elements, which usually occur singly, into a general view. He finds his starting point in the moralizing commonplace rehandled by Petronius. The first extension of the horizon is achieved by a comparison with the text from Job. The conception is then deepened by pondering the question: tragedy or comedy? (Curtius 1953, 139)

How far we have travelled from the deterministic outlook of ancient Greece! While Plato uses the *stage* metaphor to illustrate the absence of free will, John exploits its capacity to exemplify the fact that people intentionally represent themselves in a way that does not reflect their true feelings. And yet, John works unmistakably within the same framework. From its cosmological beginnings, John has followed the trail indicated by the *stage* metaphor to a distant but important quotidian end. He is one of many beneficiaries of centuries of the metaphor's use, through which vast differences in cultural context have encouraged and enabled diverse generations of writers to explore new directions in which the metaphor might be pushed and by which it might produce yet further insights. John's own exploration spans two whole chapters. By the time the device reappears in *As You Like It*, it is a cliché; Sancho Panche greets Don Quixote's 1615 usage with a somewhat contemptuous sneer (Part II, Chapter 12; quoted in Curtius 1953, 141).

Nor is it solely specific metaphors that are subject to repeat application through the history of the humanities. Curtius likewise traces the perpetual reappearance of a wide variety of specific literary topics: "Affected Modesty," "Boy and Old Man," "The World Turned Upside Down," and so on. This same phenomenon is discernible in pre-Islamic Arabic poetry. Tribal superiority, reminiscences of great battles, heroes among one's ancestors, unrequited love, the death of a loved one – this was the thematic ground that poets were expected to cover, for these were the sorts of things that made up the significant features of life.

Metaphors and persistence in theme are both a kind of framing device. What is important for our purposes here is the way in which they and other framing devices are used to accentuate the salience of certain features of human experience. When Salinger (purportedly) frames Ethel Merman as the Queen Mary entering Walden Pond, he means to draw

---

⁵ Quoted in Curtius 1953, 139.

attention not to just how goddamn loud Ethel Merman is, but to her estimable capacity to make the listener long to return to a state of pre-Merman tranquility. No matter what the context, she makes you realize how relatively quiet things were before she started singing. This is a very particular kind of experience. It is fundamentally different from just hearing a loud, persistent noise, like a siren. It is like a fire alarm you can't figure out how to shut off. On and on it blares, as you frantically try everything you can think of just to get it to stop, because how sweet will that be? How much more serene does Walden Pond seem once the Queen Mary has disappeared? It's almost worth listening to Ethel Merman just to experience the inexpressible pleasure of a Merman-free world. No mean offensive sound can achieve this. These are the kinds of auditory experiences that make memories.

These same types of lessons apply to the more well-worn themes and metaphors surveyed by Curtius and other historians. While the *stage* metaphor accentuates different features of experience when used by different authors across the ages, it always accentuates *some cluster of features or other*. That is its mandate. One writer uses it to direct our attention to the likely mismatch between outer presentation and inner reality; it is used by Martin Luther to illustrate the concept of divine predestination (Curtius 1953, 140). Each of these marks for its author an important dimension of the human condition. The pre-Islamic Arabian's world was dominated by death, by the rivalries of tribes, by the mantle borne by the descendants of ancient heroes, and by the desert. In both contexts, the author uses recognized means to orient us toward something that really matters for gaining a deeper understanding our lives. Martin Luther and John of Salisbury use the *stage* metaphor to create a vivid illustration of the distinction between manifest appearances and the veiled reality of which one must always be mindful lest he be misled. The elegy of the Arabian poetess al-Khansa' for her fallen brother, Sakhr, reminds hesitant soldiers of the immortality promised to the brave by the inexhaustible human capacity for mourning:

> Be generous, my eyes, with shedding copious tears
> And weep a stream of tears for Sakhr!
> I could not sleep and was awake all night;
> It was as if my eyes were rubbed with grit.
> I watched the stars, though it was not my task to watch;
> At times I wrapped myself in my remaining rags
> ...
> Thus shall I weep for you as long as ringdoves wail
> As long as night stars shine for travelers

> I'll not make peace with people that you fought
> Until black pitch turns white.
> ...
> He would protect his comrade in a fight, a match
> For those who fight with weapons, tooth, or claw
> Amidst a troupe of horses straining at their bridles eagerly,
> Like lions that arrive in pastures lush.[6]

Remember: if you are killed in battle, future generations will know of your valor and skill. Your absence will be felt even more strongly than your presence. Upon no one else is a comparable honor bestowed.

These kinds of framing devices won't be unfamiliar to anyone who has spent time reading literature. My purpose in drawing attention to them is to (once again) show the surprisingly deep connections between the humanities and the natural sciences. Like nature, human experience is a high-dimensionality space. There are an obscene number of ways of accurately describing it. Most of them refer to things that don't really matter. And of those that accurately describe things that do matter, only a few are able to deepen and clarify our grasp of those things, allowing us to hold them in place and reflect on them and on their connections to other things of value. The words of Al-Khansa' encourage the wavering warrior not to be distracted by the illusory riches of personal safety, while John and Luther each in their own way apprise the reader of how little control she has over what she experiences, and to not become too invested in outward appearances. Whether through thematic repetition or through metaphor, the reader's (or listener's) attention is summoned with unusual force to focus and reflect on very specific features of human life.

But recall that this is precisely the function of such devices in the natural sciences. Darwin's contemporaries were well aware of the tendency of members of a species to have slightly different traits, of those differences to sometimes cause slight differences in the performance of some important task, and of the tendency to pass traits to offspring. What they lacked was a perspective which forced them to reflect carefully and specifically on the implications of that set of facts in particular, instead of on the many other biological facts they knew. Darwin's *selection* metaphor gave it to them. This situation has an important connection to the state of scientific "crisis" described in Chapter 3, and to the experimental trials of Robert Millikan mentioned in Chapter 4. As those discussions emphasized, there is a lot of weird stuff that goes on when doing experiments. Experimental

---

[6] Translation from van Gelder 2012, 12–14.

research can't function productively unless the experimenter knows to, on the whole, ignore most of what she sees and focus only on the relevant and most promising phenomena. Similarly, someone engaged in observation or in the analysis of data needs to pay attention to specific features of experience or specific kinds of trends in order to productively separate that which is meaningful from noise. The production of scientific knowledge depends on the development and refinement of certain devices for narrowing the field of perceptual attention.

Viewed in this way, we gain a fresh perspective on the importance of exemplars for the production of scientific knowledge, for it will be observed that metaphors rely on exemplars to do most of their semantic heavy lifting. "The Queen Mary entering Walden Pond" works so well because the Queen Mary exemplifies the class of big noisy things, as does Walden Pond that of pristine peace. Compare this highly effective metaphor with, "Ethel Merman is my '76 Chevelle driving down Lincoln Blvd." What, if anything, do my '76 Chevelle and Lincoln Blvd exemplify? What features do they demand that we privilege with our attention? For which categories do they function as symbols? Lacking any implicit reference to specific properties, or specific kinds of properties, the image of my '76 Chevelle driving down Lincoln Blvd cannot productively shape my perception of Ethel Merman. In failing to evoke any determinate features, it has failed to give me any purchase on *what kind of thing Ethel Merman is* (no one actually knows). If metaphors work by directing us toward certain features, they reach the height of their potency through the use of exemplars which amplify the salience of those features.

Marking off a specific cluster of features as being particularly important for understanding a certain phenomenon is an act of classification. It tells us to conceive of that phenomenon as a member of the class defined or designated or picked out by that cluster of features (Slater 2015). By emphasizing particular features of wild populations, Darwin suggested that we classify adaptive transmutation as a kind of breeding. This kind of breeding differs from the breeding of domestic herds in that it is the conditions of existence doing the "selecting," rather than human breeders themselves – but that difference is immaterial for gaining a fundamental grasp on what is happening to species in the wild over generations. Breeding is a well-defined process characterized by a small set of features. Analogous features are instantiated in the wild. Arguably, then, the process of adaptive transmutation is the same kind of process as what goes on between breeders and their domestic herds. And, indeed, it is not uncommon to hear the nature of science itself framed in terms of developing and refining classifications of the natural world.

6.3 The Kind Makers

I'm ekeing my way toward an account of how the humanities generate knowledge of what matters to us. Does it have to be so excruciating? Do I have to keep circling back to the same themes over and over and over again? Look, I've tried to keep it relatively light. I'm not a miracle-worker. I've got lots of balls in the air here, and I'm doing my best ensure that they give the appearance of a mostly continuous ring. Plus, it's not like there is a well-trodden path for me to blissfully skip down, as there is in the case of scientific knowledge. And even then, where did that get us? Right smack in the middle of a bunch of exploded myths. I can't say my account will fare any better. In fact, I *can* say that ultimately my account *won't* fare any better. But dammit if it's not going to be clear and wide-ranging.

Human life is debilitatingly noisy – ever more so than the natural scientist's carefully curated investigate contexts. No set of statements, regardless of how exhaustive and accurate, can by itself help us to confront the enormous challenges involved in making sense of one's life and all it contains. Like the natural scientist in the field, we profit from being able to classify our experiences as *some kind of experience or other*. These acts of classification are implicit commitments to the significance of certain features of an experience, features which appear to us to get to the bottom of what that experience represents. Each branch of the humanities contributes independently to the taxonomy to which we can turn in search of resources that might allow us to organize the utter mess of human experience into a set of relatively stable and describable kinds of experience. Call these relatively stable and describable kinds of experience *experiential kinds*. Humanists develop this taxonomy by studying poignant illustrations of human experience described in literature; by examining the contours of our concepts, our implicit commitments, and their logical interrelations; by tracing the evolution of culture and ideas over time. Through their varied approaches to research, humanists uncover and refine the defining features of different kinds of human experience. They construct the means to read what lies within.

In this section, I want to look at a specific example of a humanist's effort to develop what I've called an experiential kind: Stanely Cavell's "The Avoidance of Love: A Reading of *King Lear*." This is humanistic inquiry at its best. Although my discussion presents us with just one instance of humanities research, that instance is – dare I say it? – exemplary. And by that I mean something way more confusing: it possesses, and amplifies the salience of, the defining characteristics of how the humanities generate knowledge of the defining characteristics of an experience. It is a study in experiential kind-making. After looking at Cavell's study in some detail, I step back to consider some of the key lessons it suggests. This will put us in a position to see how the humanities produce knowledge of what matters to us.

I love my wife very much. At least, I think I do. Here's what I know for sure: I have a very complicated set of feelings associated with her. Some, like an overpowering physical attraction, are easy to identify and are easily connected to being in love. Some are easy to identify despite appearing to be quite distinct from love, like the indescribable sense of triumph I feel in the rare instance in which I gain the upper hand in an argument with her. Others, like the weird cluster of negative feelings I get when I haven't heard from her in a while, are not easily identified. Most of my feelings about her fall into this latter, inexplicable category. The other night I walked into the room where she was sitting and I was struck by how much she looked the way she did the first time I saw her, twenty years ago. I proceeded to stare at her, utterly transported to that time, with what seemed like a feeling of gratitude. I won't say that it was gratitude. I don't know what it was, except for that I assume it was a symptom of my love for her. When I try to think carefully about my feelings for my wife, I don't get very far. All I see is a big casserole – a more or less homogenous ooze, peppered here and there with recognizable flecks, heavily biased toward the recent and the most memorable, both positive and negative. I do not have a perspective on these feelings which allows me to cleanly delineate one from another, nor does it allow me to see them as coherent manifestations of love as I understand it.

Cavell's reading of *King Lear* focuses on the play's multiple manifestations of the relationship between love and self-knowledge, perhaps most clearly displayed in the opening scene. There Lear announces his intent to abdicate the throne and divide his kingdom among his three daughters; the largest share to whomever loves him most. From his eldest daughters, Goneril and Regan, he gets exactly what he wants and expects from them: a public declaration of their love which, through hyperbole, shows itself to be disingenuous. His youngest, Cordelia, does not follow suit. She offers a curt but honest reply: "What shall Cordelia speak? Love, and be silent" (*I, i*, 64). She indulges him only to the point that her love permits. And because of this, argues Cavell, Lear loses his mind (Cavell 1969, 263–264).

Why? Because he is a tyrant and a bully? He is that, but tyrants and bullies meet defiance (if Cordelia is even guilty of that) with force, not self-immolation. Cavell argues instead that Lear's rage and madness descend from his confrontation with the fact that Cordelia's articulation of her love is genuine, despite her knowing and understanding him, faults and all – including the fault that he himself is incapable of love:

> he wants something he does not have to return *in kind*, something which a division of his property fully pays for. And he wants to *look* like a loved man—for the sake of the subjects, as it were. He is perfectly happy with his little plan, until Cordelia speaks. Happy not because he is blind, but because he is getting what he wants, his plan is working. (Cavell 1969, 267; original emphasis)

He offers his daughters bribes in exchange for public declarations of their affection. But Cordelia won't participate, because the whole thing is a shameful spectacle, and her love for him would never allow her to be party to his humiliation. "Why should she wish to shame him publicly? He has shamed himself and everyone knows it. She is trying to conceal him" (Cavell 1969, 269).

> Cordelia is alarming precisely because he *knows* she is offering the real thing, offering something a more opulent third of his kingdom cannot, must not, repay; putting a claim upon him he cannot face. She threatens to expose both his plan for returning false love with no love, and expose the necessity for that plan – his terror of being loved, of needing love. (Cavell 1969, 267)

Through his analysis of this and other scenes, Cavell uses *King Lear* as a spotlight for the illumination of a very subtle feature of love: its deep interconnectedness with self-knowledge. Lear is disgusted by his true self. He is ashamed. But as long as he avoids the bonds of real love, he can keep his true self at bay. Why? Because one cannot be loved unless one is known. One can *provoke* love by projecting a false image of oneself. But the object of that love is the mirage behind which hides the individual. Or one can elicit false love by manipulating others, as Lear does. The only understanding required here, though, is of the terms of the transaction. But Cordelia neither loves falsely nor truly loves a false image. She loves her father, Lear; Lear, from whom she wants nothing, and whom she endeavors to spare humiliation.

Now, whence self-knowledge? If Cordelia cannot love her father unless she knows him, then she must know him. And this, according to Cavell, is what Lear cannot abide – being *recognized*. In effect, a profession of love is tantamount to uttering, "I know who you are." To learn that one has been recognized is to be confronted with a truth that might have easily passed undetected – namely, the truth about who one is. As long as Lear is not loved, he is not recognized. And as long as he remains unrecognized, he may postpone a reckoning with himself. He may continue to hide behind the veil. Love lifts the veil, because it is an unmistakable signal that one has been recognized. To continue to lie to oneself, love must be avoided – at all costs. Now, it is part of the lore of love that it makes one vulnerable. What we normally understand by this cliché is that developing feelings of love for someone exposes one to the potential for having those feelings hurt, suffering a broken heart, etc. But reading Cavell's analysis, and reading *King Lear* through it, you can suddenly see how vulnerable one becomes by *being loved*. Viewed from this perspective, the fabric that binds us to those we love takes on a new significance. The potency of my relationship with my wife comes not only from how I feel about her, but from what her feelings for me can tell me about myself.

This is the service Cavell has provided for people like me – that is, people who are more interested in understanding themselves than in the niceties of *King Lear* scholarship. He has honed part of the morass of feelings associated with love into a set of well-defined ideas that people like me can apply introspectively to sort our experience into categories with clearly defined features. These ideas support a perspective from which I am able to see those newly clarified aspects of my experience *as* aspects of the experience of love. These aspects of love needn't be particularly subtle or complex in order to escape our notice. With love, as with many other forms of human experience, the challenge often involves being able to shift the position of the objects in our field of introspective vision. Cavell understood: "It is the difficulty of seeing the obvious, something which for some reason is always underestimated" (1969, 285). Our lives are intense. It's rarely possible to pause and reflect, even about matters in which we're relatively well versed. Reading works in the humanities brings to the fore features of everyday experience that are often either too subtle or too routine to command much attention. Cavell's "The Avoidance of Love" converts these muted background features into highly visible aspects of my experience. I now have a magnifying glass through which I can clearly and convincingly see which of my thoughts and feelings are closely associated with love, and which are part of something else. I have a deeper, richer grasp of the contents of my own feelings, memories, and experiences. I have acquired the means to read what lies within.

There's no question that this process of self-recognition can be extremely painful. I finally had to just force myself to stop thinking about it because it became too depressing. No wonder Lear went temporarily insane. Although, maybe Cavell's lens is all the more valuable for that. Who that has suffered through the torment of self-recognition would ever chance lying to himself again? But the reward is even more concrete. Cavell's framework has brought into sharp relief subtle demands of love that we can now aspire to satisfy. And here we are able to see how the application of the humanist's experiential kind is able to kindle a second-order desire, a desire that my desires take this form or that. Thanks to Cavell we come to better appreciate the contours of love and just how far beyond the bounds of love our behavior can be. That presents us with a dilemma: do we want to bring our desires more in line with the demands of love, or are we content with our love's existing imperfections? Now, I won't say that one is rationally compelled to aspire to more perfect versions of love. What I will say is that Cavell's framework gives us the means to clearly perceive what our true normative commitments are vis a vis love. Which do we value more: improving our embodiment of love's essential characteristics, or continuing in our present state? After Cavell's analysis, I can see that love is incompatible with certain of my other desires. That awareness has forced a choice between incompatible desires, and the outcome of that choice will reveal the truth about what I actually value. I can't hide behind the mists of ignorance and confusion anymore. I can't lie to myself as effectively. Finding out what matters to oneself is not always pleasant. Having a clear conception of what love requires forces us to confront the question of how much we value it.

6.4 Conclusion

We barely scratched the surface of Cavell's account. But that's primarily what we're interested here – the contours of that surface, rather than the substance within. His account is a study in experiential kind-making. It is a scholarly effort to aptly characterize a phenomenon at the center of human experience. As part of that effort, he has used literature to draw our attention to the types of manifestations to which that phenomenon and its features are often given. He has promoted the significance of certain aspects of our experience as being particularly important for understanding that phenomenon. And he has provided a formulation of that phenomenon that we can use to organize, inspect, and – were we to be so inclined – potentially remake our experience. This is what self-knowledge looks like.

The process of making experiential kinds begins with the use of exemplars to draw our attention to features of particular significance for understanding certain kinds of experience. It ends with a framework that facilitates the characterization of experience in terms of those kinds. These frameworks can take a variety of forms, and indeed what one finds across the humanities is a vast spectrum of approaches to the making of experiential kinds. Different types of experiential kinds are often best served in different ways. Some experiential kinds focus more on the representation of certain kinds of people or events than on emotions like love. A framework for representing a certain kind of person or event might be best served by looking at different manifestations of it across a range of artistic and literary works, as in Curtius's survey of the Latin Middle Ages, seeking to develop an archetype. Readers of these humanistic endeavors will not always come away with a set of propositions that can be deployed in other contexts. Rather, they acquire something like a mental image or pattern, defined not by necessary and sufficient conditions but by an intuitive grasp of telltale symptoms. We saw Robert Millikan use this sort of knowledge to guide his Nobel-prize winning study of the electron. Students of the humanities can use it to guide their reflection on everyday life.

The ultimate question is, how does the use of an experiential kind for the purposes of introspection qualify as knowledge? Isn't it possible to *misread* what lies within? All that a given experiential kind offers us is *one* way of conceptualizing our experience. Who's to say that that is the right way to do so? And who's to say that Stanely Cavell has correctly read *King Lear*?

I want to suggest a different way of looking at this question. As with scientific inquiry, the goal of introspection is not the disclosure of THE fundamental mind-independent truths, but rather the development of a perspective on the phenomenon of interest that makes its features clear enough to explore in a systematic way. Is there some ultimate, cosmically grounded truth about whether I love my wife? Maybe, but its discovery (were it to exist) lies beyond our grasp. The study of the self, like the study of nature, proceeds through classification of experience. The taxonomy that guides this process informs the general picture that results. Different taxonomies carve up experience in different ways. We refine our taxonomy through careful thinking and the cultivation of new experiences; also through happenstance. As we refine that taxonomy, the various features in our general picture become increasingly well-defined. The more well-defined those features are, the more clearly we can see whether they conflict with our other commitments. If an apparent conflict taxes us beyond our willingness to resolve it, we may move on to a new way of classifying experience. We've decided that we've misread nature, or that we've misread what lies within. And so on and so on. That is all there is to systematic inquiry, be it directed outward or inward. Certainly it is possible to misread what lies within. But, as in science, the best way to find out you are wrong about something is to develop a careful articulation of what things should be like if you are right. I might be misreading my feelings for my wife.

Indeed, Cavell's account convinced me that I have been misinterpreting certain feelings in that regard. I might be misreading my feelings about distributive justice. Through Rawls' carefully articulated framework, I at least had to come to terms with the fact that a commitment to distributive justice entails a commitment to tolerating inequalities only if they are necessary to make the worst off as well off as possible. That's a pretty high bar. Maybe I'm not as positively disposed toward distributive justice as I thought I was. On the other hand, maybe I'm even more committed now.

Being able to read what lies within requires that we be honest with ourselves. Through the cycle of refinement and comparison, the humanities can help us develop and maintain a vantage point from which we can examine our experience with a certain amount of critical distance. For, the project of introspection then becomes less focused strictly on how we feel and more on how to fit our feelings into well-defined categories; or, failing that, constructing new experiential kinds that better capture the contours of our experience. It becomes less about defending the appropriateness of an impulse or feeling and more about enabling a better cognitive grasp of those states. Feeling what lies within is not the same as reading what lies within. For reasons beyond my comprehension, there is just something about articulating a feeling that depersonalizes it to some degree. It is the difference between knowing *how* one is feeling and knowing *what* one is feeling. We will never be free from motivated reasoning; that includes the scientists among us. But, over centuries, the sciences have developed a number of tools to dampen the effects of the ever-present drive to see in nature what one wants to see. In similar ways and through relevantly similar means, the humanities encourage a kind of perspective on our inner lives that reduces the threat of self-delusion.

Toward the end of the play, Lear imagines a future in which he loves Cordelia as she has loved him, in which they live "as if we were God's spies" (*V, iii, 17*). Why *God's* spies? God's spies must give an accurate moral weighting. They must be pure. Like the angelic scribes depicted in the Qur'an, like the pure Cordelia, Lear has been purified and can now see and acknowledge things as they are, including himself as he is, as Cordelia has known him. But now, even as he and his daughter face their imminent imprisonment and death, he is content. He is more than content. He looks eagerly toward those days, days in which he no longer needs to avoid himself and, therefore, can love. As painful as self-knowledge can be, in the end it is liberating.

CHAPTER 7

Humanities Victorious?

Well, I guess that about wraps it up. The humanities produce knowledge. And they've been doing it for thousands of years. They do not produce *scientific* knowledge. That's probably OK, though. Very little of our knowledge is scientific. And the bit that is scientific bears little resemblance to the cherished Potemkin village that we've erected – the Scientific Method – in order to distract from the fact that the form and function of much of the content of scientific knowledge is ineliminably humanistic in character. I warmly invite anyone skeptical of this bold claim to attempt to refute it.

I gave an account of disciplinary knowledge spanning Chapters 2–5. This account is comprised of a handful of "moving parts" that are easily recognized in the natural sciences, even if they tend not to be especially salient in the prevailing perspective on scientific knowledge. Let's briefly review the "moving parts" of the model of disciplinary knowledge, so as to give the reader a map of the foci of coming chapters and how they relate to what has led to this point in my argument. The foundation of this model is the scholarly canon or consensus, which I have argued are two manifestations of the same phenomenon. The canon is the center of scholarly gravity. It is the source from and in accordance with which disciplinary inquiry proceeds. It is the grammar and the lexicon acquired by practitioners in development, through which they communicate and with which they produce novel terms and propositions. These novelties are attempts to articulate knowledge, which are then submitted to the scholarly community for expert vetting.

A canon, whether scientific or humanistic, is composed of exemplars. This is the second moving part. Exemplars offer a much higher-bandwidth conduit for learning than propositions. However, they do so at the "expense" of greater ambiguity. Of course, I do not think that it is an expense at all, only that it appears like one relative to the misrepresentation of scientific knowledge that confuses clarity of attempts to articulate knowledge with knowledge itself. Indeed, it can be shown to be the exact opposite of an expense. It is nearly pure profit, as Grosholz (2007) shows across an instructively broad range of episodes and traditions in the history of science.[1] Since an exemplar does not tell us why it itself is significant or what makes it an important achievement, members of the scholarly community have a certain freedom to value what they will about it, and consequently to develop perspectives on and characterizations of that value which they use to guide their own creative endeavors. This well-known capacity of works or literature, of philosophy, and of art is also of critical importance in the natural sciences, though it is not widely appreciated. One researcher might find Newton's unification of celestial and terrestrial mechanics to be the *Principia*'s most important contribution, while another draws inspiration from his use of geometrical proof to solve the problems of motion. Many aspiring natural scientists followed up Newton's exacting methods of experimentation in the *Opticks*, whereas others were rather more keen to explore suggestive affinities with heat and electricity. Their research trajectories will diverge accordingly, perhaps laying the foundation for subsidiary research traditions of their own.[2]

In this way, the canon's exemplars serve as the foundation for the community's attempts to develop a range of scholarly norms. Enter moving part #3. As members of the research community explore the limitless range of different pathways suggested by an exemplary achievement, they increasingly come to understand the meaning and value of the achievement in terms of those specific pathways that prove to be particularly fruitful. This is easy enough to appreciate in creative works of arts and literature, which often develop a reputation as a symbol of this, or a model of that. But that pattern is emblematic of the sciences too. Tappenden (2008), for example, argues that the fruitfulness of a particular concept or definition in mathematics is interpreted as evidence that that concept or definition is the "natural" framework for understanding the mathematical phenomena in question. In both contexts, the success of a particular way of interpreting what makes the exemplar exemplary endows the interpretation with a normative status. The interpretation's elevation to normative status has some powerful effects. In the first place, it constrains the range of options from which the practitioner may choose when she is attempting to use an exemplar as a guide to future research. As, for example, the witty exchanges of *Pride and Prejudice* begin to gain acceptance as its special, era-defining

---

[1] Which is not to say that the relationship between profit and ambiguity is limitlessly positive. Haufe 2024 is partly an attempt to explain why ambiguity is so productive.
[2] Cohen 1956, entire book. p163 contains a specific but telling illustration of how this worked.

feature, attempts to remake literature in its image will be judged according to that feature in some form or other. A norm of scholarly practice has emerged, though perhaps only implicitly.

The second powerful effect (and my fourth "moving part") is that the increasingly widespread appreciation of the centrality of those witty exchanges (say) inspires attempts to characterize what it is that makes those witty exchanges so valuable – attempts to understand the way in which they are central to the book's acknowledged literary achievement, and to explain how exactly they contribute to or establish the claim of *Pride and Prejudice* to the mantle of exemplar. As described in previous chapters, this too occurs in the natural sciences. In each context, an articulation is a practitioner's attempt characterize what he has derived from an exemplar so as to share it with other members of the scholarly community. This characterization is an attempt to capture the cluster of properties that stand out as particularly salient for practitioners and that appear to them to be most in need of attention and explanation (Camp 2019). A characterization of, say, how the witty exchanges contribute to the majesty of *Pride and Prejudice* will be adopted by other scholars when it appears to illuminate (part of) why they esteem that work; as the Arab prosodists of the early Middle Ages adopted the metric scheme of al-Khalil ibn Ahmed because of how it captured the exemplary poems of their time; as the SVO characterization of English grammar is able to model native speakers' intuitions for acceptable utterances. And so on. Each of these efforts constitutes an attempt to articulate the content of norms governing experts' patterns of appraisal in a given domain. Each of them is designed to give concrete expression to what it is about an exemplar that explains its disciplinary role as part of the "the price of admission to practice and the basis of participation in debate."

What has not been achieved is a vindication of the thesis that the humanities are "on a par" with the natural sciences. I believe such a thesis to be incoherent. To me, that is like saying that shrews are on a par with tigers. What would that even mean? They're not "on a par," nor is one superior to another. They're just separate lineages, lineages which share a lot of evolutionary history but which diverged long ago for predictable evolutionary reasons. Each one can do things the other can't. Tigers have a much more heavily restricted range, but they are its apex predators. Shrews live everywhere and are more extinction-proof than tigers. Plus they are way older. A bit runty, yes, although I'm not sure I want to know what an apex predatory shrew would look like. Shrews and tigers both play valuable ecological roles. Tigers are easy to admire because they're gigantic killing machines. They command respect. I developed a healthy respect for them after I saw one transition into "creep" mode upon seeing my baby deer-sized son on a tiger preserve in North Carolina (also on that visit, a tiger copiously urinated on an 8-year-old boy who simply stood there, smiling blissfully). I feel sorry for whomever cannot bring themselves to invest in and admire shrews because of how enamored they are of tigers. Shrews are fascinating once you get to know them. Dismissing shrews because they can't rip out something's larynx is just prejudiced. There's more to life than ripping out larynxes.

There is a passage in *The Structure of Scientific Revolutions* where Kuhn asserts that there are good reasons to think that acquainting students with the details of the historical development of science need not improve their scientific acumen, and can in fact be expected to make them poorer scientists (Kuhn 1962, 165–166). I have always found this to be a plausible claim, as do I find his claim that suppressing the historical details of scientific inquiry is "pedagogically unexceptionable." (Kuhn 1962, 140). For several years after I started teaching his book to students, I felt the moral gravity of this tradeoff each time I elected to assign the book as course reading. Do I dare chance weakening the scientific acuity of students merely to acquaint them with the historical pattern of scientific development? Then, quite suddenly, and through the kind of gestalt shift in which Kuhn himself had been so intensely interested, I was struck by the absurdity of the quandary. For, the moral gravity of the choice of inhibiting someone's ability to practice science can only be felt against a backdrop which presumes that to do so would be to tread unforgivably upon sacred ground. It must be borne in mind that, just as there is more to life than unburdening something of its larynx, there are dimensions of personal growth even more important than developing one's ability as a scientist. And that applies just as much to scientists as it does to the rest of us. Maintaining one's acuity as a scientist should not come at the expense of depriving oneself the opportunity to become a better human being.

Just as certainly, however, our quest to appreciate the depth and breadth of human experience ought not to distract us from our cultural and intellectual responsibility to grapple in a competent way with the natural sciences, for they too are a product of human experience and very carefully tuned judgment every bit as much as is *Tintern Abbey* (well, some of them are…). Perhaps even more importantly, though, they are the part of *communal* experience and judgment, and the way in which that communal dimension facilitates the sciences' ability to contribute to human culture has not been given due reflection by humanists as they lament the lack of genuine appreciation for the humanities.

I think there are serious problems with the humanities today, but I do not think they stem from an inherent or inveterate lack of concern with producing knowledge. Rather, the problem is a diminished capacity to produce *disciplinary* knowledge, and it is the result of certain pathologies which afflict humanities disciplines in their present configurations. In the following chapters, I look at a few symptoms of these pathologies and attempt to trace them back to their source. In each instance, I argue that the problem can be understood in terms of the absence or wholly deficient presence of one of the key ingredients involved in the production of disciplinary knowledge.

We know that these problems are not inherent to humanistic inquiry, because they appear to be a relatively recent phenomenon. It is clear from historical studies of the humanities that the ability of humanists to function as a discipline, and to enjoy the fruits thereof, is an ancient one. Kuhn himself cites theology as the kind of community that functions the way scientific communities do (Kuhn 1962, 166). Makdisi (1990) surveys a wide array of such communities beginning in the late seventh century, from grammarians to prosodists to epistolographers to philosophers, emphasizing in particular the way in which exemplars bound each community's members together and functioned as the launchpad for training and inquiry. Brown (2007) describes the disciplinary consequences of canonization of certain texts in the formative period of the Islamic legal tradition. El Shamsy (2013), focusing on related communities around the same period, discusses explicitly and at length the several points of contact between those communities and Kuhn's community-centered model of scholarly development. This is to say nothing of the development of knowledge in communities whose concerns were more distant from what we think of as the humanities. Communities of mathematicians are examined by, for example, Mahoney (1973) in the seventeenth century, Gray (2008) in the nineteenth century, and Netz (2004) in late antiquity. Netz (2020) traces the developments of communities of humanists, also at this time.

It is good news that our difficulties with producing disciplinary knowledge are a contingent defect of our present situation, and not an incurable byproduct of the scholarly attempt to understand human experience. It means that the problem is potentially soluble. What has brought us to this state? Part of the issue appears to have something to do with broader social and cultural circumstances which we did not create and which are exacerbated by modern society's embrace of a gross misrepresentation of scientific knowledge, a process which began in the eighteenth century (Gaukroger 2006, 2010, 2020). But humanists themselves bear much of the responsibility. As I observed in Chapter 2, Collini (1999) is symptomatic of the way in which humanists themselves have largely accepted this misrepresentation and have amplified critics of the humanities in their opinion that we do not produce knowledge. Small (2013) even goes so far as to balk at the notion that we do research. Seriously; look it up (page 2). Free from the weighty encumbrances of epistemic labor, many humanists have moved forcefully in the direction of what looks much more like self-expression than scholarly inquiry. There is a place for self-expression, even for scholarly self-expression. It's just that we don't need disciplines to do it. And, as a result, groups of humanists seem often to qualify as disciplines in name only; guilds or professions, maybe. It takes more than a collection of intellectuals to make a discipline, and it is important to think seriously about what we as scholars can do to fix the situation. The alternative is to risk further abetting our descent into irrelevance.

7.1 Canon across Cultures

My goal for the remainder of the book is to describe some aspects of contemporary humanities research culture and motivate the conclusion that they render the disciplines afflicted with them epistemically defective in some way. Each of these defects can be traced back to some deviation from the model of disciplinary knowledge. Ultimately, though, they are all rooted in one way or another in *the death of the tradition of mastering a relatively small set of exemplars* – which fits, given the way in which exemplars lie at the base of disciplinary knowledge on my account. Exemplars are the concrete manifestation of a discipline's idealized self-image. They teach us about what is important and how to achieve it. They are the benchmark of adequacy and the platform for further creative elaboration. They are both ancestor and archetype.

Disciplines need exemplars in order to impart scholarly values and norms. They need exemplars to function as the vehicles by which scholarly skills and techniques are transmitted. They need exemplars to act as a common reference point that binds the community of scholars together by functioning as the repository of meaning for the lexicon of scholarly thought. While the exemplars certainly mean different things to different communities of scholars across time and space, a given scholarly community – a discipline – is nonetheless picked out by the substantial overlap in its esteem for a certain set of scholarly achievements, and in its understanding of the normative constraints, however broad, that those achievements place upon the scholarly efforts of current members. It is this overlap that grounds the distinction between a discipline and a group of scholars with roughly isomorphic interests.

Relatedly, and perhaps more importantly, the relatively small set of exemplars is itself what makes it possible to gain mastery over a scholarly tradition. Taken together as a canon, these exemplars constitute something like a framework. They are concrete, yet they are also symbols. To master these works is to master the basic framework for scholarly production – "the price of admission to practice and the basis of participation in debate." But it is not simply a matter of "paying one's dues"; the "price" invoked by Grafton and Most is the effort required to absorb the scholarly norms that make it possible to contribute meaningfully to the development of knowledge in a domain. It is many years spent among the right bedouin tribes. It is many years spent in the provinces of European literature, moving frequently about from one to another. Remarking on the ancient literary context, Netz (2020, 152) observes, "One interiorized the canon, and in so doing one sensed the effect of style, of superb verbal performance as such. And, in so doing, one perfected one's own rhetoric." Makdisi (1990, 141) observes precisely the same effect in the classical Islamic literary context:

> In Islam the Koran was one of the sources of eloquence for poets and writers of artistic prose. It was regarded by the Arabs as the ideal of eloquence, a model, *the* model par excellence for poetry, oratory and the epistolary art. It was the schoolboy's first textbook, which he memorized from a tender age, his prayerbook as he grew up into adolescence and adulthood. It was the first text of classical Arabic that he memorized through constant daily repetition, so that its recitation was to him as second nature as the dominical prayer was to his Christian analogue. Consciously or unconsciously, he was affected in his language by the language and style of the Koran.

Mastery of a canon, which traditionally took the form of memorization, makes it "a part of you." It affects the substance and direction of thought and language, shaping them in ways that reflect the common spirit underlying the discipline's range of exemplars. Through this kind of mastery, scholars develop a reflex for relating novel phenomena or experiences back to the canonical framework in some way.

When every member of a community develops the same kinds of reflexive instincts, they are able to function as an intellectual unit with the capacity to engage in community-level scholarly scrutiny. They are able to converse with one another on a register occupied by them alone, partaking of a "shared world" or "commonwealth of motifs" (Netz 2020, 138, 139, respectively): "Works referred to a 'given', neutral word of myth or of history; they did so without relying on the properties of the written text ..."(147). In parallel language, and for the same reasons, one could say with Kuhn that scientists working within different research frameworks are "[p]racticing in different worlds" (Kuhn 1962, 150; one *could* say that, but *should* one?). Indeed, the sociologist of science Rudolf Stichweh explicitly identifies a scientific discipline as a closed network of communication:

> Modern scientific disciplines constitute relatively precariously constructed networks dependent on communications (conceptually) linked to other communications, and on third parties observing this process. In turn, if these third parties want to convey messages, they must be prepared to provide communications that also use such (conceptual) links. (Stichweh 2007, 9)

Without this common substrate and the unique community-level capacities it affords, a group of specialists is, in my view, no different from a group of nonspecialists in terms of their group-level properties. In other words, a discipline without a tradition of mastering exemplars is not really any kind of discipline at all.[3] Echoing Kuhn, we might say that, though those individuals may be scholars, the combined efforts of their activity amount to something less than knowledge or understanding.

This dynamic is so easily discernible in the grand literary traditions of the premodern world that it scarcely bears mention (but here goes). Netz (2020) identifies 19 authors ("give or take a few," 94) – Homer, Euripides, Plato, Thucydides, to name a few – who can be shown to constitute the Greek canon by the end of antiquity, out of which the Latin literary tradition emerges. The historical influence of these works needs no elaboration. Makdisi (1990) traces the emergence of the humanistic tradition that defined Islamic civilization to the Qur'an and seven pre-Islamic Arabian poets who lived between the fifth and sixth/early seventh centuries, whose names were and are known (al-Khansa, Imru' al-Qais, Zuhair, etc.) and whose odes were collected by Hammad ar-Rawiya (lit., Hammad "the rhapsodist") in a volume known as *al-Mu'allaqat* ("The Hanging poems") in the second Islamic century/eighth century CE (Makdisi 1990, 132, 139). Since readers are most likely less familiar with this tradition, I quote Makdisi at length from a section of his book titled "Evidential Value of Pre-Islamic Poetry for *Adab*" (the Arabic word for humanities).

---

[3] See, for example, Stichweh (2007, 10–11) on the distinction between disciplines, which he takes to be "communication complexes," and professions, which "represent not scholarly knowledge systems but action systems specializing in contacts between members of the profession and clients."

> The uses made of these collections were many, considering the value of Pre-Islamic poetry as the repository par excellence of *al-'Arabiya,* the pure classical language. From this repository are drawn the evidential examples for grammar and lexicography, and 'the other disciplines of *adab*'; for the exegesis of the Koran and of the words of the Prophet in the hadith [reports of Muhammad's sayings and doings]; for the history of the pre-Islamic Arabians and all that pertains to them. An example of the evidential use of poetry is the work of Ibn al-Yazidi (d. *c.* 2nd quarter of the third/ninth century) … a work on the rare or strange words in the Koran, in six volumes; in which each word of the Koran was supported with several verses from pre-Islamic poetry as evidential examples … To Ibn 'Abbas [d. *c.* 67–68 AH/687 CE) is attributed the saying that when a problem arises regarding the meaning of a strange word in the Koran, one should 'seek it in [pre-Islamic] poetry, for it is the Register of the Arabians. (133)[4]

Observing the unmitigated pluripotency of these foundational texts, he notes:

> The importance assigned to the classical Arabic language, the effort made to collect its vast vocabulary, the search for its strange and rare words as contained in ancient Arabian poetry, in the Koran and the Prophetic Traditions, led to the constitution of other fields that were to come under the designation of *adab,* the *studia adabiya.* Chief among these were:
> 1. philology; that is, grammar and lexicography
> 2. poetry, including the sciences of metrics and rhyme
> 3. rhetoric, as applied to the arts of letter-writing and speech-writing
> 4. history, including the genealogy of the ancient Arabians, their battles, customs, and tribal history, leading to the various genres of historiography: the diary; the annals; the chronicle; prosopography in its various genres, the classes of the society of learned and other illustrious men, and the later centennials (covering one century…); and
> 5. moral philosophy, including apophthegms, proverbs, the science of government, the rules and regulations of various occupations in the religious sciences and in government; e.g., the discipline of the secretary, of the Judge, of the Minister, and so on… (120)[5]

Similarly, Lewis (1999) documents the same phenomenon during the Han period in China: "A single group of texts triumphed … anonymous classics at the top, a constructed author 'Confucius'…interpreting them, trailed by the various authored texts that interpret Confucius" (Netz 2020, 7). As in the Islamic and Greek contexts, this Chinese canonical tradition functioned as the common core from which other writers derived both

---

[4] I have removed Makdisi's parenthetical translations of certain terms into Arabic.
[5] Here again, I remove parenthetical translations into Arabic.

literary ideals as well as the moral and political ideals instantiated in the mythical polity *Zhou Li*, the ancient exemplar to which later dynasties aspired. As Lewis describes it:

> The imaginary state of *Zhou Li* came to define the imperial order, and the textual realm fashioned in the coded judgements of the [texts of the canon] endured, while the substantial realities of actual administration all turned to dust. In this way the Chinese empire became a realm built of texts. (Lewis 1999, 362; quoted in Netz 2020, 7)

In each context, we see clear reflections of the classes of disciplinary phenomena described in our exploration of consensus and canon. These different classes all emanate from the way in which the canon, or in which scientific consensus, functions as an abstract framework that is generative yet highly restricted. Commenting on this tension, and the discomfort it induces in the contemporary humanist, Netz (2020, 95) remarks:

> It has become an established procedure in the humanities to display the heterogeneity underlying apparent units. We have learned to argue that the naïve assumption of homogeneity prevails just because of the power of words to draw an essentialist spell. Thus, we have learned to decry the error of assuming that there was something such as 'the Greeks.' 'Nonsense,' the sober contemporary humanist comments. Surely there were many varieties of being Greek? There must have been 'cultures within ancient Greek culture,' – to quote the title of an influential recent collection (Dougherty and Kurke, 2003). I do not question the particular claims made in such a volume, and by the research tradition it represents. Surely, we can point to the tension between the use of a lyre or an aulos, between the implicit ideology of an Aesop and that of a Delphi. Greeks had their tensions. And yet we should not be blinded to the facts of homogeneity. Through the centuries studied in this book, across an expanding Greek Mediterranean, the top literary field was unique and stable. In fact, the paradox was deeper: a world made of local identities, of the sense of attachment to one's own city – shaped by a universal and homogeneous canon. It was always like that: epichoric but, above all, Panhellenic.

In fact, the evidence from the natural sciences and the world-changing literary civilizations of the past is overwhelming: these traditions are *generative precisely because they are restricted.*

Netz provides a wealth of penetrating insight into how and why canons were able to define disciplines in the way I'm suggesting. He begins with an empirical observation that he and I both found surprising: for any given Greek canonical author, a library of papyri is in general no more likely to contain one of his works than another. The reason that this is surprising is that these libraries are *ex hypothesi* assumed to contain the most popular works. If an author's works are equally distributed across libraries, that suggests that what is popular is not the work, but the author himself. Possessors of small libraries seemed not to care whether their collection contained a copy of Plato's rather highly philosophical *Parmenides* or his more accessible *Meno* (Netz 2020, 119–120).

That was the first surprise. The other thing that surprised us both is that, in a random sample of 100 authors drawn from the *Thesaurus Linguae Graecae*, 79 of them were "clearly active in a single genre" – meaning, they only wrote works of history, or of philosophy, or of poetry; cross-generic authors are relatively unusual. This was true even among those authors working in the exact sciences:

> ancient scientists had an extremely strict disciplinary regime. Not a single author contributed to both medical and mathematical literature .... The same ... was true of all scientists in antiquity: they were first and foremost that thing which they were. Archimedes, Hero, Ptolemy: very different authors but certainly 'mathematicians' contributing to a particular genre, namely the exact sciences. The mix could have been different ... *Within* a generic boundary, there would have been considerable freedom. But the freedom stopped at the generic border. (Netz 2020, 134–135)

Summing up, Netz (135) remarks, "An author's career would be defined by genre. Indeed, it would be defined: authors would be aware of their choices of writing as falling into the pattern of their overall output."

The second surprise explains the first. Evidently, the ultimate function of a work was to represent a genre: works, chosen essentially at random from an author's corpus, stand in for the author. The author, in turn, stands in for the genre. Why? Because, by and large, authors stuck very closely to a single genre. Thus, if you want philosophy represented in your library, just grab something by Plato. A dash of mathematics? Anything from the Archimedes bin will suffice. And so on. Such was the primacy of genre in the ancient literary world. Nor was its predominance something that was perceived solely by the casual reader, as the strong signal coming from small libraries might suggest. Authors viewed themselves as denizens of a genre/discipline, and thus constrained by the disciplinary norms therein. Netz contrasts this with "modern literary careers," in which "an author's career is made by the *crossing* of generic boundaries":

> Genre breaking is typical to post-Romantic literature for reasons which are obvious enough: the more an author can flout generic constraints, the more he puts on display his *idiosyncratic* power. He breaks from the pack. The figure of the author, in the post-Romantic era, is made like that; the more

> powerful it is, the more so…In antiquity, genre reigned supreme: because an author was imagined as taking up a *life*. Authors were marked more by their genre, and so, conversely, authors were defined less by their works. (135–136; original emphasis)

Further evidence for the determinative role of genre in antiquity, as against its causal inertness among modern writers, comes from the style of literary criticism in the ancient world. And here in particular we can discern the function of exemplars in conveying an understanding of the conceptual content of genre/discipline-defining norms:

> The first tendency of ancient literary criticism was to set an author within very broad categories of style. The first question was: what was an author like? And the answer would be a single adjective, taken from a small, restricted repertoire. Demetrius has four types…: spare, elevated, elegant, and powerful; Dinoysius has three kinds (De Comp Verb. 21): austere, elegant, blended; Longinus' extant treatise is dedicated to a single variety, that of the 'sublime'. Hermogenes in 'On Ideas' looks, instead, for the abstract nouns that form the *elements* of style (clarity, grandeur, beauty, rapidity, character and sincerity). (150)

The vehicle for imparting the content of these literary ideals was a genre-exemplifying author:

> This variety is discussed in the terms of authors-within-genres. Hermogenes chooses one author, Demosthenes, explicitly because he is said to be paradigmatic of all types of style … Dionysius introduces each kind by stating who the paradigmatic authors are according to genre of each; for instance, the paradigmatic blended authors are …: in epic, Homer; in lyric, Stesichorus and Alcaeus; in tragedy, Sophocles; in history, Herodotus; in rhetoric, Demosthenes; in philosophy, Democritus, Plato and Aristotle. (150)

To emphasize the point, Netz tellingly notes:

> Most significantly, the discussion is never concerned with the level of the work taken as a whole. Rarely, entire poems are analyzed, but even then the analysis is focused in individual selections, ranging in size between the clause and (rarely) the paragraph. This is because the project of detecting paradigmaticity is based on the identification of features of verbal texture, which are not taken to be unique to a given author but are, rather, displayed in any given work, with many individual passages. (150)

He concludes with an important contrast between the ancient literary tradition and our own: "Modernity and antiquity are near opposites in all of that. Modern critics end up praising the genius of idiosyncrasy. Their ancient counterparts praised the master craftsman of paradigmaticity" (150).

Netz goes on to review the generative capacity of exemplars in a canon across a range of disciplines. I hope you'll forgive one last long quotation (albeit from a 900-page book!), as a means of illustrating that capacity through a specific instance taken from Euripides:

> ... there was no obvious ancient parallel to Shakespeare's Hamlet, no figure that, by virtue of a powerful treatment by a canonical author, comes to be defined as essentially *of that author*. Consider what might appear to be a leading contender: Euripides' *Medea*. It could have been Euripides' invention to have her kill her children, and it is indeed as a child killer that she is remembered from Euripides onwards. But even if this is Euripides' own invention, it does not take place in the enclosed domain of Euripides' fiction. Instead, it takes place in the shared domain of myth. That is: Euripides has, perhaps, changed the manner in which others will recall myth from that point onwards, and they were free to do so, writing their own Medea plays. There may or may not have been a previous infanticide version in a tragedy by Neophron [contemporary of Euripides]; there were perhaps seven or eight tragic authors, as well as five comic authors ..., writing versions of 'Medea' in the century *following* Euripides' *Medea* ... I do not deny that, when thinking about Medea, viewers also thought of Euripides; I do not deny that, when they thought of Medea, they thought of her ... primarily as represented by Euripides. But what they did think about was her: Medea. She remained a creature of myth, not of tragedy. (139–141)

Medea as ancestor. Medea as archetype.

7.2 A Question for the Ages

I want to pause here to pose a question, for which I possess neither answer nor insight. The question takes as its starting point the three themes that emerge out of our examination of the ancient Greek and Islamic literary contexts – viz., (1) the way in which a canon functioned to define a genre/discipline; (2) the pronounced effect that those canonical works had on constraining forms of literary production; and (3) the pronounced generative effect that those constraints appear to have had. My question is this: what intellectual casualties result from a lack of exemplars and the consequent loosening of constraints?

In order to gain a purchase on this question, think back to the earlier references to a "shared world" and a "commonwealth of motifs" in which the ancient Greek authors operated. Theirs was a world made by the Trojan War, by the ideal forms, by planes, points, and lines (the kind that never meet if they are parallel). Homer was to be credited with having brought the Trojan War to them, but it was not Homer's Trojan War, no more than Medea belonged to Euripides, despite his accentuating the salience of certain child-killing properties such as to have an epoch-defining effect on the way in which she was conceptualized by later dramatists. The *Elements* becomes our gateway to the mathematical world. The Qur'an allowed poets, grammarians, lexicographers, and philologists to enter an ideal world of literary form unveiled by God himself. The pre-Islamic poets kept the fires ablaze in the desert of their ancestors, whose names, deeds, and reputations were well preserved; they could have been contemporaries in a neighboring town. Once inside the Trojan War's world, or that of divine eloquence, or of point, line, and plane constructions, or the ancestors' desert, the intellectual could draw out new distinctions, make new connections, experiment with new perspectives, all within a framework of norms and values that would have been instantly recognizable to his congenerics or possibly to a much broader audience.

These are the same "worlds" envisioned by Thomas Kuhn in *The Structure of Scientific Revolutions*. Galileo built a Euclidean world of terrestrial motion. Kepler built a world of elliptical orbits controlled by the sun. Newton united these worlds and erected upon them an entire universe of physical reasoning and perspective, the one in which our now long-forgotten undergraduate zombies frolic for 15 blissful weeks before facing their next pre-med hurdle. During that precious time, they learn how to explore novel scenarios within the strict constraints that the Newtonian universe imposes on creative thought – for example, that the magnitude of any force is to be decomposed into the magnitude of its component forces in the vertical and horizontal direction. Max Planck's discrete packets of energy constitute yet another world for the physicist, as does Einstein's picture of relative motion, space, and time. Breaking from Aristotle's eternally stable species, Darwin inaugurated a world of perpetual organic change, one species gradually emerging from another. Natural scientists work in these worlds and in far more specialized worlds in precisely the same sense that Euripides and other ancient dramatists all meet together on a common playing field made by the myth of Medea. Just as later theorists have reshaped aspects of Darwin's evolutionary world, like his views about mass extinctions (Sepkoski 2012), Euripides' portrayal of Medea had a lasting effect on subsequent generations of writers. But they continued to work within the constraints defined by Medea in myth, in the same way the guardrails for evolutionary thought continue to be discernibly and uncompromisingly Darwinian.

But what of Darwin's impress do they retain, from the perspective of the evolutionary biologist? Most biologists have never read *On the Origin of Species*. And why should they? There are far more direct routes into the evolutionary world to which they must gain access. For their purposes, what Darwin does in 125 pages of dense yet delightful prose can be stated in a single sentence: some variations within a species are inherited by offspring and give them an ecological advantage. Doubtless there is much for the contemporary biologist to profit from in the *Origin*, but none of that is required to enter the world in which she needs to work. Where contemporary humanists see an author as the progenitor of certain works and ideas, the ancient Greeks saw him rather as a vehicle for a genre. The ancient Arabians and their successors in the Medieval and early modern periods clearly saw poets as the conveyances for the highest ideals of the Arabic language: "poetry…is the Register of the Arabians." Ancient Greek mathematicians were merely the doors through which readers gained entry to the Euclidean world. But this is not strictly an ancient phenomenon. Observe that the author of a modern scientific research article is all but nonexistent; could anything be more nearly anonymizing than the interminable lists of authors appended to modern scientific collaborations? Indeed, the literary form of a scientific research article strongly favors authorial invisibility, affording the reader as unmediated a view of the natural world as possible (however illusory that effect may be).

About ten years ago, a physicist observed to me in fascination how humanists seem to know the dates of all sorts of publications in their fields. It wasn't until reading Netz's *Scale, Space, and Canon in Ancient Literary Culture* that I was able to see why this fascinated him, it being second nature to me as a humanist. We prioritize this information because of the way in which we prioritize "the author": her mind is the native environment for the work she produces. But the natural sciences do not work this way. The native environment for a scientist's work is the discipline. She is essentially a messenger, bringing information from nature to enrich the disciplinary environment as a way of providing it with more structure. Certainly, she may hope to walk "the path to immortality," as my physicist friend put it. Perhaps she writes down an equation or isolates an effect that will bear her name. But this is exceedingly unlikely, compared against the number of scientific ideas that make it into print. Odds are she will spend her career humbly filling in more or less well-defined gaps in our knowledge, gaps of all sizes. Her contemporaries might see that a hole has been plugged, and that she was the one who plugged it. However, subsequent generations will be treated to a picture of scientific knowledge in their field which contains few if any traces of previous gaps; only advanced students and professionals will even be aware of *existing* gaps. The natural scientist contributes to the discipline and works within its conceptual and methodological boundaries. If she does her job well, disciplinary knowledge will consist of a clearer and more comprehensive version of those boundaries than when she began. It almost certainly will not record her name. As Kuhn (1962, 52) observes, everyday scientific research "does not aim at novelties of fact or theory and, when successful, finds none." This research is done in service of a world-picture, a "commonwealth of motifs" which the scientist sees as her job and *privilege* to elaborate.

It is difficult to avoid the impression that the disciplinary constraints which emerge from a canon are causally responsible for the immense creative intellectual power of these traditions, be they scientific or literary. This is the core of Kuhn's entire argument in *The Structure of Scientific Revolutions*, and I find little reason to doubt it; sometimes you just get things right. Netz and Makdisi both note the close association between constraints and generativity in their respective literary traditions. Cohen (1983, 1956) documents the same association in the historical influence of the Newtonian framework. Abd-Allah (2013), Brown (2007), and El Shamsy (2013) each argues explicitly for the generative power of canonical constraints with respect to certain dimensions of Islamic legal thought, dating from the second Islamic century/eighth century CE. The *Elements* is highly circumscribed. Nevertheless – and, by my lights, largely *because of that* – it fundamentally and forever transformed every intellectual culture it ever touched; in the words of one historian, it "shaped the world" (Wardhaugh 2021). No need to go on, though. One could spend an entire career documenting different instances of this phenomenon across the history of creative human thought. One could write an abstruse philosophical treatise just on this topic. To put it in the crass and reductive yet strangely resonant parlance of our time: this is a thing.

If it is a thing, we need to be wary of it. Humanistic inquiry is not just about timeless questions and human experience. Viewed historically, it is equally about working within the constraints of a world of ideas shaped by a small set of exemplars. Not necessarily the specific set of Western "classics" that have been associated the phrase, "the canon," but with *one or another small set of exemplars*. Had history gone entirely differently such that a different set of literary and philosophical works, artistic traditions, or religious texts appeared on Earth, some exemplary subset of those might have done equally well as a foundation from which humanism could have developed. In the remaining chapters, I articulate a few reasons to think that the causal connection between exemplar-based disciplinary constraints and creative intellectual depth is very, very real. Chapter 8 looks at the challenges for producing knowledge that arise from practitioners pursuing research topics just because they find them interesting. I argue that this convention is only consistent with the production of knowledge under certain disciplinary conditions specified by our model, conditions that are often violated by contemporary humanities disciplines. In Chapter 9, I provide a critical assessment of the significance of a recent spate of academic hoaxes as well as the humanities community's reaction to them. Here I try to show why many of the criticisms of the hoaxes are misplaced, why the hoaxes seem to be fairly easy to pull off, and why we can expect more of them given the way in which many of our disciplines deviate from the conditions required for disciplinary knowledge. I also examine the essentially nonexistent phenomenon of publication retraction in the humanities. I argue that this is a puzzle, but it's one into which I lack any real insight. Undaunted by the mists of confusion, I proceed to speculate irresponsibly about why we don't retract publications, arguing that the phenomenon can ultimately be traced back to – yes – some deviation from the model of disciplinary knowledge.

CHAPTER 8

Of Interest

8.1 Introduction

In March of 2018, Congressional Representative Lamar Smith of Texas, head of the House Committee on Science, Space, and Technology, released the latest in a series of statements over the past decade that criticized the National Science Foundation (NSF) for "funding too many projects that seem marginal or frivolous."[1] The real trouble began in 2013, when Rep. Smith, through his committee, requested all documentation related to five grants awarded by the NSF that year. When the NSF denied the request, Smith's committee came back with a similar request, only this time the scope had widened to over fifty awards. Again, the NSF denied the request. After an increasingly tense back-and-forth between Smith and the NSF, Smith ended the impasse by pointing out that the House Committee had absolute legal authority to review any NSF documents that it wanted to. At this point, Smith's committee was allowed to come to a little room at NSF headquarters to review the files, which allowed NSF to satisfy the request while making it as unpleasant as possible.

Despite the clear oversight authority granted to Congress by the NSF's charter – authority that has never before been a subject of major concern – there is a temptation among many researchers to see this as inappropriate government intrusion into a sacred domain, one which, in point of fact, already has in place a time-honored peer-review system that provides much better oversight than a Congressional committee could hope to give. As an expression of this sentiment, the presidents of the various science studies professional societies (SHOT, HSS, PSA, and SSSS) co-authored a letter in support of the NSF and against the perceived assault on peer review, which it described as "the best method" for fostering the growth

[1] Press release, Committee on Science, Space, and Technology, March 15, 2018, "An Overview of the National Science Foundation Budget Proposal for Fiscal Year 2019."

of knowledge. However, in correspondence with the NSF, Smith also pointed out that his committee had sent similar requests to all other government agencies involved in the distribution of scientific research funds (NIH, DoE, etc.), and only the NSF had objected (August 27, 2014 letter). Why was the NSF so reluctant to allow a review of their referee process?

Looking at the awards for which documentation was initially requested gives us a clue. All of these awards went to projects in the humanities and humanistic subbranches of the social sciences. And, from the perspective of people outside the relevant disciplines, the projects do not exactly inspire confidence in the intellectual integrity of the humanities. At the peak of the feud, I met with the then-current president of one of the signatory societies to ask about the letter they'd written and about the motivation for supporting the NSF's stonewalling of Congress. That president confirmed the hypothesis I formed when I first read through the list of questionable awards: it might not look good for the NSF program that funds humanities research if these award-winning projects were put on display for public appraisal.

The "NSF v. Congress" episode can be seen as just one battle in what is perceived to be a wider war on humanities scholarship. I would like to look at one front along which this war has been waged, the one exemplified by the NSF episode – namely, the quality of research topics in the humanities. Who decides whether a research topic is important? Is intellectual significance a purely subjective matter, or is there some sense in which it is constrained by forces that lie outside any particular researcher? I think that certain aspects of the culture of academic humanities have made it difficult to entertain the possibility that some research topics are genuinely insignificant, and have weakened our ability to conceive of a distinction between what interests us (or what is interesting), on the one hand, and what would be a significant contribution to scholarship, on the other. For reasons that I will articulate shortly, much of the value of scholarly research depends on this distinction being upheld.

In the remainder of this chapter, I argue that interest (or interestingness) *can* serve as a reliable guide to the detection of important research topics, but only under specific conditions. My argument begins by reflecting on a specific cultural difference between the natural sciences and the humanities that exemplifies the disparate roles that interestingness plays in the two domains. I explain how this specific difference is a symptom of a much more far-reaching contrast between them, and how this contrast tracks differences in the tendency of something of genuine scholarly significance to emerge from the pursuit of research questions that one finds interesting. Ultimately I will argue that disciplines in which consensus is a rarity, if it exists at all, do not function as intellectual communities capable of cultivating a causal link between something's being interesting and something's being important.

Polanyi recognized the centrality of this connection decades ago, writing in *Personal Knowledge* that

> Our vision of the general nature of things is our guide for the interpretation of all future experience. Such guidance is indispensable. Theories of the scientific method which try to explain the establishment of scientific truth by any purely objective formal procedure are doomed to failure. Any process of enquiry unguided by intellectual passions would inevitably spread out into a desert of trivialities. (135)

But his claim about inquiry unguided by intellectual passions needs to be qualified. Those intellectual passions cannot come from just anywhere. They need to be acquired through and molded by a robust, well-defined intellectual culture in the sense developed at the end of the previous chapter. These cultures, both scientific and literary, provided a tangible "vision of the general nature of things" which acted as a "guide for the interpretation of all future experience." Many of the natural sciences profit from the exploitation of intellectual passion because through their training, practitioners come to be passionate about the things that matter for their discipline. Inquiry guided by an intellectual passion out of step with disciplinary culture is just as likely to lead us into triviality as is inquiry unguided by passion. And the same holds for intellectual passion expressed in the absence of the kind of heavily restricted intellectual culture we surveyed earlier. Our survey of a range of highly productive intellectual cultures appears to strongly confirm Polanyi's claim: such guidance is indispensable.

8.2 Conflicts of Interest

I frequently have occasion to interact with natural scientists across a variety of disciplines – at professional meetings or conferences, colloquia, or just casually around campus. Because I am curious about the kinds of things they are researching, I will typically ask them about what they are working on. Scientists usually have several versions of this answer in their quiver. There's the professional insider's version, which often states a specific research topic, or a range of topics denoted by a single technical term (e.g., "I work on partial differential equations."). There's the professional outsider's version, which is organized around references to things generally familiar to people with graduate training in the natural sciences.

And there's the polite version: I'm a physicist/biologist, etc. If the person I'm talking to knows that I'm a philosopher of science, I tend to get something like the professional outsider's version, sprinkled with insider tidbits in direct proportion to the specificity of my follow-up questions. This packaging schema is familiar to humanists as well. (My polite version – "I teach history and philosophy of *science*" – is basically designed to conceal the fact that I am a philosopher. Trust me, it's not the kind of designation whose follow-up questions you'd want to be on the hook for answering. Think of it is the dermatology of the mind: "A dermatologist? Great! What do you think about this thing on my neck?")

During my conversations with scientists, I also make a point of asking why the thing they are working on is important. My motivation for asking scientists about the importance of what they're working on is one of professional curiosity: it is a very economical way to get up-to-date information on the current topics in a field and how they relate to one another. This strategy works, because the question is understood by them as asking what other sorts of issues their research bears on, and, again, the form their answer takes will be tailored to what they think I'm prepared to hear. The insider's version might cite other outstanding questions out of which their question emerges. The outsider's version might point to broader fields of inquiry of which that question is part. The polite version is usually a reference to its relation to some widely known area of concern outside of science ("cancer," or "climate change"). Beneath the variety of answers, however, lies a common spirit to these responses, in that each of them attempts to connect their research question with something that their interlocutor can be assumed to recognize as important. Later on, I will speculate on exactly *why* their answers take this form. For now, though, let it be observed that, for these scientists, what it *means* for their research to be important is for it to bear on issues whose importance they can reasonably expect to be recognized by members of certain groups. (Is that circular reasoning? Maybe, I don't know. That is a question for a philosopher. And, as I said, I *teach history and philosophy of science*.)

Humanists' responses to questions about the importance of their research also exhibit a range of predictable forms, although not in quite the same way as the scientists' curated adaptations of a single story. One predictable form is a very specific kind of confusion, manifested by the kind of silent, blank stare that I imagine is on my face when people speak too quickly to me in Arabic, a language in which I can "get by" but with which I have nothing like a native speaker's grasp. It is a look that says, "Based on the way you are talking to me, I must have given you the impression that I will understand what you're saying." By asking this person to articulate the importance of their research, we have lured them onto terrain with which they are constitutionally unfamiliar.

The most common reaction takes the form of what can be described as offense or hostility. One gets the impression that the very act of *asking* that question is considered to be an audacious, bellicose breach of widely observed social norms. Now, to be honest, my intention in these contexts almost always *is* to violate a widely observed social norm in the humanities. But sometimes you have to violate a norm in order to draw attention to it and subject it to scrutiny. In particular, the norm I'm seeking to violate is the one according to which we have an unimpeachable intellectual prerogative to work on whatever interests us. By asking why the research is important, we are taken to hint at the possibility that it is not. To hint at such a possibility is, I believe, to impeach the foundation of that intellectual prerogative. A characteristic expression of this hostility is the attempt to expose the incoherence of questions about the importance of some bit of research by responding to those questions with another question, which the beleaguered humanist assumes is obviously rhetorical: *who decides what counts as important?*

I want to pause for a second to reflect on what kind of disciplinary cultural norms would need to be in place in order for it to be obvious to someone that there is no defensible answer to the question "who decides what counts as important?" First, notice the contrast with the natural sciences. In all my years of pestering scientists, *not once* has someone stumbled or taken offense to a question about the importance of their research. They just answer the question. In that culture, it is in no way obvious that the question, "who decides what counts as important?" is rhetorical. The reason it is not obviously rhetorical is because there's a clear answer to it, an answer that is reflected in the spirit of the response to questions about the importance of specific topics that I surveyed above. The answer, clear as day to anyone who works in these disciplines, is that the disciplinary community decides what is important. That is why the importance of a specific topic is understood to hinge on its connection to other topics whose importance is already known. Known to whom? To the disciplinary membership. This is one of the ways in which certain disciplines in the natural sciences function like traditional cultures. There is a concept of "the known good," which practitioners have acquired through disciplinary acculturation and which they use to guide themselves toward research topics that the community has – sometimes explicitly, sometimes implicitly – recognized as being particularly significant. We looked closely in

Chapters 2 and 3 at how facts about what is important come to be fixed at the community-level, how practitioners gain access to those facts, and how those facts can change over time.

The rhetorical version of the question, "Who decides what counts as important?" presumes one of two things: either (1) that there is no fact of the matter as to which research topics are important, or (2) that because importance is entirely subjective, a topic becomes important simply by being of interest to some researcher. Perhaps it presumes some hybridization of these: there is *only* a fact of the matter regarding a topic's importance insofar as some researcher is interested in it. It is not obvious to me whether such a position can be cogently defended. It is clearly false in the context of the natural sciences, a point for which I argue in more detail below.

8.3 Scholarly Traditions

The existence of community-level or cultural facts depends on the presence of a community with the kind of structure that is capable of hosting those facts. That structure inheres in what we typically refer to as cultural norms, or traditions, or practices. Different sets of traditions facilitate the development of yet other traditions, forming something like a cultural "scaffold" in which the existing set of traditions constrains the set of subsequent possibilities for future cultural expression (Wimsatt 2013). There are lots of different mechanisms by which these structures get perpetuated from one generation to the next. Some do so simply by resting at the foundation of lots of other practices, such as our use of fossil fuels. (This is not the only mechanism perpetuating the use of fossil fuels. Evil also plays a significant role.) Probably the great majority of cultural norms persist through cultural osmosis, unconsciously absorbed as a byproduct of being immersed in a given environment. No one has to instruct a British lad in the subtle art of understatement.

Different mechanisms perpetuate cultural practices with varying degrees of fidelity, and the fidelity of these mechanisms bears significantly on the long-term stability of the culture. One particularly high-fidelity mechanism is direct enforcement. We instruct novices in the how-to of specific practices. In that instructional context, those practices acquire normative significance. Oftentimes, the normative significance is itself directly enforced: we do things *this* way, rather than *that* way, because *that* way is bad and *this* way is good. Explicit instruction through exemplification is one of the primary means by which, for example, a sense of aesthetic value is acquired (Clune 2021). Once a practice has been imbued with normative significance, group members have a motivation both to learn the practice *and* transmit it to others. As the practice gets taught from member to member, or from generation to generation, its normative significance travels along with it. In this way, the spread of practices through direct instruction creates communities whose members are bound together by a shared understanding that the relevant practice is widespread because it *ought* to be. For such a community, the existence of certain normative facts – facts about how things *ought* to be, for example – are fixed by that shared understanding (see Chapter 2).

I have just sketched a general picture of how a tradition of direct instruction can give rise to communities capable of grounding normative facts about what their members ought to do. I want to use this sketch to examine what I take to be a highly instructive contrast between cultural practices in the natural sciences and the humanities with respect to how research topics are *selected*. In general, the cultural norms governing research topic selection give us a lot of insight into how research importance is understood in a discipline, as long as we can justifiably assume that scholars do not regularly waste their research time on purpose (if we can't help ourselves to that assumption, then we need to have a different conversation). The topic selection process reflects part of a discipline's understanding of research importance, because it is designed to ensure that the questions pursued by members satisfy disciplinary standards for intellectual significance. I'm going to focus specifically on the selection of dissertation topics, partly because it is a particularly well-defined selection process, and partly because it incorporates aspects of the cross-generational transmission process sketched above.

Let's begin with the natural sciences. First, I want to acknowledge that, like every cultural tradition, the dissertation topic selection process admits of a variety of permutations across a variety of disciplines. I'm going to focus on a particular style of topic selection, because it appears to be overwhelmingly the most widely employed style. If you are a graduate student in the natural sciences, how do you decide what to work on for your dissertation? The short answer is that you don't decide at all. You are assigned a topic by a professor in your department. It is also fairly routine for departments to make the following distinction: if you come into the department with external funding, you are allowed to choose with whom you work; if you are funded by the department, you will be assigned an advisor, who will assign you a topic (or a small set of topics from which you are allowed to choose). In these disciplines, it is standard for graduate students to have no decision-making power whatsoever regarding what they will write their dissertation on. In fact, the freedom to choose research topics is routinely *not* extended even to postdoctoral researchers, who are hired because (1) they possess a particular skill that the Principal Investigator's (PI's) chosen topic requires but that she herself lacks, or because (2) the PI's topic requires the effort of multiple practitioners of the same specialty. The denial of research freedom to doctoral students and postdoctoral researchers normally lasts for roughly ten years, a figure which converges nicely with the historical study conducted by historian of science Larry Holmes in which he found that it takes, on average, ten years for someone to make the transition from new graduate student to independent creative investigator (Holmes 2004). (I will add parenthetically – since I don't have a sense of how common it is – that senior researchers involved in large collaborations like LIGO and LHC are often assigned specific topics as well.)

It is tempting to think that the practice of assigning dissertation topics is a practical necessity born of the constraint imposed by the need for laboratory space for research in these disciplines. This is incorrect. Only *some* research in the natural sciences requires laboratory or field work, yet the practice of topic assignment is general across all different kinds of research. (Topic assignment is also practiced in mathematics.) Why, then, would these disciplines resort to such authoritarian measures, if not out of practical necessity? Plainly speaking, it is because members of the disciplinary community have identified certain topics as the topics that ought to be worked on, due to their particular degree of importance, and they do not have confidence that a graduate student will be able to accurately assess a topic's degree of importance.

When I describe this tradition to my fellow humanists, they are uniformly surprised (I'll give you a moment to collect yourself). There is also often a sense of visceral revulsion that this news tends to induce, one which was crystalized for me in 2019 when, in response to hearing it, a senior historian shot back in horror, "Why not have arranged marriages, too?!" Long have I meditated on these words. The tone of shocked offense in her voice is seared into my mind. I think it's worth reflecting on this episode for a bit, because of the way in which it exemplifies certain deeply entrenched features of disciplinary culture in the humanities.

First, let it be observed that the United States is not exactly a model of marital bliss. Is our own cultural approach to marriage really so vastly superior to arranged marriages that one could safely assume that the question, "Why not have arranged marriages, too?" would be understood rhetorically? Much of the world does it. Maybe we should give it a go? In truth, I don't think the rhetorical force behind this historian's question was supposed to reside in the differential prospects for a successful marriage between the two systems. She actually meant something much more instructive. She felt that "Why not have arranged marriages, too?" was an appropriate response to hearing that scientists assign topics to their students because, to her, the two processes are, in important ways, analogous. She holds both to be scared rites of self-realization. In her disciplinary culture, a graduate student's dissertation topic selection is treated as a rite of passage, and is frequently accompanied by all the self-doubt, soul-searching, and other varieties of mental anguish that are standardly associated with the transition to a new phase of life. The graduate student selects a topic that interests him deeply and about which he feels he has something new to say. Special priority is typically given to research questions that are maximally distant from anything anyone has asked before. In short, selecting a dissertation topic is a deeply *personal* matter. (This recalls the fetishization of idiosyncrasy in modern humanities disciplines to which Netz alluded in the previous chapter.) To violate that personal prerogative would be quite like telling an artist what he has to paint. Or, telling someone whom to marry. My interlocutor's attempt to ask the "arranged marriages" question rhetorically was based on the presumption that being assigned a dissertation topic is obviously a gross violation of basic disciplinary cultural norms protecting the right of an individual to self-actualize, as obvious and as gross of a violation as assigning them a marriage partner.

Despite the attempt to make it rhetorical, the question, "Why not have arranged marriages, too?" actually does have an answer, one which draws instructively upon the same principles that deprived the question, "Who decides what counts as important?" of its own rhetorical force. In point of fact, there are lots of cultures that have a system of arranged marriages. Certain features of their community structures make such a system possible. One such feature is, plainly, the preexisting tradition of arranged marriages. In these cultures, you can literally ask someone to arrange a marriage for you (could be a friend, relative, or person in the community with a good track record). I can't do that in American culture – not *really*. The idea of asking my parents to find someone for me to marry, for example, is bizarre and counterintuitive (especially given that I am already married). But, for anyone who comes from a culture in which this is routine, it doesn't seem bizarre at all. It can seem perfectly natural. There are other interesting parallels, if you think about it for a while.

In the same way that our regional culture lacks the community structures that make a cultural system of arranged marriages possible, I believe that contemporary humanities disciplines generally lack the substrate of cultural norms that make it possible to distinguish between *personal interest* and *disciplinary importance*. In our disciplinary culture, scholarly research (like marriage) is conceptualized as an act of self-actualization or self-expression. The goal of an act of self-expression is to create an external representation of one's personal value commitments. Within this framework, the distinction between something's being important, and something's being important *to me*, evaporates. For, in the context of self-expression, my highest priority is to produce a representation of something that I hold dear; it is only by doing this that I can successfully engage in self-expression. What's most important in this context is whatever holds value *for me*.

Scholarly research functions as an act of self-expression in the humanities in that it is routinely treated as a vehicle for articulating one's thoughts on a subject that is of immense personal interest to him. Is it any wonder, then, that practitioners might have a hard time conceptualizing the importance of a research topic in any way other than whether it is of interest to the person investigating it? We should expect the question, "Why is this important?" to barely make sense to a contemporary humanist. When we treat scholarly research as if it were predominately a platform for self-expression or self-actualization, we make it conceptually impossible to draw a distinction between what is important, on the one hand, and what is interesting to oneself, on the other. For instance, I am interested in Charles Darwin's conception of natural law. That interest alone functioned as sufficient justification for spending four months out of a two-year postdoc researching the topic. It never occurred to me to so much as *think* about whether that was an important topic. I'm not actually sure the question of whether it was important would have made sense to me. Embarking on this project was simply me exercising my discipline-sanctioned scholarly prerogative to pursue what interests me. To ask whether the subject of an act of self-expression is important is, at best, to misunderstand what self-expression is about. At worst, it is a personal attack.

Now, I am not questioning the value of self-expression. As a recovering teenager, I appreciate the degree of centrality that acts of self-expression can come to command in a person's life. They are among the most distinctive features of the human experience. Their effects on our culture are inestimable. What I *am* questioning is whether it makes sense for us as a scholarly community to use interestingness to oneself as the primary determinant of scholarly importance or priority. There are costs to blurring or collapsing the conceptual boundary between interestingness and importance.

Apart from the obvious disadvantage of undermining our ability to conceive of a variety of research importance whose scope extends beyond our own feelings, I believe it has fundamentally weakened our ability to make lasting contributions to human culture. Relatedly, it has inhibited – perhaps even erased – the capacity of groups of scholars to function as disciplinary communities. Like any culture, functional disciplinary communities require widespread agreement on a broad range of normative commitments – commitments about *how* research ought to be undertaken, about what sorts of topics are important, and so forth. This widespread agreement on normative issues provides an invaluable background against which an individual can develop their own sense of normative understanding; it may even be essential. When our selection of research topics is driven not by a sense of importance whose source is external, but by our own internally cultivated individual sense of interestingness, we undermine our ability to develop the kind of shared understanding of importance that can support the development of deeper, richer humanistic inquiry.

It is tempting to think of replying along the following lines: the culture of the humanities recognizes a sense of research importance that is sourced at the community-level and conceptually independent of personal interest. It's just that, with sufficient training, one's interests come to be driven by the community's scholarly priorities. Following one's interests thus becomes a way to research important topics: because the importance of a topic is what is causing us to be interested in it, we can use our interests to reliably guide us to important topics.

I think that this sort of reply actually makes a lot of sense in principle. It is the qualifying background to Polanyi's observation above. Now, let us try to think about what kind of conditions would need to be satisfied to develop an instinctive interest in the scholarly issues that the community has deemed important. At a minimum, it would require there to be widespread agreement across community members with respect to which topics are important; if we are going to cultivate an instinctive interest in important topics, there has to be some fact of the matter about what topics are important – a fact that is determined by widespread scholarly agreement. Second, it would require that there be some mechanism for imparting that interest to members of the disciplinary community.

Regarding the first requirement, we do see lots of cases in the natural sciences in which members of a discipline display consensus on the importance of certain topics. For many disciplines, it is possible to make lists of such topics; different members' "top 10" lists are likely to show substantial overlap. The general agreement among practitioners with respect to which topics are important is what makes it possible, in principle, for others to learn what those topics are. It is, I believe, no coincidence that these are also disciplines in which all available textbooks tend to cover the same content, often right down to the order in which topics are presented.

This leads us to the second requirement – viz., the existence of a mechanism for transmitting an instinctive interest in important topics. Disciplines in which there is widespread agreement on such issues display an impressive ability to propagate that agreement. In fact, I think the transmission process is so familiar that it easily escapes our notice. In these disciplines, practitioners routinely pass down the facts about topic importance through direct instruction. This instruction can be explicit, as in, "This is an important topic. That is not an important topic." It can also be implicit, as when a doctoral advisor assigns a topic to a graduate student. The fact that the advisor is working on such topics, and that she assigns related topics to her limited supply of graduate students, is itself a signal that the assigned topic is an important one – again, assuming that we can help ourselves to the presumption that the advisor is not in the business of intentionally wasting her time and the time of her students. I think that it is fairly typical for practitioners in these sorts of disciplines to develop an intuitive interest in or sense of the discipline's important topics, in much the same way that members of norm-saturated cultures come to discriminate on matters of value in the prevailing cultural mode.

It is worth observing that neither of these conditions can be effective without the other: consensus on important topics makes little difference to the historical trajectory of research if those topics are not being inherited by subsequent generations of scholars. Similarly, a tradition of direct instruction in the importance of certain topics will not have much effect if everyone is being instructed in the importance of *different* topics – or, to put it only slightly differently, if the prevailing disciplinary understanding of importance is indistinguishable from interestingness to oneself. In the absence of a substantial base of agreement on the importance of certain topics, all that I end up teaching my students is that certain topics appeal to me. In a way, I also end up teaching them – sometimes by explicit instruction – that the proper way to select a research topic is to pursue what most interests them.

It is far from clear that any such system of norms exists in the current cultural manifestation of humanities disciplines; it is far from clear that any such system *could* exist. The difficulty is not simply that our disciplines lack consensus on the range of important topics. It's actually significantly deeper than this. The difficulty, it seems to me, is that, to the extent that we *do* transmit a sense of how to detect a kind of importance that does not reduce to mere self-expression, it is through the pursuit of *novel topics solely for the sake of their novelty*. Using a combination of referee reports and interviews, Michèle Lamont's (2009) study of *How Professors Think* examined the review practices of grant proposal referees for major humanities grants. This investigation showed that humanists' estimations of a research topic's *significance* are strongly tied to only one other feature of a research proposal – *originality*. Now, these data are extraordinarily opaque, so it is important to not be overconfident in what they might mean. But it is suggestive that no other evaluation criteria were as dominant, nor as closely associated with one another. Humanists tend to regard a research project as highly significant if, and *only* if, it is highly original.

In the current culture of our disciplines, a project's intellectual merit is often conceived of in terms of how much of a break it is with previous research. Different methodologies applied to different topics interpreted with different theories derived from different frameworks. To do something very different is a reliable way of doing, by our lights, something very important. The notion that "importance" in humanities research is defined chiefly in terms of novelty or difference obviously would, if true, explain why *significance* and *originality* estimates are so tightly correlated among humanists; both estimates are tracking the same underlying property. It could also explain why graduate students are subject to so few constraints when choosing a dissertation research topic. Plainly, if the only constraint on importance is that the topic be sufficiently novel, then the goal of working on something important has been satisfied as soon as one has chosen a topic on which no one has worked before. Precisely because most questions have never been asked, ensuring that students ask novel questions does not require a great deal of oversight.

A conception of scholarly importance focused predominately on self-expression and novelty is incompatible with the existence of a disciplinary culture capable of transmitting a substantive community-defined sense of importance to future generations of researchers. Now, that might not be something in which we can see any particular value. But it is something that lots of previous generations of humanists (and artists) held on a pedestal. As the studies of early literary communities clearly show, there is nothing inherent in humanistic research that requires a focus on novelty or scholarly self-actualization. That is a contingent feature of our current disciplinary cultures, and it is worth reflecting on the extent to which it is in the long-term interest of the humanities to continue to perpetuate this conception of importance. Might it not be better to instead try to reconfigure our cultural norms in a way that promotes community-centered intellectual growth? In the remainder of this chapter, I examine this question in depth.

8.4 Novelty, Destroyer of Worlds?

My key point here will be that the rise of novelty as the master norm has made intellectual passion an unreliable guide to research importance. In order for intellectual passion to effectively serve as a guide to important research topics, an intellectual community needs to reliably transmit its constellation of intellectual norms and values – its "world," its "commonwealth of motifs" – to the next generation of researchers. The sense of importance that feeds their passion needs to be shaped by this inheritance. But if the dominant norm is novelty, their sense of importance comes to be associated with *deviating* from the very constellation that defines the intellectual community as a discipline. As scholars seek to stake out new deviations, they weaken the disciplinary fabric, degrading and ultimately destroying the constraints that have, historically, proven to be highly generative for all sorts of intellectual communities. Novelty is the anti-norm.

My strategy for establishing this point will be to look in some detail at how the resistance to novelty facilitates intellectual *depth*. For obvious reasons, novelty and depth very typically act at cross-purposes to one another. I begin by examining how depth is facilitated by shared scholarly interest in particular research topics or themes. I then look at the roles variously played by a shared interest in research strategies or methodologies, and by a shared sense among scholars regarding what *increases* in depth tend to look like. As I hinted above, though, novelty also has implications for a discipline's ability to replicate itself, and this too strongly affects whether scholars are able to achieve depth.

8.4.1 Shared Passions

The history of mathematics and of the natural sciences both attest to a strong association between a shared sense of what research topics are important, on the one hand, and the ability to achieve greater intellectual depth, on the other. Knorr (1975), for instance, shows that ancient Greek mathematicians were fixated on the problem of incommensurable magnitudes (what became our irrational numbers) from the fifth century BCE until the fully mature expression of the theory by Eudoxus (d. 355 BCE), a member of Plato's circle. This fixation, argues Knorr, was not merely productive of the development of the working theory of irrational quantities that appears in Book X of the *Elements*, but of the *Elements* in its entirety. Cohen (1985) and Damerow (1991) show how preoccupation with the seemingly innocent problem of an object in free fall defined the conceptual framework through which classical mechanics came to be articulated over the course of the early – mid-seventeenth century. Ospovat (1981) and Rehbock (1983) examine the period from Goethe and Buffon (mid-eighteenth century) to Darwin, in which the problems of morphology, embryology, biogeographic distribution, and adaptation occupied the majority of naturalists' interest, culminating in their stunning unification in the *Origin* in 1859. Rocke (1984) shows how the development of atomic theory from the early mid-nineteenth century was driven almost exclusively by the question of how to empirically track the basic proportions that constituted different substances (e.g., is water H_2O or HO?). Kuhn (1957) describes how astronomers since antiquity were concerned primarily with a small family of problems associated with celestial motion. Heilbron (1979) traces the development of the science of electricity through the struggle to understand a small set of its behaviors (e.g., attraction, repulsion, conduction, insulation) over the seventeenth and eighteenth centuries. Sepkoski (2012) describes the emergence of paleobiology as an autonomous evolutionary discipline centered around the problems of extinction and diversity as evolutionary phenomena. This, too, is a thing.

Each of these problems admits of a variety of dimensions, all of which served as hosts for more specialized lines of inquiry. The problem of free fall was not simply, "What's up with free fall?" but actually denotes a cluster of questions that challenged practitioners' understanding of terrestrial motion; they wanted to know, for example, why a ball dropped from the crow's nest of a moving ship should fall directly below, rather than some distance behind (in fact, many doubted that this would happen at all), or why heavy and light objects fell at more or less the same rate (this too was disputed). In this way, scientific research problems form a sort of genus, which over time give rise to several species or subgenera, radiating out like an evolutionary tree. At the base of the tree sits the phenomenon – free fall, or electrical attraction – which exemplified the kinds of things that matter for a discipline, that fall under its purview and demand explanation by its practitioners. As described in Chapters 3 and 4, exemplars leave themselves open to a range of understandings of their significance. Just as dramatists found myriad ways of exploring the moral significance of

Medea, practitioners in the natural sciences take some salient phenomenon as their starting point and endeavor to extract whatever we might be able to learn from it.

And the lessons are potentially limitless. For, problems are perpetually reconceptualized, subsumed under new frameworks and consequently generative of new understanding and further inquiry. Galileo and Newton both ruminate on the problem of free fall, both accept (their versions of) the expression $\frac{1}{2}at^2$, but they view the problem in radically different ways. For Newton, orbit and free fall are manifestations of the same phenomenon (gravitational attraction), whereas Galileo sees them as different kinds of "natural motion," an Aristotelian notion of which Galileo seems not to have been able to unburden himself (Westfall 1971, Chapter 1). Similarly, Netz suggests that Medea acquires a new meaning for audiences after Euripides' *Medea*, even while his version is ultimately a stand-in for the canonical Medea of Greek myth. His Medea is a subgenus, perhaps a dominant one; so too is Newton's version of free fall. This sequence of genus-generating problem followed by generative reframing after reframing is ubiquitous across the history of science and mathematics (see Haufe 2024 for why).

Viewed from this perspective, it is easy to see why Kuhn (1962, 10) writes of exemplary scientific achievements that they serve "for a time implicitly to define the legitimate problems and methods of a research field for succeeding generations of practitioners." Much of what made these achievements influential has to do with the convincing and comprehensive vision of inquiry that they offered, rather than a convincing and comprehensive picture of the natural world. They gave practitioners a clear sense of what it would be like to do research within the framework on display. We know this was their primary concern because we find lots of instances in which communities of mathematicians or natural scientists discover that there is some fundamental problem with a framework and yet continue to use it, or adapt it to fit their needs. Newton's appeal to gravitational action at a distance was not well-received – not even by Newton, who "[s]hortly after completing the *Principia* ... wrote a strong letter to Richard Bentley declaring that no person in his right mind could believe that a body can 'act where it is not'" (Newton 1999, 62). Nevertheless, his geometrical approach to the problems of motion quickly became the *lingua franca* for the discipline, as did the menu of problems which he had selected for treatment (many of which he himself had inherited from earlier generations). More than anything, it is this perception of "future promise" that solidifies some scientific contribution's claim to exemplary status.

With that status obtained, the exemplar's normative powers begin to manifest themselves. For, they "implicitly define the legitimate problems" in the sense that a research topic needs to be perceived by the community as broadly consistent with the *kinds* of problems exemplified by the exemplar in order to be taken seriously by the community. Indeed, insofar as one was trained in the practice of inquiry, interest in these problems largely defined one's membership in the associated communities. One could not, for example, claim to be a geneticist in the early twentieth century and fail to acknowledge the paramount importance of biological inheritance as a scientific problem. Notice, though, that this is entirely possible in our own time. A contemporary geneticist need only be interested in one of the many extremely narrow problems associated with, say, protein folding in order to qualify as a geneticist; she need not have any research (or even peripheral) interest in the general phenomenon of biological inheritance per se, and she may have little if any understanding of how patterns of inheritance affect population structure over time. Similarly, it would have sounded contradictory during antiquity to claim to be an astronomer but to deny any relevance to or interest in the phenomenon of stellar parallax, whereas the opposite is probably true today – that is, a graduate student hoping to further our understanding of stellar parallax would probably be looked at as incredibly ignorant, even deranged; definitely not fit for a research career in astronomy. In any case, such a person would, in failing to acknowledge the fact that stellar parallax is not a legitimate puzzle, place himself quite beyond the boundaries of the community of astronomers. So tightly does the disciplinary community constrain what is to count as an important problem – a problem worthy of intellectual interest and research effort – that one's very status as a practitioner of the specialty associated with that community depends on his implicit avowal of the community's research themes.

We can see in this convention how restricting the range of legitimate research topics facilitates the attainment of significantly higher degrees of intellectual depth of the sort surveyed in the first paragraph of this section. By defining community membership partly in terms of whether someone takes up certain prescribed sorts of research topics, the disciplinary community ensures that it is principally *those* topics that get addressed. The relative degree of focus that a small, reasonably well-defined problem set affords is what explains the community's ability to achieve greater depths of understanding. It is this focus that allows the devotion of an unprecedented amount of intellectual energy to a mere handful of topics, energy which might previously have been distributed across a large and heterogenous "desert of trivialities." It makes sense that the rapid progress that ensues following major advances in scientific theory is associated with a contemporaneous demotion of many of the issues with which the community was previously engaged to the dustbin of scientific irrelevance. This phenomenon is all the more evident in cases where historically disparate schools of thought are united (or better, conquered) by a sufficiently impressive theoretical achievement. The unwieldy herd of puzzles with which schools once occupied themselves is whittled down to a small, well-behaved collection of topics whose importance is acknowledged by all members of the newly established intellectual community. This relationship between focus on a narrow bandwidth of topics, on the one hand, and mastery over those problems, on the other, is well-described by the old saw, "Jack of all trades, master of none."

Highly productive scholarly communities have always worked in this way. They actively resist the introduction of gratuitously novel research topics, and it is not difficult to see why. Acquiring a truly deep understanding of a phenomenon, whether it be natural, mathematical, philosophical, moral, or literary, requires successive generations of a community of specialists pouring all their energy into developing a picture of the phenomenon that is able to command broad ascent within the community. Although there are many instances of this in the humanities, there is also a cross-disciplinary fixation on researching highly obscure topics that have hitherto escaped our notice. There are lots of disciplines in which someone who does this is simply not taken seriously, to the point where they are viewed as not part of the discipline at all. The humanities disciplines used to be among them, judging from the heavily restricted genre parameters within which premodern humanists worked. This is the expected result when practitioners are guided by the ideal of intellectual service to a specific domain of inquiry, rather than their designs for self-expression.

History also suggests another expected result: knowledge and understanding. On a purely practical level, it is simply not plausible to think that a scholarly community of finite size can exercise genuine expertise over an endlessly proliferating field of research topics. In this context, any effort to exercise the kind of community-level scrutiny required to produce genuine knowledge or understanding will necessarily be pathetically shallow, if it exists at all. We need to have the intellectual courage to declare certain questions as illegitimate research topics in order to preserve the integrity and the intellectual credibility of our disciplines. We need to impart a sense of topic legitimacy and illegitimacy to succeeding generations in order to preserve our capacity to pursue anything of intellectual depth.

In Netz's terms, we need to stop treating a discipline as a forum for exploring authorial idiosyncrasies and instead return to thinking of ourselves as mere vehicles for disciplinary knowledge. The natural sciences have largely succeeded in this.

8.4.2 A Shared Commitment to a Set of Strategies for Inquiry

The above quote from Kuhn also stresses the way in which exemplars implicitly define the legitimate *methods* of a research field, and here too we find an association with increased intellectual depth that is causally explicable, and which is predictably rooted in the community's essential role in the production of knowledge. Back in the Introduction, I mentioned a couple of cases in which the work of modern scientists was initially rejected on account of having employed the method of hypotheses in their research. Although they look bizarre by contemporary lights, these objections illustrate a key feature of the process by which disciplinary knowledge is produced – namely, that, at any given time, only certain approaches to inquiry are understood to result in knowledge. This reflects Goodman's profound insight, mentioned in Chapter 4, that an inference is valid when it conforms to the accepted norms of inference. There is no higher court.

Just as we can find scores of historical instances right down to the present day in which practitioners shared an interest in a narrow set of research topics which they as a community deemed legitimate, the causal efficacy of a shared commitment to certain strategies for inquiry also emits a signal that is broadcast loud and clear across the history of science and mathematics. One instructive example comes from Newton, who chose to frame the mathematics of *Principia* in the geometry of the ancients, rather than in the more direct and analytically powerful calculus, which he had invented some twenty years earlier. Why? The argument made by his biographer Westfall (1980) and accepted by others is that it was because proofs done in classical geometry were comprehensible to and trusted by all mathematicians at the time. On the other hand, the calculus, which Newton had not published and which he had shared with practically no one, would have been all but unrecognizable as a method of mathematical inquiry. As Newton correctly surmised, the relevant issue was not whether the method was valid in some cosmic sense, but whether it conformed to the accepted norms of mathematical practice (which it clearly did not). That was 1687. It took almost one hundred fifty years before anyone was able to provide rigorous mathematical foundations for the calculus, which Cauchy and others achieved in mid-nineteenth century (Grabiner 1981; Kitcher 1983). And yet mathematicians and physicists had become dependent on the unfortified version during that interim period. What mattered was whether there were norms of mathematical inference against which it could be judged to produce valid inferences, not whether the inferences were valid, "full stop." "Full stop" validity is not a thing; not even in mathematics (see Tappenden 2005 for a Goodman-inspired "new riddle of deduction").

Many scholars have noted a large-scale shift in the standards for knowledge that occurred during the seventeenth century (Hacking 1975; Shapiro 1983, among several others). This transition is typically understood as a movement away from the requirement that conclusions hold with demonstrative certainty, to a gentler standard according to which some degree of probability was epistemically sufficient. That fits, doesn't it? After all, this is also the period in which experimental, observational, and more generally empirical methods of investigation begin their rise to the apex of scientific inquiry. We can't rightly go round claiming that something like Boyle's air pump reveals the secrets of nature while also insisting that revealing the secrets of nature requires indubitable methods of inquiry, now, can we? Shapin and Schaffer (1985) paint a sympathetic picture of Hobbes as something like a dinosaur that accidentally survived the Chixalub meteorite, raging against the inadequacies of the increasingly popular experimentalists:

> Those Fellows of Gresham who are most believed, and are as masters of the rest, dispute with me about physics. They display new machines, to show their vacuum and trifling wonders, in the way that they behave who deal in exotic animals, which are not to be seen without payment. All of them are my enemies. (Hobbes *Dialogus Physicus*; quoted in Shapin and Schaffer 1985, 12)

Harrison (2007) makes the further, nearly unbelievable claim that this transition from certainty to probabilism was in fact motivated specifically by early modern attempts to come to grips with some of the epistemic deprivations inflicted on human beings as a result of the Fall from the Garden of Eden; *nearly* unbelievable. The historical evidence marshaled by Harrison in support of this claim leaves little room for doubt. But the seventeenth century is not the only time the conversion from certainty to probabilism occurred. Weiss (1998, Chapter 5) looks at a variety of dimensions of Islamic legal reasoning that experienced this same shift, as well as the pressures that led to it. El Shamsy (2013) dates the resolution of this explicitly epistemological debate as firmly within the second Islamic century/late eighth century CE, by which time appeals to certainty stand out as "idiosyncratic" (58).

These examples, and the many others that could be adduced, point to the way in which well-functioning disciplinary communities appear to require norms governing what sorts of inferences count as valid or acceptable. The factors driving this requirement are straightforward. Disciplines need a means by which to distinguish inferences that are valid from those that are not. To put it another way, such communities need to be able to draw a distinction between legitimate and illegitimate inferences. The hypothetical inferences of Darwin and Le Sage were deemed illegitimate because they violated the norms governing acceptable inference, norms which precluded the use of hypotheses. A discipline needs these norms in order to discharge its duties as the intellectual filtration system that separates the ideas worthy of community adoption from those of insufficient gravity. Without a shared sense of whether some research has been adequately supported, this filtration process cannot be carried out. This shared sense is a large part of what makes the "review" in "peer review" meaningful. When members of a discipline are possessed of substantially divergent conceptions of what qualifies as adequate support for a claim, there is little substance to the mechanism of community-level scrutiny. As I've tried to show, this doesn't just hold for "big picture" issues like the rationalism-empiricism or probabilism-certainty divides. Every scale of "method" from philosophical conceptions of knowledge to tabletop experimental methods is subject to this same constraint. Plainly, how could the physics community come to be convinced of the results of Millikan's oil-drop experiments unless there is widespread agreement on the question of whether oil-drop experiments can disclose behaviors of the electron that are relevant to calculating its charge?

When research methods proliferate for their own sake, they do so to the detriment of the disciplinary community's ability to engage in meaningful scholarly scrutiny. While a break with widely employed or traditional methods is often praised for its originality (see discussion of Lamont 2009 above), what is generally left unconsidered is the fact that methods are used in the service of producing knowledge and understanding. And in order for that to occur, there needs to be community-level recognition that these methods produce epistemically acceptable results, that they genuinely result in deeper understanding – that they are *legitimate*. This is why, as Kuhn (1962, 169) observes, "Novelty for its own sake is not a desideratum in the sciences..." We are fortunate to have some very good data on grant proposal referee practices in the natural sciences, which come from a statistical analysis of nearly 40,000 referee reports on proposals submitted to the National Institutes of Health (Eblen et al. 2016; Lindner et al. 2016).

There are many things one could say about these data, but what matters for present purposes is how closely a referee's estimation of a proposal's "Significance" is correlated with his estimation of its other qualities. Here, we find that when a referee thinks that a project is significant, he almost always thinks it also has a high probability of completion (this is the "Approach" score). This is because Significance is defined by NIH partly in terms of the probability that the proposed research will add to existing knowledge. If the probability of completion is low, for example, the probability of adding to existing knowledge is correspondingly low. The part of Significance not covered by probability of completion has to do with the referee's estimation of the research question's importance, a measure defined by the referee's knowledge of how many other topics and fields the project promises to bear upon, as well as how long its effects will be felt in the relevant disciplines. These two factors – importance and probability of completion – determine almost all of a proposal's overall score. In contrast with humanities grant refereeing, significance and originality are not at all closely correlated in the natural sciences, and a proposal's originality score has almost no effect on its overall score.

Just so we're clear: there is no inherent problem with novel methods *per se*. Novel methods are often necessary. For what seem to be clear and defensible epistemic reasons, though, we tend not to see them in the natural sciences unless circumstances call for something new, or unless they provide a marked advantage over existing methods. Novelty tends to take care of itself. By investing in further development and elaboration of existing methods, we provide the disciplinary community with the opportunity to refine their use, and we provide it with the means for engaging in the kind of community-level scholarly scrutiny that makes possible the production of genuine knowledge and understanding. In the context of inquiry, refinement is the process by which deep insight is eventually extracted from an initial, roughly defined kernel of profundity. In science, the process of refinement is familiar across several different dimensions of inquiry. Scientific theories undergo a process of refinement as the lines of investigation associated with them begin to mature. The contemporary theory of natural selection, for example, is a highly refined version of the one outlined by Darwin in the *Origin*. The latter is not equivalent to the contemporary theory. It is a special case. But evolutionary biologists recognize the contemporary theory as preserving at its core the essential insight out of which our modern, considerably more powerful understanding has grown. And indeed, as Einstein remarked, "No fairer destiny could be allotted to any physical theory, than that it should of itself point out the way to the introduction of a more comprehensive theory, in which it lives on as a limiting case" (1916/2015, 91).

Because of the many deep challenges that confront attempts to craft a satisfactory relationship between theory and nature, the process of theory refinement typically requires the efforts of an entire community of researchers, spanning multiple generations. For this reason, theoretical novelty is generally opposed unless it offers great immediate gains of some kind. Outside of these very particular circumstances, novelty tends to disrupt the theory refinement process; it promotes the diffusion of the community's cognitive effort when increasing depth rather requires that it be highly concentrated.

A closely related refinement process focuses on the maturation of the scientific problems themselves. Darwin's *Origin*-al problem of explaining how "favorable variations" are preserved had by the early twentieth century evolved into the problem of explaining changes in gene frequencies, and several present indications suggest that this may also be not quite the best question to ask.[2] An instructive analogy here is that of an archeological excavation. The initial detection of a scientific problem can come from any number of sources, but is typically a vague perception of significance. Appreciating the scope, significance, and specific contours of the excavation site is a dynamic process that will often span multiple lifetimes, involving multiple modes of expertise and iterative feedback between current understanding and future research. Simply put, a successful excavation is rarely something that can be achieved by a single researcher, a single type of expert, or even a single generation.

Similarly, the pursuit of a deep scientific problem is a multi-generation effort that requires the resources of different groups of experts. As with scientific theories, what appears to be a well-defined problem from the perspective of one generation comes to be seen by the next generation as a helpful but only roughly specified first step. Along the way, the refinement process may result in the assignment of the problem to different disciplines.[3] Although inherited variations were a problem for "naturalists" during Darwin's time, it has now become the purview of an extraordinary breadth of specialties, ranging from paleobiology to physics; "naturalists" no longer exist as an identifiable research community.

In broad outline, then, the importance of refinement in scientific inquiry lies in its contribution to the development of inquiry beyond the most rudimentary stages, which I take to be wholly positive; it is hard to imagine

---

[2] See, for example, Dupré (2012) and Wagner (2014).
[3] Laudan (1977) observes that new discoveries regularly resist assignment to a given specialty.

what a persuasive argument *against* this sort of development would look like. If the epistemic importance of refinement is not unique to science, humanists' preoccupation with novelty is a threat to the development of humanistic inquiry at multiple levels – in general, any level of inquiry in which refinement is possible. If we care about insight and understanding as much as we claim to, we need to take seriously the possibility that genuine insight – the sort of insight we take to be the signature of humanistic inquiry – can only be achieved through the concentrated efforts of a community of researchers spanning several generations.

8.4.3 A Discipline's Self-Replication

Most problems worth working on are very hard to solve, and the course of inquiry into these problems typically raises unforeseen puzzles of far greater moment. Because of the depth and complexity of problems, the competing demands on the lives of researchers, and the predictable unavailability of an off-the-shelf toolkit that can be readily applied, a disciplinary community will need to exist for several generations if it is to refine its grasp of the research questions it has set for itself. It therefore must have some mechanism in place by which it replicates itself.

Generally speaking, the community achieves this through the training of graduate students. Whatever else these students receive from their teachers, they must above all inherit, observe, and enforce the constraints on membership in the disciplinary community discussed above. That is, they must (a) explore the set of research questions that defines the community of which they are becoming members and (b) pursue answers to those questions in a way that the community has deemed acceptable. The disciplinary community only exists as long as the membership conditions are instantiated. The membership conditions will of course evolve as inquiry evolves; changing conditions is consistent with *some* set of conditions being instantiated at a given time. The student enters the community by satisfying the membership conditions that are operative at the time of entry.

In our time, different knowledge communities replicate themselves with greater or lesser success, and the difference in fidelity of copying manifests itself in the degree of progress that a discipline exhibits over time. At a very general level, one way this difference shows up is in the freedom that graduate students have over their dissertation topics. The emphasis on novelty for its own sake, the student's lightly if not unconstrained freedom to choose his own topic, his lack of a cultivated, intuitive sense of what a good problem is – all of this increases the probability that, for every generation g of the knowledge community, generation $g + 1$ will be characterized by a set of research topics that has little to do with the set of topics that characterized generation *g*. This is a recipe for stagnation in the growth of knowledge for a discipline. By building into to the disciplinary structure a mechanism that ensures that the same research problems do not get passed down from one generation of researchers to another, the discipline virtually guarantees that no measurable progress will be made toward *refining* our understanding. Each generation must essentially reinvent the disciplinary community anew, ensuring that the deep challenges taken up by a parent generation are rarely given more than the superficial treatment that a single individual can hope to achieve during the span of his career (cf. Kuhn 1962, 13). With no problem inheritance, the disciplinary community cannot survive beyond a single generation.

Each of these pathologies contributes to what I see as the fundamental problem we face in the humanities. With each gratuitous novelty, be it of problem or of method, we loosen the ties that bind us together as scholars in a shared world. This shared world is composed of the norms regarding what is of intellectual importance, norms that supervene on widespread agreement across a community of scholars. Our knowledge of these norms – knowledge of what matters – is derived from intense engagement with exemplars. But it is more than that. The very possibility of such knowledge seems to require restricting our scholarly attention to what can be achieved within the constraints imposed by those exemplars. When we abandon them, we compromise our ability to acquire humanistic knowledge. More importantly, we transform the very nature of inquiry. Under these conditions, it no longer makes sense to imagine refining one's judgment in a shared world, such that deeper knowledge and understanding become genuinely possible. That world has evaporated.

8.5 Conclusion

There is one further observation made by Netz (2020) that bears on the question of whether using interestingness to oneself as a guide for selecting research problems is well reasoned. He notes that the works which comprise the ancient literary canon were all distinguished by both their prestige *and* their popularity. In a similar spirit, Philip Kitcher (2011, 248–249) recounts an episode in the history of musical performance:

> Once upon a time, in a country not too far away, the most prominent musicians decided to become serious about their profession. They encouraged their promising students to devote hours to special exercises designed to

strengthen fingers, shape lips, and extend breath control. Within a few years, conservatories began to hold exciting competitions, at which the most rigorous études would be performed in public. For a while, these contests went on side by side with concerts devoted to the traditional repertoire. Gradually, however, interest in the compositions of the past – and virtually all those of the present – began to wane. Serious pianists found the studies composed by Chopin, Liszt, Debussy, and Ligeti insufficiently taxing, and they dismissed the suites, concertos, and sonatas of Bach, Mozart, Beethoven, Brahms, and Prokofiev as worthy of performance only by second-raters.

Popular interest in the festivals organized by the major conservatories quickly declined, although the contests continued to be attended by a tiny group of self-described cognoscenti. A few maverick musicians, including some who had once been counted among the serious professionals, offered performances of works their elite ex-colleagues despised. When reports of the broad enthusiastic response to a recital centered on the late Beethoven sonatas came to the ears of the professionals, the glowing reviews produced only a smile and a sniff. For serious pianists, the fact that one of their former fellows had now decided to slum it was no cause for serious concern. Compared to the recent competition in which one pianist had delivered *Multi-Scale 937* in under 7'10" and another had ornamented *Quadruple Tremolo 41* with an extra trill, an applauded performance of the *Hammerklavier* was truly small potatoes.

As time went on, the outside audience for "serious performance" dwindled to nothing, and the public applause for the "second-raters" who offered Bach, Chopin, and Prokofiev became more intense. The smiles of the cognoscenti became a little more strained, and the sniffs were ever more disdainful.

Both observations underscore an important lesson for our own time. The desolation of our disciplinary world is not the only casualty of the search for increasingly obscure forms and topics of inquiry. The further we stray from the canonical neighborhoods on which the great traditions of humanistic inquiry were built, the more difficult we make it to engage with the broader nonspecialist public whose investment in those great traditions allowed them to define civilizations.

It's not a matter of survival in a "marketplace" that trends toward the reductive and the scientistic (well, it partly is that). Mostly, it is a matter of allowing nonspecialists to partake of the bounty of ideas that have enriched countless lives. Ideas that have transformed entire cultures. Ideas that inspire. The humanities are valuable. Actually, they are more than valuable: they are invaluable. They have proven this through a pedigree far older than and just as distinguished as any other human endeavor. But when we insist on straying ever further beyond the bounds of genre and discipline, we deprive nonspecialists of the opportunity to be affected by them.

It is easy to excuse our ascent to greater esoteric heights through appeals to analogous trends in the natural sciences and in mathematics: "No one understands them, either. That's just the intellectual's lot in life." This response papers over a few important differences. First, as Kitcher (2011) points out, there is normally a fairly direct route from the esoteric research problem with which some natural scientist occupies herself back to a more general issue of identifiable human concern. This is not very surprising, if you think about it. In an era in which roughly 20% of natural science grant proposals receive funding, there is a high value placed on proposals that are able to articulate their "broader impact" in a clear and convincing way.[4] This is especially true at the higher levels of administrative review, once a proposal has survived the scrutiny of specialist review panels. (In that regard, maybe our disciplinary cultures have been weakened by the fact that doing good research in the humanities does not normally require millions of dollars. Because it is possible to do our inexpensive research without having to convince lots of other people that it's good (besides a couple of referees every now and then), we're more or less free to do whatever we want.)

This apology for nonspecialist incomprehensibility ignores another point: does anyone honestly think that the natural sciences and mathematics would be in this position if they had a choice? Because of it, they've been reduced to relying on Professor McInquiry and related stunts in order to keep nonspecialists interested. I guarantee that no practicing scientist swells with pride at seeing how the wonders of liquid nitrogen are still a hit at parties. It would be great if we could tell the kids that they might, if they are lucky, get the opportunity to count 15,000 ants just like Edward O. Wilson did. Or about the indescribable rush one gets from looking at spreadsheets. So many spreadsheets. Hard as it may be to imagine, that kind of thing does not resonate with someone who is in the position to consider a life in the sciences. We in the humanities are fortunate in that we do not routinely face the demands of mathematical hyperprecision that necessitate an appeal to generally inaccessible formulae and multi-million dollar apparatus. We should be taking advantage of our relative freedom in this regard. Where there is no absolute need to mint fresh jargon or appeal to "theory," maybe don't? Take every opportunity to make direct contact with areas of perennial human concern; for real, not in a hand-wavy sort of way. The premodern humanities cultures thrived on precisely these grounds. The modern natural sciences thrive on these grounds. We can, too.

---

[4] www.niaid.nih.gov/grants-contracts/fy-2020-award-data. Accessed March 13, 2022.

CHAPTER 9

The Hoax and the Humanities

9.1 The Emperor's New Articles

Imagine a twist on Hans Christian Andersen's classic tale in which not weavers but writers pay a visit to the emperor, offering to produce journal articles on his behalf, articles which cannot be understood by the dull and unenlightened. Eager to advance his academic career, the emperor greedily accepts the offer, and the writers set up a sumptuous study in which they appear to be very busy generating profundities. In fact, they *are* very busy, but with the business of generating nonsense, rather than knowledge, wisdom, or insight. The emperor's inner circle periodically checks in to see how things are going, unable to make heads or tails of the articles but nevertheless approving enthusiastically, lest they be taken for fools. The finished articles are then shown around to various academic administrators, who, keen to avoid offending the emperor and his coterie of initiates, politely nod as they attempt, unsuccessfully, to understand the meaningless strings of words cobbled together and pressed into a mold vaguely reminiscent of research. In the original tale, the emperor doubles down after being exposed, proceeding proudly and undeterred as the world around him laughs on. I don't think we need to go into a lot of detail regarding what the moral is here. Suffice it to say that it has not been customary to read this as a parable about the importance of standing up for what you believe.

In this chapter, I want to take a close look at two distinct but related phenomena in the humanities, each of which marks a stark contrast with the natural sciences for reasons that are not altogether clear. The first involves a recent episode in which several deliberately nonsensical articles were published as part of an effort to expose a certain family of humanities disciplines as intellectually hollow. This episode is, in fact, only the latest in a series of similar events that now appear to be occurring with increasing frequency. Examining the details of this particular case, I will argue that the general phenomenon it illustrates does in fact represent a serious problem in the humanities. But it also suggests the possible form a solution to that problem might take. I do not expect my proposed solution will convince or even resonate with all of my fellow humanists. Ultimately, though, my primary goal is simply to get us to take the phenomenon of the academic hoax seriously, because this recent episode is not a fluke, or a failure of the refereeing process, or any of the other excuses to which we might appeal in order to drain it of significance. This will happen again, because it exploits deeply entrenched features of our current culture of research. Rather than dismiss our detractors as mean-spirited lackwits and frauds, as the emperor did, we should pause to ensure that there's really something there.

The second phenomenon is the general absence of article retraction in the humanities. Retraction plays an important epistemic role in science. The discovery of published material worthy of retraction can have serious consequences for large groups of scientists, and can cast a pall over an author's career as well as those of co-authors unrelated to the retracted article. The high costs associated with retraction are meant to serve as a safeguard against practices that might put a publication in the crosshairs. Now, why is the retraction rate in the humanities holding steady at around 0%? Is this cause for celebration, cause for concern, or an insignificant by-product of the fundamental difference between scientific knowledge and humanistic knowledge? More broadly, what does the fact that humanities articles do not get retracted tell us about the nature, significance, and accumulation of contemporary humanistic inquiry?

The explanation for the general absence of retractions in the humanities might be rooted either in (a) the fact that epistemic function of retraction in science is performed by other means in the humanities, or (b) some difference between humanistic knowledge and scientific knowledge that makes the absence of retractions in the former epistemically unimportant. Either of these explanations would preserve whatever integrity humanistic knowledge has, since in either case, the absence of retractions in the humanities would not be problematic from the standpoint of the well-foundedness of humanistic knowledge. In fact, I'm going to argue that the epistemic function performed by retraction in science does not satisfy any distinctive epistemic demands that arise specifically in scientific contexts. Rather, the function it performs is of a very general sort; it's the sort of function demanded by any species of knowledge worthy of the distinction. This suggests that the epistemic pedigree of humanistic claims is in peril unless the function performed by retraction in science is discharged in the humanities through other means. It will turn out that the conditions under which retractions could possibly occur are extraordinarily bizarre from the perspective of mainstream humanities research methodology. This is a symptom of a fundamental problem with the way in which research claims in the humanities are typically supported, *not* an indication of a fundamental difference between scientific and humanistic knowledge. It is a problem that can be fixed, but only by paying attention to the epistemic significance of retraction in science and by looking for opportunities to incorporate the conditions that make it relevant into humanistic practice.

9.2 The Art of the Hoax

First, the facts: three people, Helen Pluckrose, Peter Boghossian, and James A. Lindsay, co-wrote twenty papers over ten months. These papers were submitted for publication in "ranked peer-reviewed journals in [a] field, the higher the better and at the top of their subdisciplines whenever possible," none of which was a "pay-to-publish" journal. Second, seven of those papers were accepted (one of which received an award as an exemplary piece of scholarship); seven others were "still in play" when the hoax was called to a halt. The remaining six were "retired as fatally flawed or beyond repair." Seven out of twenty papers (35%) were accepted after just ten months of writing. That is a staggering success rate, especially for such a short amount of time. And it is reasonable to assume that at least one of the seven papers still under review would eventually have been accepted.[1] In their words:

> The primary purpose of this project was to draw greater public and scholarly attention to how commonplace this scholarship is in these disciplines. In particular, because much of this scholarship is of such low quality, we believe it to be grossly inadequate to its declared task of furthering the cause of social justice, that is, fostering a more fair society, especially in terms of minimizing prejudice, discrimination, and the material [sic] and their psychosocial impacts … As a secondary purpose, we wanted to obtain a first-hand view of the scholarly procedures and standards in these disciplines in order to ensure that our own criticisms of that scholarship are duly informed and accurate. We sought an "outsider within" experience … of how the peer-review process in these subdisciplines works, to see how we would be directed by editors and expert reviewers, and to determine what we could (and couldn't) get away with and why. The result was that 7 of

---

[1] https://areomagazine.com/2018/10/02/academic-grievance-studies-and-the-corruption-of-scholarship/.

these 20 papers had been accepted, and 4 published, by the time we were discovered by the popular press … and decided to prematurely terminate our project. At least four of the seven other papers that were still under review arguably stood a very good chance of going on to be published in the scholarly literature …. (Pluckrose et al. 2021, 1917)

The authors describe their papers as "all outlandish or intentionally broken in significant ways"; "sophistry"; and "a forgery of knowledge that should not be mistaken for the real thing." According to them, "[t]he goal was always to use what the existing literature offered to get some little bit of lunacy or depravity to be acceptable at the highest levels of intellectual respectability within the field" – specifically, the "fields of scholarship loosely known as 'cultural studies' or 'identity studies' (for example, gender studies) or 'critical theory'."

Let's take a moment to let this sink in before moving on, because only by appreciating the essential, indisputable facts of the case will we be able to have a productive discussion about its significance. The authors intentionally engaged in sophistry, made ludicrous, depraved, and poorly supported claims, and wound up getting seven papers accepted in ten months, including one award-winning paper. By their lights, "We shouldn't have been able to get *any* papers this terrible published in reputable journals, let alone seven."[2]

9.3 Clearing the Brush

9.3.1 Fake Data

I want to look at some features of the hoax and the surrounding commentary that have inhibited our ability to sufficiently appreciate what was achieved and why it's important. First, a number of commentators have argued that the hoaxers falsified data, and are thus guilty of academic fraud.[3] This is correct. A few of the papers claimed to have collected data, when in fact no such data had been collected. There's no question that this constitutes fraud. But it would be hasty and unfortunate to simply conclude based on the falsification of some data that there is nothing to be learned from the hoax. First of all, many of the papers did not report any data. So, even if we decide that there's nothing to be learned from papers that falsify data, that still leaves us with several papers from which we could potentially learn a great deal. In this connection, it's worth wondering

---

[2] https://areomagazine.com/2018/10/02/academic-grievance-studies-and-the-corruption-of-scholarship/
[3] www.insidehighered.com/news/2019/01/08/author-recent-academic-hoax-faces-disciplinary-action-portland-state. Retreived September 16, 2023.

whether those papers with manufactured data would have been accepted had they contained no data reports whatsoever. Based on the fact that several data-free papers were accepted, there's good reason to think that the papers with cooked data might have been accepted without it. But, in general, the existence of falsified data in some papers cannot impugn the larger study itself.

Second, it's important to look closely at the content of the data claims, because doing so helps to illustrate the nature of some of the problems to which the authors were hoping to draw attention. One paper on dog parks claimed to have "closely and respectfully examined the genitals of slightly fewer than ten thousand dogs." Think about that: 10,000 dogs. Now, it is neither reasonable nor realistic to expect referees to be able to detect all instances of data fraud. But it is certainly reasonable to expect referees to spot flagrant, statistically freakish claims. The claim to have personally and carefully examined the genitals of 10,000 dogs is implausible on its face. Far less outlandish claims have raised concern with referees before, and those concerns have frequently led to retractions. This should have been flagged for verification. In fact, according to the authors, a number of empirical studies reported in their articles were specifically designed to set off alarm bells. The fact that no alarm bells went off is significant.[4]

To summarize: (1) falsified data only appears in a subset of the published papers; (2) there's good reason to think that some of those papers would have been accepted without *any* data; and (3) the falsified data were often designed specifically to look troubling, and yet failed to trouble anyone. We can't dismiss the hoax on account of the fact that some data were fake. That's a total nonsequitur. We can dismiss the conclusions drawn from the data. But the falsified data simply aren't relevant to anything beyond the inferences they're employed to support. It would be epistemically irresponsible to extend their reach beyond the credibility of those inferences.

(Just as an aside, I think it's a regrettable feature of the hoax that they faked data. It introduced a lot of noise and confusion into the study. It *is* a good way to test whether referees are capable of detecting enormous lies. But it would have been better to have found some other way to do this.)

---

[4] I have learned from Patricia Princehouse, a historian of science and professional breeder of many prize-winning dogs, that a professional dog show judge might examine the genitals of as many as 10,000 dogs in a given year. I didn't say it was impossible.

9.3.2 "Grievance Studies"

Another set of confounding factors is the authors' professed attempt to test for ideological bias in certain fields, and to label that set of fields, "grievance studies." I think this latter factor is another regrettable choice on their part, since they needlessly generated additional hostility by using name-calling in an attempt to minimize the significance of certain disciplines. It may be that the problems addressed by these disciplines are genuinely insignificant, but slinging mud is not the way to show that, and it probably alienated audience members who might otherwise have been ready to listen. Bad on the authors for that.

The question of whether the hoax does a good job of testing for ideological bias turns out to be more complicated. To review, for each paper, the authors' claim to have been testing one or another version of the following hypothesis: *a ridiculous paper will be accepted for publication in certain subdisciplines if it panders to ideologies that prevail in those subdisciplines.*[5] What we know is that all the papers pandered to the relevant ideologies, and that 35% of them got accepted. We certainly can't infer from that that ideologically pandering papers will be accepted, or even that they will tend to be accepted. Indeed, it's really not clear *what* we can infer about the causal role of referee ideology from the acceptances, because all of the papers are a combination of two factors: a mimicry of disciplinary language, and an ideological spin. If they wanted to test for the causal role of ideological bias, they should have submitted two versions of the paper: one that panders to bias, and one that doesn't. They didn't do this, and so the acceptances aren't very informative on the question of whether ideological bias plays a role in the referee process.

Having said that, the referee reports – which the authors published in full on their website – do not exactly discourage the inference that being on the approved side of certain social issues elicits positive responses from referees. The referees rarely, if ever, object to the consistently strident ideological tone of the papers. In several instances, referees are explicit about their approval of the social or political stance taken in an article. I have to say that, as someone who has refereed lots of papers and read lots of reports, I was pretty shocked by how blatantly political the refereeing process reflected in these reports seems to be at times.[6] Now, I understand

---

[5] https://areomagazine.com/2018/10/02/academic-grievance-studies-and-the-corruption-of-scholarship/.
[6] Two sample referee comments: (1) "yes, privileged folks are fragile but are we re-centering them by focusing on their objections?"; (2) "the author quotes Cooper as lauding visibility as a political strategy. I think at the very least, the perils of visibility politics for queer communities in the wake of

that refereeing is a complicated social and psychological process, and that what referees say to authors is not always representative of precisely what they think about a paper. But if we're going to try to explain away the apparent politicization of the refereeing process, we need some alternative explanation for why referees were so enthusiastic and explicit in their affirmation of the papers' sociopolitical ambitions. We can't just express a general skepticism. What alternative could there be, besides trying to indicate to either the authors, the editor, or both, that the article's political tilt is a point in its favor? Are there different alternative motivations for these comments for each referee, for each paper? That would be a very poor alternative explanation.

I am not convinced that ideological pandering contributed to referees' favorable impressions of these articles. But I am also not convinced that it *didn't*. In general, referee reports should be viewed as a unique and valuable glimpse into the epistemology of a discipline. The default assumption is that referees will appeal to a discipline's epistemic norms in arguing for or against publication, and the process is designed to encourage this. Practitioners probably have less motivation to lie in referee reports than they do in any other dimension of inquiry. These reports are a good way of taking the epistemological temperature of a discipline, because referees are charged with evaluating articles relative to the epistemic norms of the discipline. We should treat with the utmost seriousness any trends that prevail in a discipline's refereeing practices. If it looks like there is a tendency for referees to be positively disposed toward an article based on whether that article subscribes to a certain sociopolitical ideology, then that is a problem.

9.3.3 The Imperfections of Peer Review

Another widely expressed complaint regarding the hoax is that it proves a point that is already universally acknowledged – namely, that the peer-review process is imperfect, or that it is not designed to detect fraud, or in any event the hoaxers have misunderstood the point of peer review.[7] This objection does not hold up under scrutiny.

Let's begin by acknowledging that referees come to the refereeing process with a variety of goals in mind. We are looking to see if the research potentially adds to existing knowledge (i.e., doesn't reproduce something

---

the neoliberalization of mainstream LGBT political machinery needs to be a serious consideration as the author leans on what I might suggest is a naïve hope for visibility politics."
[7] https://slate.com/technology/2018/10/grievance-studies-hoax-not-academic-scandal.html. Retrieved September 16, 2023.

already on the books). And we are tasked with judging whether some research is important enough to warrant publication even if it is novel and well done. Some referees and editors take a more constructive approach than others, trying to help develop a piece so that it satisfies the community demands on scholarship.

But this is not all that we do. We must evaluate a submission's reasoning. And we must consider any reported results with skepticism. Not blind, unwarranted skepticism, but enough skepticism to discourage researchers from taking shortcuts, being careless, and overplaying their hand. Part of the reasoning behind sending submissions to experts in the relevant area of specialization is that expertise can often be relied upon to detect anomalies in a study that warrant further scrutiny. Because of their highly developed knowledge of certain systems or phenomena, experts will have an intuitive sense of how plausible a data set is, or how likely it is that researchers actually obtained the result they claim to have obtained. An expert on randomness, for example, can reliably distinguish a truly random sequence from a sequence that was concocted to appear as if it were a random sequence. An expert on Charles Darwin will be able to tell with high probability whether a piece of correspondence attributed to Darwin is genuinely his. An intuitive ability to sense significant deviations from a system's normal behavior is a big part of what real expertise gives someone and why it is valuable.

To say that expert peer review is not designed to detect fraud is perfectly true, but it's also beside the point. Because most research is not conducted in a public setting, there is nothing we can do to prevent fraud in principle. Nor has anyone ever supposed that we could. But to say that it is not the job of expert peer review to spot potential fraud or unintentional error is a dereliction of scholarly duty, pure and simple. There is enormous pressure to produce results, and it would be implausible to suggest that a convention of good faith is all that is needed to keep everything above board. The presumption that experts are able and willing to scrutinize submissions is one of the most powerful incentives researchers have to be careful and honest in their work. When it becomes known that expert peer reviewers are not minding the fence – or not *capable* of minding the fence – we can expect fraud to occur more often.

9.3.4 "Bad Faith"

In this connection, the last bit of brush I would like to clear relates to the several accusations of "bad faith" that have been directed toward the hoaxers' efforts (e.g., Kafka 2018). Note that the "bad faith" accusations raise concerns that are entirely distinct from those raised by the "fake data" accusations. The latter are about the reliability of the claims that enlist the fake data for their support. By contrast, the "bad faith" accusations are concerned with the hoaxers' hidden intentions and lack of sincerity.

More than anything, I think the charge of insincerity gives us a glimpse into how important the hoax's accomplishment really is. What exactly is the significance of the fact that the authors did not believe the nonsense they were writing? It is instructive to contrast this case with another highly publicized accusation of research misconduct in the humanities: the Sokal Hoax. Physicist Alan Sokal published what he described as a "parody" in a cultural studies journal, *Social Text*. As an attempt to expose the weakness of constraints on what could be asserted in cultural studies, Sokal's article aimed to test those constraints by "employ[ing] scientific and mathematical concepts in ways that few scientists or mathematicians could possibly take seriously," but which, he later found, were deemed acceptable by the journal's editors. Stanley Fish, then executive editor of the press that publishes *Social Text*, responded in a *New York Times* op-ed with an accusation of fraud:

> In a 1989 report published in *The Proceedings of the National Academy of Science*, fraud is said to go "beyond error to erode the foundation of trust on which science is built." That is Professor Sokal's legacy, one likely to be longer lasting than the brief fame he now enjoys for having successfully pretended to be himself. (Fish 1996)

Ultimately, Fish's accusation rested on the fact that "Alan Sokal put forward ... a line of argument he says he never believed in." Now, in science, fraud can only occur when a report deliberately misrepresents the existence of support on which the report is allegedly based.[8] So, if (1) one has to misrepresent the existence of support for a claim in order to commit fraud; and (2) the charge of fraud is grounded in the fact that Sokal misrepresented his personal belief in his own incoherent rambling, then it turns out that, for Fish, whether Sokal's claims were properly supported depends on whether he sincerely believed them. To put it in the language of the National Science Foundation, Sokal was guilty of "making up" a certain attitude toward certain propositions and then implicitly "reporting" that attitude by asserting those propositions. There's no

---

[8] The National Science Foundation labels this type of misconduct "fabrication: ...making up data or results and recording or reporting them" (url: www.nsf.gov/oig/_pdf/cfr/45-CFR-689.pdf; last accessed December 9, 2015).

question that Sokal did not believe what he was saying, but in order for that to rise to the level of fraud, his sincerity itself must somehow function as *support* for what he is saying.

The idea that whether Sokal's and Pluckrose et al.'s claims were properly supported depends on how sincere they were when making them should surprise us. Indeed, if they were *trying* to make ridiculous or meaningless claims, it should count in their favor that they did not believe them. The fact that other people found value in the hoaxers' intentional nonsense would seem to reflect poorly on the receptive audience, not the hoaxers. As Fish noted in his op-ed, trust is an essential part of science, and a presumption of sincerity is part of what makes trust possible. But it would be a mistake to think that a scientist's sincerity forms part of the evidence base for her report. Whether her report is properly supported depends on whether the data she alleges to have obtained in support of it (1) actually exist, and (2) are judged to be probative.[9] However, in this case, the fraud accusation rests solely on Sokal's insincerity. Are the conditions under which fraud was possible in the Sokal case simply an aberration, or does the case reveal a fundamental difference between the sciences and the humanities that makes sincerity probative in the latter but not in the former? The "bad faith" objection leveled at the Pluckrose et al. hoaxes suggests that Sokal's case is representative of how to commit fraud in the humanities.

To see how irrelevant the "bad faith" charge is, let us try to think about what would have to be different in order for the hoaxers' project to have been done in good faith: literally nothing, except that they would need to have believed what they were saying. But maybe they did! Maybe it's actually a meta-hoax, where they claim to have been insincere but were in fact perfectly sincere. Or, what if an army of scholars came forward and announced that they never believed the stuff they were saying? Not that their data were fraudulent – no worries there – just that they personally did not believe the inferences that were drawn from them in the work they published. Alternatively, recall the 2016 dust-up around a paper on "feminist glaciology" that was suspected of *being* a hoax until the author publicly confirmed his sincerity.[10] What difference do the authors' intentions make to *our* warrant for accepting those inferences? That warrant is determined by our appraisal of the relation that the

---

[9] Boghossian and Nagel (1996) make this point in their contribution to a forum on the Sokal Hoax.
[10] www.science.org/content/article/qa-author-feminist-glaciology-study-reflects-sudden-appearance-culture-wars. Retrieved September 16, 2023.

evidence bears to the conclusions. *Our* warrant is not affected by what the *authors* think about the data's relation to the conclusion. Imagine if we found out that Pythagoras did not believe his own proof for the Pythagorean theorem, yet in any case chose to promulgate the theorem. Would that cause us to second-guess the theorem? Of course not. Would Pythagoras be guilty of fraud? Of course not. We can look at the premises and decide for ourselves whether they support the conclusion. The author's sincerity or lack thereof is simply not relevant.

The "bad faith" objection is a last-ditch effort to avoid the obvious and most damaging implication of the successful hoaxes – namely, that maybe the only difference between real scholarship and nonsense in certain disciplines is whether or not the author believes what he's saying. If he believes it, it's genuine research; if not, it's parody. The "bad faith" objection is a tacit admission that, in these disciplines, we cannot tell the difference between real scholarship and sophistry, and that we need the authors to promise that they are being genuine.

It's important to remember that this issue simply does not arise in every discipline. Yes, we need researchers to be honest, but what we need them to be honest about is the *existence of their data and the methods used to collect it*, not whether they believe their sentences to be meaningful. The question of whether a researcher is being honest about their intentions or similarly irrelevant details of context doesn't enter into the assessment of an argument, and so we generally don't worry about it when we're evaluating research. And it's a good thing, too, because the broader context of inquiry is incredibly messy. Consider the simple fact that many research projects have literally hundreds of contributors. Do we need assurances that they're all motivated by the same "good faith" intentions? Well, they're not. I can guarantee that on any particular research project, there are several investigators who think that the research problem is just plain stupid. They're simply following a protocol.

To appreciate the irrelevance of contextual details that do not affect the reliability of the data, consider these few excerpts from my favorite Twitter feed, "Overly Honest Methods"

"We used that technique because my student had a crush on the technician"
"Incubating your ELISA plates an extra three hours just because that's the time it took to see Ghostbusters"
"Sample was warmed to approximately 37°C, in my armpit."
"Sections were 6 microns thick because I am not skilled enough with a microtome to cut 5 micron sections."

In these cases, nothing changes (or, at least, nothing *should* change) when we find out that, for example, Technique A was used *because* of a student's love interest. It's mildly entertaining, but it's irrelevant to our assessment of the research. For, what really matters is *that* Technique A was used, not why. If we are worried about the efficacy of Technique A, our worries will not be quelled by the confidence of a particular researcher.

Contrary to what the "bad faith" objections presume, then, there is no blanket assumption in research that all claims are made in good faith. The "good faith" assumption is very narrowly restricted to claims about what data there is and how that data was obtained. This restricted scope is entirely appropriate, because the communal growth of knowledge requires that we be able to rely on others' data, and only the researcher knows for sure whether she is accurately reporting her observations and the methods she used to collect them. But the communal growth of knowledge certainly does *not* require that we be able to rely on others' inferences from the data. Unlike the raw data themselves, the validity of an inference from data is something that is available to anyone who bothers to scrutinize it on the printed page. We do not need inferences to be made in good faith, because knowing that an argument is sincere or insincere cannot help us to distinguish warranted claims from unwarranted ones. Nor do we need to know whether a particular author thinks that the issue they are addressing is of major intellectual significance. Both of these issues are settled at the community level. If we find ourselves wondering whether an author is sincere before we make up our own minds, something has gone badly wrong.

A variant of the "bad faith" objection might prove tempting. This objection goes as follows: "Just because the authors attempted to generate meaningless sentences does not imply that they were successful. It is possible to produce meaningful sentences by accident. Therefore, it is possible to accidentally produce articles that are worthy for publication."

I first want to acknowledge the possible cogency of this objection. There is some room for debate as to whether, say, an inscription or utterance can carry meaning despite a lack of any such intent on the part of an author – whether, for example, a bottle of ink that has spilled in such a way as to accidentally form a series of marks that looks just like the English sentence, "Snow is white," carries meaning in the way ink marks would had they been written out that way by an author. If such accidents of meaning are possible, then accidentally publication-worthy articles are apparently possible.

Ultimately, though, I think this objection does more harm than good. If things have devolved to the point where we are attempting to delegitimize the hoax by insisting that the authors *might* have failed to produce nonsense due to the fact that semantic content is partially determined by interpreters, we have arrived at a very dark place. Indeed, the objection really misses the forest for the trees. The relevant concern should not be whether accidental meaningfulness is possible, but rather what it says about our disciplines and our intellectual integrity if we are willing to defend our peer review system by appealing to the possibility that sometimes sentences can be meaningful by accident.

9.4 How to Retract an Article in the Humanities

The accusations of fraud leveled at the hoaxes direct us to a related phenomenon which seems to hold across humanities disciplines – namely, the mysterious absence of retracted publications. Even if you think it's obvious why articles don't get targeted for retraction, or accused of fraud, there is still the question of whether the fact that fraud is nearly impossible is a symptom of an epistemically healthy form of inquiry.

In this section, I attempt to articulate the epistemic role of retraction in the natural sciences. I argue that the epistemic niche occupied by retraction is not unique to the sciences; its contribution to the growth of knowledge and understanding can be understood in very general terms relevant to humanities scholarship. The absence of retraction thus emerges as a puzzle, for which I offer a potential solution. Before we begin, I want to stress the highly speculative nature of the argument I'm making. I am morally certain that there are better hypotheses for the absence of retractions than the one I offer here. As in my discussion of the hoaxes, my goal is to motivate the idea that we should worry about whether research practices in the humanities include some mechanism that can do for our claims what retraction does for science. The expectations that make retraction possible in science form part of the explanation for why scientific knowledge is so valuable. The fact that no such demands are placed on humanists' claims might alert us to something fundamental about the nature and importance of the humanities.

9.4.1 A Science without Retraction

We can start to understand why the possibility of retraction is important in science by imagining a world in which there were no retractions issued in science. The fact that our world is not like this tells us something about the epistemic conditions under which research is carried out and which necessitate the practice of retraction. Broadly speaking, there are two epistemic conditions whose instantiation would obviate the need for retractions. One is unachievable: the set of conditions under which scientists simply made no errors. The other is undesirable: the set of conditions under which error is possible but insufficiently worrisome to compel the development of a practice of retraction. The practice of research retraction, I argue, was an outgrowth of the seventeenth-century cultural shift in natural philosophy known colloquially as the Scientific Revolution. A critical dimension of this cultural shift was that the possibility of error became sufficiently worrisome.

We used to live in a world where there were no scientific retractions. As far as I can tell, the first retraction of a factual claim in what we would recognize as a scientific publication occurs in 1684 (see below), during the ferment of the principles of Baconian natural philosophy. That ferment included a number of features familiar from contemporary scientific research conditions, including the demand that support for claims about nature be empirical and that it be publicly accessible. The limit version of this latter demand is the standard of *reproducibility*, to which (legend tells) all experimental assertions are held in principle (but to which very few are held in practice).

The experimental natural philosopher's revolutionary demand for public accessibility of support was at that time contrasted with two species of inquiry against which the emerging experimental natural philosophy would define itself. One was the *speculative* approach to inquiry characteristic of the Scholastics and various other classically oriented scholarly communities whose decline began in the sixteenth century and continued to accelerate for the next hundred years or so. The other was the community of alchemists, who would outlive speculative philosophers but who were similarly marginalized as contributors to natural philosophy. The public accessibility criterion targeted distinct but related aspects of these two scholarly communities. Let us look at them in turn.

As concerns speculation, the familiar complaint was that the Ancients' preferred method of inquiry was not discriminating enough to provide the sufficient foundation for knowledge. We are well-acquainted with this criticism as a principal fault line during the Scientific Revolution. But as Peter Harrison has shown, the denigration of speculative, ratiocinative approaches to inquiry and the concomitant epistemic elevation of "experiment" was a well-established contrast several centuries before it was to be pressed into the service of experimental natural philosophy. For example, the contrast is already widespread in the Middle Ages, where it is represented in medicine as a distinction between, on the one hand, medical treatments that were theoretically deduced from accepted medical (principally Galenic) doctrine ('*via rationis*'), and, on the other, those that (for better or for worse) lacked doctrinal justification – the latter being referred to as *experimenta* (Harrison 2011, 415).

It is not all that surprising that partisans of experimental natural philosophy would have observed the broad distinction between speculative and experimental knowledge that would become so important in the mid seventeenth century. What *is* surprising is that the distinction is equally if not more clear in medieval theology, where "speculative" knowledge of God is occasionally contrasted with "experimental" knowledge of God. Here is Aquinas:

> There is a twofold knowledge of God's goodness or will. One is speculative and as to this it is not lawful to doubt or to prove whether God's will be good, or whether God is sweet. The other knowledge of God's will or goodness is effective or experimental and thereby a man experiences in himself the taste of God's sweetness, and complacency in God's will, as Dionysius says of Hierotheos (*Div. Nom.* ii) that "he learnt divine things through experience of them." It is in this way that we are told to prove God's will, and to taste His sweetness.[11]

Elsewhere, Aquinas and others emphasize the unique discriminating capacity of experiment, as in the case where Adam and Eve's knowledge of God's moral authority is tested by the "experiment" with the forbidden fruit. This distinctive experiential dimension of religious knowledge would become an important focus during the Reformation, where "experimental religion" is strongly and favorably posed against the speculative brand of religious knowledge associated with the Catholic Church (*ibid.*). As Harrison has shown elsewhere, the rise of experimental natural philosophy in the mid-seventeenth century can be convincingly traced directly to the Protestant emphasis on the superiority of knowledge rooted in experience (Harrison 2007).

The problem with speculation had been that the religious knowledge gained through it was nothing more than, as one clergyman put it, "a Head knowledge, or an aery, empty, notionall, speculative knowledge."[12] This same weakness – along with its associated remedy through experiment – was a dominant theme in the early methodological prescriptions of the Royal Society of London, who, according to its first secretary and erstwhile promoter, Henry Oldenburg, "aimes at the improvement of all usefull Sciences and Arts, not by *mere speculations*, but by exact and faithfull Observations and Experiments."[13] The general superiority of experimental knowledge in both the religious and (natural) philosophical

---

[11] *Summa theologiae*, 2a2ae. 97, 2; quoted in Harrison 2011, 416–417.
[12] T. Hall 1658: 244; quoted in Harrison 2011, 419.
[13] Oldenburg to Norwood, 10 February 1667/8, Oldenburg 1965–1986, IV, p. 168, quoted in Hunter 1989, 47. (Also quoted in Anstey 2005, 220; my emphasis.)

domains, as well as the connection between them, was affirmed by Thomas Sprat, co-founder of the Society and author of its well-known *History*:

> The spiritual Repentance is a careful survay of our former Errors, and a resolution of amendment. The spiritual Humility is an observation of our Defects, and a lowly sense of our own weakness. And the Experimenter for his part must have some Qualities that answer to these: He must judge aright of himself; he must misdoubt the best of his own thoughts; he must be sensible of his own ignorance, if ever he will attempt to purge and renew his Reason. (Sprat 1667, 367, quoted in Harrison 2011, 428)

Being as it was "a Head knowledge," a "notionall knowledge," the speculative natural philosopher would remain unable to "purge and renew his Reason," since he had no means by which to "doubt the best of his own thoughts." This link between merely "notional knowledge" and epistemically inferior inquiry was passionately drawn in Joseph Glanvill's contemporaneous defense of the Royal Society, where it was once again contrasted with the epistemic superiority of "experimental" knowledge:

> the *Modern Experimenters* think, That the *Philosophers* of elder Times, though their *Wits* were excellent, yet the way they took was not like to bring much *advantage* to *Knowledge* or any of the *Uses* of *humane Life*; being for the most part *that* of *Notion* and *Dispute*, which still runs round in a *Labyrinth* of *Talk*, but *advanceth nothing*. And the *unfruitfulness* of those *Methods* of *Science*, which in so many *Centuries* never brought the World so much *practical, beneficial Knowledge* as would help towards the *Cure* of a *Cut finger*, is a palpable Argument, That they were *fundamental Mistakes*, and that the *Way* was not *right*. (Glanvill 1668, 7–8; quoted in Anstey 2005, 222)

The "palpable Argument" provided in the form of the fruitlessness of speculative natural philosophy deserves notice. What was fundamentally at stake in these debates was not only the method by which the aims of inquiry might best be satisfied, but also the question of what those aims should be. The fact that a criticism of speculative natural philosophy can rest without further explanation on the grounds that "those Methods of Science" were culpable for "so many Centuries" of "unfruitfulness" signals that the reigning epistemic metric of the day was fruitfulness, and that speculative natural philosophy did not measure up.

Speculation was subject to many forms of abuse in the seventeenth century. But for the steadily growing community of experimental natural philosophers, the inherently subjective quality of the data it provided occupied a special place in epistemic Hell. A principal advantage that experiment held over speculation was to move the support for assertions from outside the individual into the public domain where it could be authenticated by others. This was no less the case in religious contexts. It is the sense of "experiment" that is used in the context of the attempt to authenticate the submission of Adam and Eve in the Garden, and in the context if Joseph's attempt to authenticate his brothers' claims to have changed their scheming ways (Genesis 42:15; quoted in Harrison 2011, 417). Thomas Sprat went so far as to root the special epistemic significance of the performance of miracles in their ability to provide public access to what could otherwise only be authenticated by a single individual (Jesus):

> Had not the appearance of *Christ* bin strengthen'd by undeniable signs of *almighty Power*, no age nor place had bin oblig'd to believe his Message. And these *Miracles* with which he asserted the *Truths* that he taught (if I might be allow'd this boldness in a matter so sacred) I would even venture to call *Divine Experiments* of his *Godhead*. (Sprat 1667, 352; quoted in Harrison 2011, 429)

It's important to emphasize here that Sprat is making a much stronger claim than merely that miracles have the power to convince witnesses. Rather, he asserts that the epistemic obligation of observers to believe the message of Christ rests on their having been granted access to more than just his testimony; there is no reason to expect observers to accept Christ merely on his say-so. Miracles allow "the Truths that he taught" to be independently authenticated by observers. Harrison (2011, 431) summarizes the anti-speculative thrust of experimental religion thusly:

> experimental religion was not grounded in experiences that were merely 'subjective' and incapable, in principle, of corroboration. Rather, such experiences were shaped by devotional traditions, most obviously, but not solely, exemplified in formal spiritual exercises. These regimens were designed to bring discipline to devotional practice and guarantee that religious experiences converged upon a common object.

As experimental natural philosophers would come to appreciate, the worry that claims derived through ratiocination depended for their support upon a wholly externally inaccessible species of evidence was seen as a fatal impediment to religious knowledge. This claim is confirmed by the fact that, like their descendants in natural philosophy, experimental religionists tended to target arguments from religious authority for these same criticisms. As in scientific contexts, these arguments place observers at an epistemically unacceptable distance from the evidence.

The other publicity problem that experimental natural philosophy sought to remedy derived, interestingly, from the very experimental tradition from which it descended – viz., alchemy. The direct influence of practicing alchemists on Robert Boyle's experimental approach is now well documented (Newman and Principe 2002). Boyle made no secret of his esteem for alchemical approaches to the study of nature, going out of his way in *The Sceptical Chymist* to praise their understanding of experimental practice and recommend them as an important source of guidance for the study of nature:

> And thus much I shall here make bold to add, that we shall much undervalue Chymistry, if we imagine, that it cannot teach us things farr more useful, not only to Physick but to Philosophy, than those that are hitherto known to vulgar Chymists. And yet as for inferiour Spagyrists themselves, they have by their labours deserv'd so well of the Common-wealth of Learning, that methinks 'tis Pity they should ever misse the Truth which they have so industriously sought. And though I be no Admirer of the Theorical Part of their Art, yet my conjectures will much deceive me, if the Practical Part be not much more cultivated than hitherto it has been, and do not both employ Philosophy and Philosophers, and help to make men such. (Boyle 1661, 9)

When it came to the secretive nature of alchemical investigation, though, he was somewhat less complimentary:

> one of the chief designes of this sceptical discourse was, not so much to discredit chymistry, as to give an occasion and a kind of necessity to the more knowing artists to lay aside a little of their over-great reservedness, and either explicate or prove the chymical theory better than ordinary chymists have done, or by enriching us with some of their nobler secrets to evince that their art is able to make amends even for the deficiencies of their theory. (Ibid., 9)

In *Leviathan and the Air Pump*, Shapin and Schaffer contrast this image of the "alchemist's closet" with the ideal of public demonstrations of effects alleged to have been achieved experimentally, an ideal which became a foundational aspect of influential academic societies like the Royal Society and the Accademia del Cimento. Indeed, Heilbron (1979, Chapter 2) contends that such demonstrations were part of an academic society's mandate virtually by definition. Although various social and cultural roles have been attributed to these demonstrations,[14] their significance from an epistemic perspective is obvious: *to show whether there was any substance to reports regarding a given experimental effect.*

---

[14] Shapin 1994, Chapters 3 and 4.

9.4.2 Public Experimentation and the Emergence of Retraction

The tradition of public experimentation that emerged in the seventeenth century directly addressed the two major epistemological hang-ups that had come to haunt speculative natural philosophy. First, its experimental aspect dealt with the problem of the inherently subjective quality of evidence derived through speculation by shifting the evidentiary focus to what lay *outside* the head. On the other side, it sought to ameliorate some of the worries associated with alchemy, whose secretive nature had, by Boyle's lights, delayed the much-needed diffusion of experimental techniques into natural philosophical inquiry.

The potency of experimentation as an antidote to worries about speculative natural philosophy is an obvious and well-established point, and so not worth exploring in any depth here. It is, however, worth emphasizing how important the public dimension appears to have been for the rise of experiment as an essential aspect of the effective study of nature. The importance of witnesses that could validate – as well as help to calibrate – experimental claims was a critical component of the Royal Society's approach to the Baconian accumulation of knowledge (Heilbron 2011, 176). Reports of the experiments performed there were to be published in the *Philosophical Transactions of the Royal Society* in its role as recorder of verified experimental effects. These reports routinely include the roster of Royal Society fellows who were in attendance when the experiments were performed. These events, and their write-ups, have sometimes been interpreted by contemporary analysts through a framework that tends to unduly inflate the importance of their sociocultural aspects. Consequently, the common-sense Baconian epistemology behind them is often ignored, and the character of the events and their role in the deep change then occurring within natural philosophy has been distorted. But natural philosophers at the time were under no such delusions. They were explicit, as was Bacon, that the purpose of expert witnesses fulfilled the same function in experimental philosophy that it did in law – namely, to prevent error and the propagation of error. The early Royal Society proceeded very self-consciously in the shadow of Bacon, believing with him that future inquiry proceeds upon the path trodden by previous investigations. As such, natural philosophers had not only a sacred duty to the truth and to God, but to future inquiry, to make sure they got things right. As noted by Shapin and Schaffer (1985, 77–78), Robert Boyle's lament that his air pump results had not been replicated reflected his recognition that, in failing to deliver on the expectation of public accessibility, the ability of the air pump results to contribute to natural philosophy had been compromised.[15]

Not everything published in the *Philosophical Transactions* was a report on a public demonstration at the Royal Society. An important source of scientific communication then concerned letters, often from abroad, reporting on observations made outside Gresham College. It is in the context of one such letter that, in 1684, the journal published its first retraction, issued by Irish polymath William Molyneux.[16] The *Transactions* had previously published a letter from Molyenux containing *inter alia* a response to a query posed by Edmund Halley as to "whether *Lough Neagh* stone were not *Magnetical*, for he was told it was; but upon trial I find it is not, for it will not stir a *Needle*, or *Steel filings*, neither will it apply to the *Magnet*, in powder or calcined" (Molyneux 1684a, 554). But subsequent investigation by Molyneux showed that Lough Neagh stone did in fact become magnetic when calcined. He therefore authored the following "ingenious retractation," which is sufficiently short and illustrative as to warrant its full reproduction here:

> Tis now a good while since, I gave you some account of our *Lough-Neagh* Stone and its petrifying qualities, which I hear you have thought worth to insert in one of your *Transactions*; in which discourse I must desire you to correct one *Paragraph*, and undeceive the World in a *particular* there mention'd; which is that *Lough-Neagh Stone*, neither crude nor calcined, would apply to the *Magnet*: that it will not do so *crude*, I still affirm; but that it does not apply *calcin'd*, I must retract: for I find by further trial that it applies *calcin'd* most briskly, and in great quantities, to the *Magnet*: The occasion of my former error being, that I did not *calcine* it long enough. If upon a fit opportunity you would do me justice in this *particular*, you will much oblige me, and vindicate my credit. (Molyneux 1684b, 820)

Molyneux's desire to "undeceive the World" nicely captures the new Baconian ethos of preventing the propagation of error that made retraction

---

[15] Heilbron (2011, 177) argues that, beyond the epistemic agenda of practitioners, the publicly accessible aspect of experimentation would eventually result in its inextricable association with natural philosophy in the mind of the broader public:

> The assimilation of experimental philosophy with natural philosophy was accomplished by the distinctive science of the eighteenth century, electricity, and by the creation of new audiences for the demonstration of natural knowledge. As the practice of witnessing experiments diminished at the major learned societies in favor of reports printed in their publications, a new audience grew up consisting of well-off people curious enough about the latest findings in natural philosophy to spare an evening for it from cards. Their expectations put an even higher premium on experiments easily seen and appreciated by groups.

[16] William Molyneux is known to contemporary scholars as the progenitor of Molyneux's Problem – the question, discussed in Locke's *Essay Concerning Human Understanding*, of whether a blind person could, upon recovery, visually identify shapes known previously only by touch.

an important device, one which could substitute to a degree the epistemic safeguard provided by demonstration in front of a group of qualified natural philosophers. It is significant in this regard that the word "retraction" becomes a stable feature of English-language publications starting in 1655, marking the midpoint between when the founding members of the Royal Society began meeting regularly (1645), and when the first issue of *Philosophical Transactions* was published (1665).[17]

The practice of retraction emerged along with other safeguards such as rosters as a proxy for first-hand observation of the empirical support for factual claims. Like rosters from public demonstrations at the Royal Society, retraction gave the community of inquiry some indication that claims of fact had been subject to an appropriately rigorous process of empirical validation. Most importantly, these safeguards contributed to the prevention of error propagation by helping to affirm a principle that has since come to be associated with the distinctive epistemic character of scientific inquiry – namely, *were an error to arise, it would be corrected*.[18]

9.4.3   Explaining the Absence of Retraction in the Humanities

We can begin to better understand the special epistemic conditions that promote the institution of retraction by dividing the notion of error propagation into two distinct phenomena: error and propagation. Baconian natural philosophy conceived of each stage of inquiry as the foundation for subsequent investigation. On this model, inquiry was conducted with the intention that its results would propagate across the scientific community. Since each result was in principle destined to be taken as an assumption with which to guide future investigation, it was crucial that only well-supported empirical claims remain in the published literature. This suggests two conditions that we should expect to see satisfied in any domain in which retraction plays an important epistemic role:

(1) that it be possible for empirical claims to not be well supported, and
(2) that results tend to propagate to future stages of inquiry.

---

[17] Google N-gram view of "retraction, retractation" for the period 1500–2000. Results retrieved December 5, 2015.

[18] *cf.* the Retraction Guidelines published by the Committee on Publication Ethics:
"Retraction is a mechanism for correcting the literature and alerting readers to publications that contain such seriously flawed or erroneous data that their findings and conclusions cannot be relied upon. Unreliable data may result from honest error or from research misconduct" (url: http://publicationethics.org/files/retraction%20guidelines.pdf; last accessed December 9, 2015).

We should be able to explain the absence of retraction in the humanities via the failure of either (or both) of these conditions.

A closer look at instances of retraction in science illustrates how the first condition contributes to retraction's epistemic function in science. A scientific research publication often reports either a measurement, or a calculation, or an observation of phenomena. The part of the *Phil Trans.* letter that Molyneux eventually retracted, for instance, reported his observation of the phenomenon that Lough Neagh stone did not magnetize when calcined. A more recent retraction by Melchor et al. (2013) withdrew their initial (2002) report of Late Triassic age estimates for "bird-like footprints" in Argentina.

A further distinction relates to the source of potential error. Retractions of scientific publications divide evenly into (a) those issued on account of unintentional error, and (b) those issued on account of scientific misconduct (Steen et al. 2013). But the warrant for retraction is not dependent on the source of potential error. Both examples cited above involve unintentional error (as far as we know). Subsequent experimentation led Molyneux to reinterpret his original data. For Melchor et al.,

> radiometric dating of the sedimentary sequence containing these bird-like footprints ... indicated a Late Eocene age. Further geological studies suggest that the region suffered a complex deformation during the Andean orogeny, including block rotation. In consequence, our previous inferences about the possible implications of this finding for the fossil record of Aves are no longer supported.

Obokata et al. (2014), on the other hand, offers an example of a highly publicized recent case of retraction on the basis of scientific misconduct. Among the various reasons for retraction included the discovery that the original article had published images that had been intentionally manipulated, constituting a direct breach of general research ethics and of the journal *Nature*'s guidelines for data presentation. Although the official investigation into Obokata did not find that she

> deliberately mislead other researchers or lead them to incorrect interpretations of the data, our conclusion is that she was aware of the danger. It is evident that her purpose in creating the composite image was to articulate the T-cell receptor gene rearrangement band and that she did so without applying scientific consideration or procedures. We therefore conclude that this was an act of research misconduct corresponding to falsification. (Obokata et al. 2014; Supplementary Information 1, 5)

Whether on the basis of misconduct or unintentional error, in each case, *retraction was warranted when events subsequent to publication undermined the support for the original report.* In Molyneux's case, the support for his original report was undermined upon his observation that Lough Neagh stone did indeed magnetize when calcined; subsequent geological investigation undermined the support for Melchor's et al. original age estimate; and the support for Obokata's et al. original report of how to acquire pluripotent stem cells was undermined in light of their falsification of images.

I now invite the reader to imagine a scenario in which the general conditions for fraud as defined in the Sokal or Pluckrose et al. hoaxes were successfully realized in some other context in the humanities. Let us begin with the famous paper by Gettier (1963) in which the theory that knowledge is justified true belief is widely regarded as having been refuted. Gettier describes a case in which a man, Smith, is justified in believing the true proposition,

(e) The man who will get the job has ten coins in his pocket

despite the fact that he is wrong about which man the proposition is true in virtue of (Smith thinks its Jones, but it's really Smith himself).

> In our example, then, all of the following are true: (*i*) (e) is true, (*ii*) Smith believes that (e) is true, and (*iii*) Smith is justified in believing that (e) is true. But it is equally clear that Smith does not know that (e) is true.

That's Gettier's argument against the theory that knowledge is justified true belief.

Now let us suppose that tomorrow Gettier were to convene a press conference, during which he announces that his 1963 report that it was "clear that Smith does not know that (e) is true" was an outright fabrication: at the time he considered the example, Gettier himself was not altogether convinced that Smith did not know that (e) was true. In fact, Gettier shamefully admits during the press conference that when his paper went to press, he actually thought that Smith *did* know that (e) was true. His assertion of clarity was totally insincere; he "made it up." On Stanley Fish's model, the conditions for humanistic fraud have been satisfied: Gettier, like Sokal, "put forward … a line of argument he says he never believed in." Assuming, as the scientific community does, that research fraud warrants retraction, it would be appropriate to call for Gettier to retract his paper.

But this conclusion is at odds with the epistemic function of retraction. If, as the Committee on Publication Ethics has stated, "[r]etraction is a mechanism for correcting the literature and alerting readers to publications that contain such seriously flawed or erroneous data that their findings and conclusions cannot be relied upon"[19] – the same sentiment reflected in the original Baconian impetus – then there is no basis for retraction, in either the Gettier hypothetical or the Sokal case. For Stanley Fish, the fact that Sokal's conclusions can't be relied upon turns on Sokal's insincerity. But that's just wrong. What makes Sokal's conclusions unreliable is that neither they, nor the premises on which they are based, make any sense. Nothing about the "seriously flawed or erroneous data" contained in his publication would have been affected, had he been sincere. For precisely the same reason, Gettier's tearful mea culpa would have failed to undercut the reliability of his conclusion that knowledge is not justified true belief. Whatever the reliability of that conclusion depends on, it has nothing to do with the conviction with which Gettier asserted it, any more than my conviction that $1 + 1 = 2$ constitutes part of the support that ensures its reliability.

So, both Sokal and (hypothetical) Gettier are safe from satisfying the conditions for fraud-based retraction. And the lesson generalizes: the sorts of things that could be fabricated in most types of humanities research make no difference to how well-supported humanists' claims are. What's not clear is whether that result is a cause for celebration or, instead, deep concern about the epistemic foundations of our disciplines. Why would outright fabrication, when it is possible, generally fail to undermine humanists' conclusions? What are the epistemic implications of the fact that we generally do not employ the kinds of evidence that it would be possible or profitable to fake?

9.4.4   *When Results Tend to Not Propagate*

The other condition that the emergence of retraction requires is that the results of inquiry tend to propagate – that is, that they tend to be read, understood, and used by other researchers. Given that retraction is an important institution within science, we would expect scientists in general to have convincing grounds for thinking that their research will probably be used by others. And given that retraction does not meaningfully exist in the humanities, we might expect humanists in general to have convincing grounds for thinking that their research will probably *not* be used by others. Is there any indication that either of these predictions is correct?

---

[19] Committee on Publication Ethics: http://publicationethics.org/files/retraction%20guidelines.pdf; last accessed December 9, 2015.

One way to test the predictions is to examine citation behavior across the disciplines. We expect researchers to cite the articles they use to guide their own research, and so whether an article has been cited gives us some information about whether the research reported therein has been used in further inquiry. By looking at disciplinary citation trends, we can get a sense of how probable it is that an article will be cited. This, in turn, gives us some sense of what researchers in a given discipline can reasonably expect regarding the probability that their research will be used by others.

Figure 1 (Larivière et al. 2008) shows trends in the percentage of articles with at least one citation after two years and after five years, for medicine, natural sciences and engineering, social sciences, and humanities. These data suggest that

Division	2 Years (%)	5 Years (%)
Medicine	80	88
Natural Sciences and Engineering	60	73
Social Sciences	55	68
Humanities	<10	<18

medical researchers, scientists/engineers, and social scientists can all reasonably expect their research to be used in further inquiry after five years, albeit some more reasonably than others. Thus, we would expect retraction to be an established phenomenon within the relevant disciplines, which indeed it is (Grieneisen and Zhang 2012). Now, although the humanities numbers do not take citations of books into account (Larivière et al. 2008), they do tell us something about the probability of an article's being cited. Limiting our focus to articles, we can see that it would be unrealistic for a researcher in the humanities to expect the research published in her article to be used in further inquiry, since even after five years the chance of being cited is still less than 1 in 5.[20] Accordingly, based on our model we (correctly) expect retraction not to be an established phenomenon within the relevant disciplines. Admittedly, these data are coarse-grained, and bibliometrics can itself be a dirty business (see, for instance, Werner 2015). But there's no reason to think that the data radically underestimate the percentage of humanities publications that are cited at least one time. In point of fact, raw data on citations may easily *over*state the degree to which humanities

---

[20] Kieran Healy corroborates this for philosophy articles on his blog. See Figure 3 at http://kieranhealy.org/blog/archives/2015/02/25/gender-and-citation-in-four-general-interest-philosophy-journals-1993-2013/; last accessed August 8, 2022.

research builds on previous humanistic inquiry, since many citations are critical – that is, they are not used to indicate the original source for facts which subsequent research may henceforth treat as assumptions. In any case, at least from this perspective, the conclusions that humanists can realistically expect to have their research used by no one, and that scientists can expect their research to be used by someone, seem fairly secure.

I want to stress that this is nothing more than a speculative hypothesis. There could be any number of explanations for why the vast majority of humanities articles are never cited. I do think it is worth trying to come up with a reasonably durable explanation, because the empirical fact that articles are rarely cited strongly suggests that they are not viewed by anyone as part of a disciplinary effort to advance knowledge and understanding. They're just some articles. Some of them are interesting, some of them aren't. Why don't humanists generally need other peoples' articles in order to do what they do? What, if any, are the epistemic upshots of the fact that the vast majority of material published in humanities articles plays no role in subsequent inquiry? And what difference does it make to humanistic knowledge whether or not the kinds of evidence humanists publish can be faked? It is tempting to think that there is something fundamentally different about humanistic inquiry that explains why it tends to not build on previous humanistic achievement. That is possible. But a more economical, more conservative explanation lies in contingent social features of our disciplines, such as the focus on novelty mentioned in the previous chapter. Given how closely our conception of research excellence is tied to novelty, it is no wonder that humanists generally do not build on the previous efforts of other humanists.

9.4.5 Epistemological Upshots, If Any?

Our discussion of retraction began with a look at the historical conditions that led to the institutionalization of retraction as an important safeguard for the epistemic well-foundedness of inquiry. Specifically, retraction arose in parallel with a handful of mechanisms, distinctive to modern scientific inquiry, which are designed to prevent the propagation of error. Some of these mechanisms focus more on the prevention of error, others on error propagation. We inferred from the absence of retraction in the humanities that humanists are generally unconcerned with the threat of error propagation, and proposed two (nonexclusive) candidate explanations for their devil-may-care attitude. One is that the sorts of evidence that humanists appeal to tend to be either impossible or unprofitable to fake. This means that cases in which humanists' claims are actually not supported in the manner suggested are very unlikely to occur. The other candidate explanation is that humanists are generally unconcerned with error *propagation*, because humanists' tendency to not build on previous humanistic research ensures that the probability of humanities results propagating is very low.

Here, I want to raise some general questions, in the hope that they may be taken up by subsequent research (however, given the citation rates, that hope is probably ill fated). First, is there a convincing way of conceiving of humanistic depth that makes refinement and consensus irrelevant, or even antithetical to its achievement? The developmental pattern of scientific inquiry is one in which increasing refinement and consensus are often purchased at the expense of accessibility – that is, at the expense of the ability of the majority to appreciate the meaning of what has been achieved scientifically. It is possible that a shrinking range of accessibility, while important and necessary for scientific progress, is directly opposed to the central objectives of humanistic inquiry. After all, if research in the humanities is generally oriented toward the promotion of contemplative reflection and appreciation of value and meaning, it is not clear how successful humanistic inquiry could hope to be by following a research trajectory wherein results became increasingly inaccessible. As I suggested in the previous chapter, it might be better to think of the esotericism of specialized scientific research as a necessary evil, rather than a hallmark of mature inquiry generally.

Second, what precisely are we to make of the aberrantly low citation rate for humanities articles? I argued above that it is a consequence of an intellectually unhealthy focus on novelty, but it need not be so in order to function as a signal of some deep problem or other in our disciplines. In an essay in *The Chronicle of Higher Education*, English professor Mark Bauerlein provides a stark assessment of the costs and consequences of producing literary research, arguing that, essentially, these low citation rates (citations which are often not substantive) strongly suggest that the resources that go into producing a literary research article ($25K and 100+ hours, by his estimates) are without warrant. This is a different issue from that concerning whether humanities research can be valuable without being profitable. Rather, the point is that current research in the humanities research seems to have little effect on *anyone* – nonspecialists don't read it, and readers apparently find the vast majority of it to not be significant enough to draw on substantively in their own research (Bauerlein 2011).

Third, is there any epistemic significance attached to the fact that humanistic research is often based on evidence that would be either impossible or unprofitable to fake? One cannot fake the deductive validity of an argument, for example. One cannot fake the reasonableness of an interpretation of a work of literature (assuming the claims upon which the interpretation are based are true). One *can* fake the intuitiveness of a conclusion, to some degree, but doing some seems not to undermine the conclusion's support in a meaningful way. It's not obvious why this should weaken a discipline's epistemic foundations. On the other hand, there is no question that the seventeenth-century shift toward appealing to the kind of evidence that *could* be faked was one of the most significant developments in the history of inquiry – not *because* the evidence could be faked, but because the evidentiary focus had shifted to empirical support, and empirical support happens to be fakable. The epistemology of the humanities needs further development before any of these questions can be meaningfully addressed.

CHAPTER 10

Conclusion

Let us try to envision an alternate reality in which the humanities are glorified as the pinnacle of intellectual achievement, while the sciences are maligned and distrusted, practitioners having to beg for the cultural table scraps that are too insignificant for humanists to bother with. This happy scenario (if it is a happy one) is no fantasy. As Rachel Laudan (1993) shows in her review of histories of science to 1913, the genre of history of science arose in the seventeenth century through practitioners' attempts to demonstrate the legitimacy of science and mathematics as species of knowledge, as a way of "pressing their claims against humanist dominance of the institutions of intellectual authority, particularly educational institutions" (Laudan 1993, 2). This largely successful campaign was achieved by writing narratives of progress – stories about scientific communities' confrontation with and eventual victory over challenging intellectual puzzles whose importance was carefully explained to a scientifically uninformed readership. By describing and explaining the sciences' history of progress, practitioners were able to impart to readers a sense of how, historically, difficult problems have been chipped away at and eventually solved to the satisfaction of communities of specialists. These causal histories of science would subsequently give rise to attempts to formulate abstract characterizations of how the sciences produce knowledge, because science's demonstrated knack for solving extremely difficult problems naturally engendered a desire to know the secret to its success.

Although histories of progress *per se* are probably not the right model for how to articulate the value of the humanities, there is a lesson in these efforts to convince a public skeptical of the legitimacy of scientific knowledge. Ultimately, what impressed readers about the history of science was not merely that it had produced lots of important results, but that it produced lots of important results that were *very difficult to obtain*. The argument for increasing the representation of the sciences in curricula rested precisely on the fact that producing scientific knowledge required lots of training in the particular cognitive tools that have been successfully employed in its pursuit; no one would have been motivated to devote more instructional time to science if scientific knowledge was easy to generate. Perhaps more than any other theme, the history of science showed that there is something special about these tools, because they are causally responsible for science's impressive history of solved problems. If we see value in that history of success, went the argument, we ought to embrace the value of learning the skills on which that history depends. And if we value learning those skills, we need to devote an appreciable amount of an individual's education to them, because they do not come easy.

The lesson for us humanists is that, if we want to convince a general public that it is important to devote serious study to the humanities, it had better be the case that whatever is valuable about the humanities can only be obtained by devoting serious study to it. And if that's correct, it ought not to be the case that the production of humanistic scholarship is utterly trivial – that, for example, someone with zero training in a given humanities discipline could win awards for their exemplary scholarship. As a general rule, when we see that people with no training in a discipline can simply cobble together some jargon that survives multiple rounds of expert scrutiny, we should question whether the production of knowledge in that discipline requires any training whatsoever. To put it another way, we should wonder whether there is any meaning to the notion of *expertise* in that discipline. After all, if expertise in that discipline is not required to produce knowledge, and if it's not an effective tool for *vetting* knowledge claims, precisely what is it that distinguishes someone with expertise from someone who lacks it? And what exactly is the argument for why anyone ought to devote serious study to the body of work in that discipline? If even professional-grade scholarship can be generated not just by a novice, but by a novice who is *trying* to sound ridiculous, why should anyone waste her time immersing herself in that discipline's literature?

Part of the reason the natural sciences continue to demand a major investment of students' time, even at the undergraduate level, is because they are hard. Everyone knows that professional-grade scientific research cannot be generated by a novice, let alone by a novice who is trying to sound ridiculous. The things we find valuable about scientific inquiry are hard-won. Professional scientists know this. Aspiring scientists know this, and they are reminded of it several times a semester when they get their graded exams back. Because there is no shortcut, they invest thousands upon thousands of hours into acquiring and honing the tools that will allow them to contribute to scientific knowledge. No discipline whose professional research standards can be routinely met by people with no disciplinary training can expect to make similar demands on students' time.

It is crucial to separate this point from the regrettable fact of contemporary life wherein students seek scientific training because they think scientific training will give them a better chance at getting a good job. Suppose the fortunes were reversed. Suppose that students thought that being a really capable humanist was the only way to get a good job. The point would still stand that, apparently, being a really capable humanist often requires no training. And if *producing* award-winning humanities scholarship requires no training, surely no training would be required merely to *appreciate* the humanities. Unlike in science, the range of shortcuts here is ostensibly limitless.

It could be that much of the reason why the humanities are currently undervalued is because, much of the time, they do not appear to pose genuine intellectual challenges. Rather, they pose pseudochallenges: they demand that aspirants adopt a certain manner of speech or use of certain *en vogue* terms. To be fair, the sciences also make demands on our language. As Michael Gordin (2015) has recently shown, those demands have increasingly come to favor native English speakers; they used to favor those who knew Latin, and before that, Arabic. But they also make demands on capacities that are not dependent on language alone – demands on our analytical, logical, and computational capacities; demands on our capacity for abstraction; on our ability to creatively solve problems; on our ability to survey and weigh a large body of evidence – in sum: demands on our judgment. These are challenges that no change in language can solve. They are real, and they can only be confronted by strengthening the non-linguistic tools that their solutions require.

The weaknesses exposed by the hoaxes are not limited to the specific disciplines the authors targeted. Quite generally, we have not been sufficiently attentive to our duty to distinguish between important and unimportant research problems, and we are failing to impart a faculty of discernment to our students. We have been increasingly lax in our responsibility to bring clarity to complex and nebulous problems that fall within our purview as humanists. We have increasingly come to favor novelty over depth, because it is always easier to meet the loose, underdeveloped standards for good work on a new topic than it is to meet the well-developed standards for good work on a well-developed area of research. It is not always laudable to ask a question that no one has ever asked before. Some questions are just not worth asking; or, at least, they're not worth asking in a research context. We need to return to the level of rigor and intellectual seriousness that has defined the humanities since antiquity. If our distinctive contribution to human culture is going to be valuable, we need to hold ourselves to an intellectual standard that can only be met by seasoned specialists. Being good at humanistic research has never been easy. Let us hope it never becomes so.

References

Abd-Allah, Umar F. *Mālik and Medina: Islamic Legal Reasoning in the Formative Period*. Leiden: Brill, 2013.

Al-Tabarani, Abu al-Qasim Sulayman. *Al-Mu'jam al-Kabir*. 11 volumes. Beirut: DKI, 2007.

Anstey, P. R. Experimental versus Speculative Natural Philosophy. In *The Science of Nature in the Seventeenth Century*, edited by P. R. Anstey and J. A. Schuster. 215–42. Netherlands: Springer, 2005.

Baggott, J. E. *The Quantum Story: A History in 40 Moments*. Oxford and New York: Oxford University Press, 2011.

Bain, Jonathan, and John D. Norton. What Should Philosophers of Science Learn from the History of the Electron. In *Histories of the Electron: The Birth of Microphysics*. 451–65. Cambridge, MA: MIT Press, 2001.

Bauerlin, M. The Research Bust. *The Chronicle of Higher Education*. December 4, 2011.

Bode, Adam, and Geoff Kushnick. Proximate and Ultimate Perspectives on Romantic Love. *Frontiers in Psychology* 12 (April 12, 2021).

Boghossian, P., and T. Nagel. Letter. *Lingua Franca* 6(5) July/August 1996.

Boyd, Richard. Metaphor and Theory Change. In *Metaphor and Thought*, edited by Andrew Ortony. 481–532. Cambridge, UK: Cambridge University Press, 1979.

Broad, William J., and Nicholas Wade. *Betrayers of the Truth*. New York: Simon and Schuster, 1983.

Brown, Harvey R. *Physical Relativity: Space-Time Structure from a Dynamical Perspective*. Oxford and New York: Clarendon Press; Oxford University Press, 2005.

Brown, Jonathan A. C. *The Canonization of Al-Bukhari and Muslim*. Boston: Brill, 2007.

Brush, Stephen G. *Choosing Selection: The Revival of Natural Selection in Anglo-American Evolutionary Biology, 1930–1970*. Philadelphia: American Philosophical Society, 2009.

Brush, Stephen G., and Ariel Segal. *Making 20th Century Science: How Theories Became Knowledge*. Oxford and New York: Oxford University Press, 2015.

Camp, Elisabeth. Imaginative Frames for Scientific Inquiry: Metaphors, Telling Facts, and Just-So Stories. In *The Scientific Imagination*, edited by Arnon Levy and Peter Godfrey-Smith. 304–36. New York: Oxford University Press, 2019.

Caporael, Linnda R., James R. Griesemer, and William C. Wimsatt. *Developing Scaffolds in Evolution, Culture, and Cognition.* Cambridge, MA: The MIT Press, 2014.

Cavell, S. The Avoidance of Love: A Reading of King Lear. In *Must We Mean What We Say?: A Book of Essays*, edited by S. Cavell (Cambridge Philosophy Classics). 246–325. Cambridge, UK: Cambridge University Press, 1969/2015.

Chemla, Karine. The Value of Generality in Michel Chasles's Historiography of Geometry. In *The Oxford Handbook of Generality in Mathematics and the Sciences*, edited by Karine Chemla, Renaud Chorlay, and David Rabouin. 47–89. New York: Oxford University Press, 2016.

Clune, Michael W. *A Defense of Judgment.* Chicago: University of Chicago Press, 2021.

Cohen, G. A. *If You're an Egalitarian, How Come You're So Rich?* Cambridge, MA: Harvard University Press, 2000.

Cohen, G. A. *Rescuing Justice and Equality.* Cambridge, MA: Harvard University Press, 2008.

Cohen, I. Bernard. *Franklin and Newton; an Inquiry into Speculative Newtonian Experimental Science and Franklin's Work in Electricity as an Example Thereof.* Philadelphia: American Philosophical Society, 1956.

Cohen, I. Bernard. *The Newtonian Revolution.* Cambridge, UK: Cambridge University Press, 1983.

Cohen, I. Bernard. *The Birth of a New Physics.* New York: W. W. Norton & Company, 1985.

Collini, Stefan. *English Pasts: Essays in Culture and History.* Oxford and New York: Oxford University Press, 1999.

Creager, Angela. Model Organisms. In *Kuhn's Structure of Scientific Revolutions at Fifty*, edited by Robert Richards and Lorraine Daston. 151–66. Chicago: University of Chicago Press, 2016.

Curtius, Ernst R. *European Literature and the Latin Middle Ages.* New York: Pantheon, 1953.

Damerow, Peter, Gideon Freudenthal, Peter McLaughlin, and Jürgen Renn. *Exploring the Limits of Preclassical Mechanics: A Study of Conceptual Development in Early Modern Science: Free Fall and Compounded Motion in the Work of Descartes, Galileo and Beeckman.* New York: Springer, 1991.

Darwin, Charles. *On the Origin of Species.* London: J. Murray, 1859.

Darwin, Charles. *On the Various Contrivances by Which British and Foreign Orchids Are Fertilised by Insects, and on the Good Effects of Intercrossing.* London: J. Murray, 1862.

Darwin, Charles. *The Descent of Man, and Selection in Relation to Sex.* London: J. Murray, 1871.

Daston, Lorraine. On Scientific Observation. *Isis* 99, no. 1 (2008): 97–110.

Devitt, M. Intuitions in Linguistics. *The British Journal for the Philosophy of Science* 57, no. 3 (2006): 481–513.

Dougherty, Carol, and Leslie Kurke. *The Cultures within Ancient Greek Culture.* New York: Cambridge University Press, 2003.

Dupré, John. *Processes of Life: Essays in the Philosophy of Biology*. Oxford and New York: Oxford University Press, 2012.
Eblen, Matthew K., Robin M. Wagner, Deepshikha Roy Chowdhury, Katherine C. Patel, and Katrina Pearson. How Criterion Scores Predict the Overall Impact Score and Funding Outcomes for National Institutes of Health Peer-Reviewed Applications. *PLoS ONE* 11, no. 6 (July 1, 2016): e0155060.
Einstein, Albert, Hanoch Gutfreund, and Jürgen Renn. 2015. *Relativity: the special & the general theory*. 100th anniversary edition. Princeton: Princeton University Press.
El Shamsy, Ahmed. *The Canonization of Islamic Law: A Social and Intellectual History*. New York, NY: Cambridge University Press, 2013.
Elton, William R. *Æsthetics and Language*. Oxford: Blackwell, 1954.
Engels, Eve-Marie, and Thomas F. Glick. *The Reception of Charles Darwin in Europe*. London and New York: Continuum, 2008.
Farkas, Katalin. 2018. Know-How and *Non-Propositional Intentionality*. In *Non-Propositional Intentionality*, edited by Alex Grzankowski and Michelle Montague, 95–113. Oxford University Press.
Fish, Stanley Eugene. *Is There a Text in This Class?: The Authority of Interpretive Communities*. Cambridge, MA: Harvard University Press, 1980.
Fish, Stanley Eugene. Opinion: Professor Sokal's Bad Joke. New York Times. May 21, 1996.
Fleck, Ludwig. *The Genesis and Development of a Scientific Fact*. Chicago: University of Chicago Press, 1935/1981.
Galison, Peter. *How Experiments End*. Chicago: University of Chicago Press, 1987.
Gaukroger, Stephen. *The Emergence of a Scientific Culture: Science and the Shaping of Modernity, 1210–1685*. Oxford and New York: Clarendon Press and Oxford University Press, 2006.
Gaukroger, Stephen. *The Collapse of Mechanism and the Rise of Sensibility: Science and the Shaping of Modernity, 1680–1760*. Oxford and New York: Clarendon Press and Oxford University Press, 2010.
Gaukroger, Stephen. *Civilization and the Culture of Science: Science and the Shaping of Modernity, 1795–1935*. Oxford and New York: Oxford University Press, 2020.
Gayon, Jean. *Darwinism's Struggle for Survival*. New York, NY: Cambridge University Press, 1998.
Gettier, Edmund L. Is Justified True Belief Knowledge? *Analysis* 23, no. 6 (1963): 121–23.
Gingerich, Owen. Circles of the Gods: Copernicus, Kepler, and the Ellipse. *Bulletin of the American Academy of Arts and Sciences* 47, no. 4 (1994): 15–27.
Gleick, James. *Genius: The Life and Science of Richard Feynman*. New York: Pantheon Books, 1992.
Goodman, Nelson. *Fact, Fiction & Forecast*. London: University of London, 1954.
Goodman, Nelson. *Languages of Art; an Approach to a Theory of Symbols*. Indianapolis: Bobbs-Merrill, 1968.
Goodstein, David L. In Defense of Robert Andrews Millikan. *Engineering and Science* 63, no. 4 (2000): 30–38.

Goodstein, David L. In Defense of Robert Andrews Millikan. *American Scientist* 89, no. 1 (2001): 54–60.
Gordin, Michael D. *Scientific Babel: How Science Was Done before and after Global English*. Chicago and London: University of Chicago Press, 2015.
Grabiner, Judith V. *The Origins of Cauchy's Rigorous Calculus*. Cambridge, MA: MIT Press, 1981.
Grafton, Anthony, and Glenn W. Most. How to Do Things with Texts: An Introduction. In *Canonical Texts and Scholarly Practices: A Global Comparative Approach*, edited by Anthony Grafton and Glenn W. Most. 1–13. Cambridge, UK: Cambridge University Press, 2016.
Gray, Jeremy. *Plato's Ghost: The Modernist Transformation of Mathematics*. Princeton, NJ: Princeton University Press, 2008.
Grieneisen, Michael L., and Minghua Zhang. A Comprehensive Survey of Retracted Articles from the Scholarly Literature. *PLoS ONE* 7, no. 10 (2012): e44118.
Grosholz, Emily. *Representation and Productive Ambiguity in Mathematics and the Sciences*. Oxford and New York: Oxford University Press, 2007.
Gross, Steven. Linguistic Intuitions: Error Signals and the Voice of Competence. In *Linguistic Intuitions*, edited by Samuel Schindler, Anna Drożdżowicz, and Karen Brøcker. 13–32. Oxford: Oxford University Press, 2020.
Gross, Steven, and Jennifer Culbertson. Revisited Linguistic Intuitions. *The British Journal for the Philosophy of Science* 62, no. 3 (2011): 639–56.
Guillory, John. *Cultural Capital: The Problem of Literary Canon Formation*. Chicago: University of Chicago Press, 1993.
Gutting, Gary. *What Philosophers Know: Case Studies in Recent Analytic Philosophy*. Cambridge, UK and New York: Cambridge University Press, 2009.
Hacking, Ian. *The Emergence of Probability: A Philosophical Study of Early Ideas about Probability, Induction and Statistical Inference*. Cambridge, UK and New York: Cambridge University Press, 1975.
Hall, Edward T. Proxemic Theory. *Theory of Communication* (1966): 60–67.
Hampshire, Stuart. Logic and Appreciation. In *Aesthetics and Language*, edited by William Eton. 161–69. New York: Oxford University Press, 1954.
Harrison, Peter. *The Fall of Man and the Foundations of Science*. New York: Cambridge University Press, 2007.
Harrison, Peter. Experimental Religion and Experimental Science in Early Modern England. *Intellectual History Review* 21, no. 4 (2011): 413–33.
Haufe, Chris. *How Knowledge Grows*. Cambridge, MA: MIT Press, 2022.
Haufe, Chris. *Fruitfulness*. New York: Oxford University Press, forthcoming.
Häussler, Jana, and Tom Juzek. Linguistic Intuitions and the Puzzle of Gradience. *Linguistic Intuitions: Evidence and Method* (2020): 233–54.
Heilbron, John L. *Electricity in the 17th and 18th Centuries: A Study of Early Modern Physics*. Berkeley: University of California Press, 1979.
Heilbron, John L. Natural Philosophy. In *Wrestling with Nature*, edited by Peter Harrison, Ronald Numbers, and Michael Shank. Chicago: University of Chicago Press, 2011.

Heilbron, John L. Was There a Scientific Revolution. In *The Oxford Handbook of the History of Physics*, edited by Jed Z. Buchwald. 2–24. New York: Oxford University Press, 2013.
Heilbron, John L., and Thomas S. Kuhn. The Genesis of the Bohr Atom. *Historical Studies in the Physical Sciences* 1 (1969): vi–290. https://doi.org/10.2307/27757291.
Hesse, Mary B. *Models and Analogies in Science*. Notre Dame, IN: University of Notre Dame Press, 1966.
Holmes, Frederic Lawrence. *Investigative Pathways: Patterns and Stages in the Careers of Experimental Scientists*. New Haven: Yale University Press, 2004.
Holton, Gerald. Subelectrons, Presuppositions, and the Millikan-Ehrenhaft Dispute. *Historical Studies in the Physical Sciences* 9 (1978): 161–224.
Hull, David L. *Darwin and His Critics; the Reception of Darwin's Theory of Evolution by the Scientific Community*. Cambridge, MA: Harvard University Press, 1973.
Hull, David L. Darwin's Science and Victorian Philosophy of Science. *The Cambridge Companion to Darwin* (2003): 168–91.
Hunter, Michael. *Establishing the New Science: The Experience of the Early Royal Society*. Woodbridge, Suffolk: Boydell Press, 1989.
Huss, John. The Shape of Evolution: The Mbl Model and Clade Shape. In *The Paleobiological Revolution: Essays on the Growth of Modern Paleontology*, edited by David Sepkoski and Michael Ruse. 327–45. Chicago: University of Chicago Press, 2009.
Isenberg, Arnold. Critical Communication. In *Aesthetics and Language*, edited by William Elton. 131–46. Oxford.
Joy, Lynn S. Scientific Explanation from Formal Causes to Law of Nature. In *The Cambridge History of Science*, edited by Katherine Park and Lorraine Daston. 70–105. New York: Cambridge University Press, 2006.
Kafka, Alexander C. "Sokal Squared": Is Huge Publishing Hoax "Hilarious and Delightful" or an Ugly Example of Dishonesty and Bad Faith? *Chronicle of Higher Education* Oct. 3, 2018.
Kitcher, Philip. *The Nature of Mathematical Knowledge*. New York: Oxford University Press, 1983.
Kitcher, Philip. Darwin's Achievement. In *Reason and Rationality in Natural Science*, edited by N Rescher. 127–89. Lanham: University Press of America. Google Scholar, 1985.
Kitcher, Philip. *Science, Truth, and Democracy*. New York: Oxford University Press, 2001.
Kitcher, Philip. Two Forms of Blindness: On the Need for Both Cultures. *Technology in Society* 32, no. 1 (2010): 40–48.
Kitcher, Philip. Philosophy Inside Out. *Metaphilosophy* 42, no. 3 (2011): 248–60.
Knorr, Wilbur Richard. *The Evolution of the Euclidean Elements: A Study of the Theory of Incommensurable Magnitudes and Its Significance for Early Greek Geometry*. Dordrecht, Holland; Boston: D. Reidel Publishing Co., 1975.
Kohn, David. Darwin's Keystone: The Principle of Divergence. In *The Cambridge Companion to the Origin of Species*, edited by M. Ruse and R. Richards. 1–25. New York: Cambridge University Press, 2008.

Kuhn, Thomas S. *The Copernican Revolution; Planetary Astronomy in the Development of Western Thought.* Cambridge, MA: Harvard University Press, 1957.
Kuhn, Thomas S. The Function of Measurement in Modern Physical Science. *Isis* 52, no. 2 (1961): 161–93.
Kuhn, Thomas S. *The Structure of Scientific Revolutions.* Chicago: University of Chicago Press, 1962.
Kuhn, Thomas S. *The Structure of Scientific Revolutions.* 2nd edition. Chicago: University of Chicago Press, 1970.
Lakatos, Imre, and Alan Musgrave. *Criticism and the Growth of Knowledge.* Vol. 4. Cambridge University Press, 1970.
Lamont, Michèle. *How Professors Think: Inside the Curious World of Academic Judgment.* Cambridge, MA: Harvard University Press, 2009.
Lange, Marc. Aspects of Mathematical Explanation: Symmetry, Unity, and Salience. *The Philosophical Review* 123, no. 4 (2014): 485–531.
Lange, Marc. Explanation, Existence and Natural Properties in Mathematics: A Case Study: Desargues' Theorem. *Dialectica* 69, no. 4 (2015): 435–72.
Larivière, Vincent, Yves Gingras, and Éric Archambault. The Decline in the Concentration of Citations, 1900–2007. *Journal of the American Society for Information Science and Technology* 60, no. 4 (2008): 858–62. doi.org/10.1002/asi.21011
Laudan, Larry. *Progress and Its Problems.* Berkeley: University of California Press, 1977.
Laudan, Larry. The Medium and Its Message: A Study of Some Philosophical Controversies about Ether. In *Conceptions of Ether: Studies in the History of Ether Theories, 1740–1900,* edited by George N. Cantor and Michael J. S. Hodge. 157–85. New York: Cambridge University Press, 1981.
Laudan, Larry. The Demise of the Demarcation Problem. In *Physics, Philosophy and Psychoanalysis,* edited by Robert S. Cohen and Larry Laudan. 111–27. D. Reidel Publishing Company, 1983.
Laudan, Rachel. Histories of the Sciences and Their Uses: A Review to 1913. *History of Science* 31, no. 91 (1993): 1–34.
Lindner, Mark D., Adrian Vancea, Mei-Ching Chen, and George Chacko. NIH Peer Review: Scored Review Criteria and Overall Impact. *American Journal of Evaluation* 37, no. 2 (2016): 238–49.
Lewis, Mark Edward. *Writing and Authority in Early China.* Albany: SUNY Press, 1999.
Ludlow, Peter. *The Philosophy of Generative Linguistics.* New York: Oxford University Press, 2013.
Lycan, William G. *On Evidence in Philosophy.* New York: Oxford University Press, 2019.
Macdonald, Margaret. Some Distinctive Features of Arguments Used in Criticism of the Arts. In *Aesthetics and Language,* edited by William Elton. Oxford: Blackwell, 1954.
Mahoney, Michael. *The Mathematical Career of Pierre de Fermat, 1601–1665.* Princeton: Princeton University Press, 1973.
Makdisi, George. *The Rise of Humanism in Classical Islam and the Christian West.* Edinburgh: University of Edinburgh Press, 1990.

Melchor, Ricardo N, Silvina de Valais, and Jorge F Genise. Bird-Like Fossil Footprints from the Late Triassic. *Nature* 417, no. 6892 (2002): 936–38.

Melchor, Ricardo N., Silvina de Valais, and Jorge F. Genise. Retraction Note: Bird-like Fossil Footprints from the Late Triassic. *Nature* 501, no. 262 (2013): 262–62.

Miller, George A., and Noam A. Chomsky. Finitary Models of Language Users. In *Handbook of Mathematical Psychology*, Volume II, edited by R. Duncan Luce, Robert R. Bush, and Eugene Galanter. 419–49. New York and London: John Wiley & Sons, Inc., 1963.

Millikan, R. A. On the Elementary Electrical Charge and the Avogadro Constant. *Physical Review* 2, no. 2 (1913): 109–43.

Molyneux, William. A Letter from the Learned and Ingenious Mr. Will. Molyneux Secretary to the Society of Dublin, to Will. Musgrave L. L. B. Fellow of New Colledge, and Secretary to the Philosophical Society of Oxford, for Advancement of Natural Knowledge; Concerning Lough Neagh in Ireland, and Its Petrifying Qualitys. *Philosophical Transactions* 14, no. 155–66 (1684a): 552–54.

Molyneux, William. An Ingenious Retractation of the 7th and Last Paragraph of Mr. William Molyneux's Letter in the Philosophical Transact. Numb. 158. Pag. 554. Concerning Lough Neagh Stone and Its Non Application to the Magnet upon Calcination. Being an Abstract of a Letter of the Same Ingenious Gentleman Dated from Dublin Novemb. 25. 1684. *Philosophical Transactions* 14, no. 155–66 (1684b): 820.

Nasim, Omar W. *Observing by Hand: Sketching the Nebulae in the Nineteenth Century*. Chicago and London: University of Chicago Press, 2013.

Netz, Reviel. *The Transformation of Mathematics in the Early Mediterranean World: From Problems to Equations*. Cambridge, UK and New York: Cambridge University Press, 2004.

Netz, Reviel. *Scale, Space, and Canon in Ancient Literary Culture*. Cambridge, UK and New York: Cambridge University Press, 2020.

Newell, D. B., F. Cabiati, J. Fischer, K. Fujii, S. G. Karshenboim, H. S. Margolis, E. de Mirandés, et al. The CODATA 2017 Values Of h, e, k, and N_A for the Revision of the SI. *Metrologia* 55, no. 1 (2018): L13–16.

Newman, William, and Lawrence Principe. *Alchemy Tried in the Fire*. Chicago: University of Chicago Press, 2002.

Newton, Isaac, I. Bernard Cohen, and Anne Miller Whitman. *The Principia: Mathematical Principles of Natural Philosophy*. Berkeley: University of California Press, 1999.

Niaz, Mansoor. An Appraisal of the Controversial Nature of the Oil Drop Experiment: Is Closure Possible? *The British Journal for the Philosophy of Science* 56, no. 4 (2005): 681–702.

Nussbaum, Martha C. *Upheavals of Thought*. New York: Cambridge University Press, 2000.

Nussbaum, Martha C. *Not for Profit: Why Democracy Needs the Humanities*. Princeton, NJ: Princeton University Press, 2010.

Obokata, Haruko, Yoshiki Sasai, Hitoshi Niwa, Mitsutaka Kadota, Munazah Andrabi, Nozomu Takata, et al. Retraction: Bidirectional Developmental

Potential in Reprogrammed Cells with Acquired Pluripotency. *Nature* 511, no. 7507 (2014): 112.

Olenick, Richard P., Tom M. Apostol, and David L. Goodstein. *The Mechanical Universe: Introduction to Mechanics and Heat.* Cambridge, UK: Cambridge University Press, 2008.

Olesko, Kathryn M. The Foundation of a Canon: Kohlrausch's Practical Physics. In *Pedagogy and the Practice of Science: Historical and Contemporary Perspectives*, edited by David Kaiser. 323–56. Cambridge, MA: MIT Press, 2005.

Ording, Philip. *99 Variations on a Proof.* Princeton, NJ: Princeton University Press, 2019.

Oreskes, Naomi. *Why Trust Science?* Princeton, NJ: Princeton University Press, 2019.

Orr, H. Allen. The Genetic Theory of Adaptation: A Brief History. *Nature Reviews Genetics* 6, no. 2 (2005): 119–27.

Ospovat, Dov. *The Development of Darwin's Theory.* New York: Cambridge University Press, 1981.

Overbye, Dennis. A Tiny Particle's Wobble Could Upend the Known Laws of Physics. *New York Times,* April 9, 2021.

Pennock, Robert T. *An Instinct for Truth: Curiosity and the Moral Character of Science.* Cambridge, MA: The MIT Press, 2019.

Planck, Max. On the Theory of the Energy Distribution Law of the Normal Spectrum. *Verhandl. Dtsch. phys. Ges.*, 2, 237.

Pluckrose, Helen, James Lindsay, and Peter Boghossian. Understanding the "Grievance Studies Affair" Papers and Why They Should Be Reinstated: A Response to Geoff Cole. *Sociological Methods & Research* 50, no. 4 (2021): 1916–36.

Polanyi, Michael. *Personal Knowledge.* Chicago: University of Chicago Press, 1958.

Poincaré, Henri. The Future of Mathematics. *The Monist* 20, no. 1 (1910): 76–92.

Provine, William B. *The Origins of Theoretical Population Genetics.* Chicago: University of Chicago Press, 1971.

Quine, Willard V. Two Dogmas of Empiricism. *The Philosophical Review* 60, no. 1 (1951): 20–43.

Rawls, John. *A Theory of Justice.* Cambridge, MA: Belknap Press of Harvard University Press, 1971.

Rehbock, Philip F. *The Philosophical Naturalists: Themes in Early Nineteenth-Century British Biology.* Madison, WI: University of Wisconsin Press, 1983.

Reisch, George A. Aristotle in the Cold War: On the Origins of Thomas Kuhn's the Structure of Scientific Revolutions. *Kuhn's Structure of Scientific Revolutions at Fifty: Reflections on a Science Classic* (2016): 12–30.

Reisch, George A. *The Politics of Paradigms: Thomas S. Kuhn, James B. Bryant Conant, and the Cold War "Struggle for Men's Minds".* Albany: State University of New York Press, 2019.

Renn, Jürgen. Classical Physics in Disarray. In *The Genesis of General Relativity*, edited by Jürgen Renn, Michel Janssen, and Matthias Schemmel. 21–80. Dordrecht: Springer, 2007.

Rey, Georges. A Defense of the Voice of Competence. In *Linguistic Intuitions*, edited by Samuel Schindler, Anna Drożdżowicz, and Karen Brøcker. 33–50. Oxford University Press, 2020.

Rocke, Alan J. *Chemical Atomism in the Nineteenth Century: From Dalton to Cannizzaro*. Columbus: Ohio State University Press, 1984.

Rocke, Alan J. *Image and Reality: Kekulé, Kopp, and the Scientific Imagination*. Chicago: University of Chicago Press, 2010.

Rowling, Joanne K., *Harry Potter and the Half-Blood Prince*. New York: Arthur A. Levine Books, 2005.

Rudwick, Martin J. S. *The Meaning of Fossils: Episodes in the History of Palaeontology*. London and New York: Macdonald and Co.; American Elsevier, 1972.

Ruse, Michael. *The Darwinian Revolution: Science Red in Tooth and Claw*. Chicago: University of Chicago Press, 1979.

Russell, Bertrand. 1910–11. Knowledge by Acquaintance and Knowledge by Description. *Proceedings of the Aristotelian Society* 11: 108–128.

Sepkoski, David. *Rereading the Fossil Record*. Chicago: University of Chicago Press, 2012.

Shapin, Steven. *A Social History of Truth*. Chicago: University of Chicago Press, 1994.

Shapin, Steven, Simon Schaffer, and Thomas Hobbes. *Leviathan and the Air-Pump: Hobbes, Boyle, and the Experimental Life: Including a Translation of Thomas Hobbes, Dialogus Physicus De Natura Aeris by Simon Schaffer*. Princeton, NJ: Princeton University Press, 1985.

Shapiro, Barbara J. *Probability and Certainty in Seventeenth-Century England: A Study of the Relationships between Natural Science, Religion, History, Law, and Literature*. Princeton, NJ: Princeton University Press, 1983.

Sibley, Frank. Aesthetic Concepts. *The Philosophical Review* 68, no. 4 (1959): 421–50.

Slater, Matthew. Natural Kindness. *British Journal for the Philosophy of Science* 66, no. 2 (2015): 375–411.

Small, Helen. *The Value of the Humanities*. Oxford: Oxford University Press, 2013.

Smith, George E. J.J. Thomson and the Electron: 1897–1899 an Introduction. *The Chemical Educator* 2, no. 6 (1997): 1–42.

Sorokowska, Agnieszka, Piotr Sorokowski, and Peter Hilpert. Preferred Interpersonal Distances: A Global Comparison. *Journal of Cross-Cultural Psychology* 48, no. 4 (2017): 577–92.

Sprouse, Jon. A User's View of the Validity of Acceptability Judgments as Evidence for Syntactic Theories. In *Linguistic Intuitions: Evidence and Method*, edited by Samuel Schindler, Anna Drożdżowicz and Karen Brøcker. 215–32: Oxford University Press, 2020.

Sprouse, Jon, and Carson T. Schütze. Grammar and the Use of Data. In *The Oxford Handbook of English Grammar*, edited by Bas Aarts, Jill Bowie, and Gergana Popova. 40–58. Oxford: Oxford University Press, 2020.

Stalnaker, Robert. Intellectualism and the Objects of Knowledge. *Philosophy and Phenomenological Research* 85, no. 3 (2012): 754–61.

Steen, R. Grant, Arturo Casadevall, and Ferris C. Fang. Why Has the Number of Scientific Retractions Increased? *PLoS ONE* 8, no. 7 (2013): e68397. doi:10.1371/journal.pone.0068397.

Stichweh, Rudolf. The Sociology of Scientific Disciplines: On the Genesis and Stability of the Disciplinary Structure of Modern Science (Jul 26, 2007): 1–13.

Strevens, Michael. *The Knowledge Machine: How Irrationality Created Modern Science*. New York: Liveright Publishing Corporation, 2020.

Tappenden, Jamie. Proof Style and Understanding in Mathematics I: Visualization, Unification and Axiom Choice. In *Visualization, Explanation and Reasoning Styles in Mathematics*, edited by Mancosu Paulo, Klaus Frovin Jørgensen, and Stig Andur Pedersen. 147–214. Dordrecht: Springer, 2005.

Tappenden, Jamie. Mathematical Concepts: Fruitfulness and Naturalness. *The Philosophy of Mathematical Practice* (2008): 276–301.

Ter Haar, Dirk. *The Old Quantum Theory*. Oxford and New York: Pergamon Press, 1967.

Thomson, Joseph John. LVII. On the Masses of the Ions in Gases at Low Pressures. *The London, Edinburgh, and Dublin Philosophical Magazine and Journal of Science* 48, no. 295 (1899): 547–67.

van Gelder, Geert Jan. *Classical Arabic Literature: A Library of Arabic Literature Anthology*. New York: New York University Press, 2012.

Wagner, Günter P. *Homology, Genes, and Evolutionary Innovation*. Princeton and Oxford: Princeton University Press, 2014.

Wallace, Bruce. *Fifty Years of Genetic Load: An Odyssey*. Ithaca: Cornell University Press, 1991.

Wardhaugh, Benjamin. *Encounters with Euclid: How an Ancient Greek Geometry Text Shaped the World*. Princeton: Princeton University Press, 2021.

Weiss, Bernard G. *The Spirit of Islamic Law*. Athens: University of Georgia Press, 1998.

Werner, Reinhard. The Focus on Bibliometrics Makes Papers Less Useful. *Nature* 517 (2015): 245.

Westfall, Richard S. *Force in Newton's Physics: The Science of Dynamics in the Seventeenth Century*. New York: Macdonald and Co.; American Elsevier, 1971.

Westfall, Richard S. *Never at Rest: A Biography of Isaac Newton*. Cambridge, UK and New York: Cambridge University Press, 1980.

Wimsatt, William. Entrenchment and Scaffolding: An Architecture for a Theory of Cultural Change. In *Developing Scaffolds in Evolution, Culture, and Cognition*, edited by Linnda Caporael, James Griesemer, and William Wimsatt. 77–105. Cambridge, MA: MIT Press, 2013.

Index

Abd-Allah, Umar Faruq, 176
Academic fraud, 208–209, 212–217, 227–228
Academic hoax, 205–217
Accademia del Cimento, 222
acceptability judgments, 122, 124, 125, 127–132, 134–136
al-Sibawayh, 49–50
Andersen, Hans Christian, 205
Anderson, Carl, 88
Anomalies, 57
Anstey, Peter, 219, 220
Aquinas, Thomas, 219
Arranged marriages, 185–186
Austen, Jane, 27

Bacon, Francis, 218–225
Bauerlein, Mark, 231
Bedouins, 58–59, 167
Bentley, Richard, 193
Betrayers of the Truth, 77
Bod, Rens, 95
Boghossian, Peter, 207
Book of Grammar, 49
Boyle, Robert 197, 222–223
Broad, William 77–78, 84, 109, 118
Brown, Harvey, 5
Brown, Jonathan AC, 165, 176
Brush, Stephen, 28, 37

Camp, Elisabeth, 147, 163
canon and canonization, 43–70, 96, 161–177, 202–204
Cavell, Stanely, 154–160
Chasles, Michel 61
Chomsky, Noam, 12–14
Citation practices, 229–231
Clune, Michael, 50, 55, 58, 91–95
Collini, Stefan, 20–27
Committee on Publication Ethics, 227
Communities (research/intellectual/scholarly/disciplinary), 4, 6, 12–14, 18–20, 22, 27–69, 73–83, 92–93, 130, 161–168

as arbiter of legitimate problems, 182–196
as arbiter of legitimate methods, 196–201
of astronomers, 112–119
early modern scientific, 217–225
metaphors and, 147–153
replication of, 201–202
Consensus, 19, 28–70, 170, 188–189
Copernicus, 87, 112–119

Dalton, John, 8
Damerow, Peter, 25, 192
Darwin, Charles 3, 6, 31–34, 43–44, 145–153, 192
Disciplinary knowledge, 12–16, 20, 37, 48, 62–67, 85–87, 89–96, 161–166, 176–177

Einstein, Albert, 21, 23, 25, 174, 199
El Shamsy, Ahmed, 64, 165, 176, 197
Elements, 174, 176, 192
Enlightenment, 12
Epicycle, 113–115
"Essay on the Principle of Population," 31
Euclidean, 113, 174
Eudoxus, 192
Euripides, 168, 173–174
Exemplars, 13–14, 49–62, 65–69, 74–76, 96–108, 120, 130–135, 143, 153, 161–176, 183, 192, 202
Experiential kinds, 147–160
Expertise, 15, 58, 90–93, 109–110, 119, 137, 200, 223

Farahidi, al-Khalil ibn Ahmad, 130, 163
Feynman, Richard, 7
Fish, Stanley, 64, 67, 213–214
Fleck, Ludwig 12–13

Galileo, 11, 24, 174, 193
Galison, Peter, 39
Garrett, Merrill, 124
Gaukroger, Stephen, 166
Gettier, Edmund, 104–105, 133–136, 227–228
Gingerich, Owen, 111–118
Glanvill, Joseph, 220

Goodman, Nelson, 94, 98, 145–147, 196
Goodstein, David 84
Gordin, Michael, 235
Grafton, Anthony, 10, 47, 167
Grammar, 49–51, 110, 120–129, 133, 140–142, 163
Gray, Jeremy, 165
Grosholz, Emily, 162
Gross, Steven, 122–125
Guillory, John 60, 62–64, 75
Gutting, Gary, 64

Hacking, Ian, 3, 197
Halley, Edmund, 224
Hampshire, Stuart, 91
Harrison, Peter, 95, 197, 218–221
Heilbron, John, 4, 192, 222, 224
History (Royal Society of London), 220
Hobbes, Thomas, 66, 197
Holmes, F.L. 60, 185
Holton, Gerald, 82–86
Homer, 168, 173
House Committee on Science, Space, and Technology, 178
How Professors Think, 190
Hull, David, 32
Hume, David 93–94

Ibn 'Abbas, Abdullah, 169
Isenberg, Arnold, 133, 135

Jenkin, Fleeming, 33–34

Kepler, Johannes, 109, 111–118, 174
Kitcher, Philip, 44, 202–204
Knorr, Wilbur 191–192
Kuhn, Thomas, 12–14, 26, 43, 52–61, 64, 66–67, 72–74, 77–78, 87–95, 117, 164–165, 168, 174, 176–177, 192, 193, 196, 198, 202

Lamont, Michéle, 190
Laudan, Larry, 200
Laudan, Rachel, 11, 233
Le Sage, George-Louis, 3, 198
Leviathan, 47–51
Lindsay, James A., 207
Lord Kelvin, 71–72, 106
Lycan, William, 37, 64–65, 75

MacDonald, Margaret, 91
Makdisi, George, 58–59, 64, 130–131, 165, 167, 176
Malthus, Thomas, 31–32
Mathematics,
 fruitfulness in, 162
 understanding in, 22, 89–96, 196, 197

maximin, 103
Macdonald equation, 5
Medea, 173–174, 193
Meno, 28
Metaphor, 43, 143–153
Millikan, Robert, 77–92, 102, 109
Milton, John, 114
Molyneux, William, 224, 226–227
Moral arbitariness, 103–104
Most, Glenn, 47
Mysterium cosmographicum, 117

Nasim, Omar, 3
National Institutes of Health (NIH), 179, 198–199
National Science Foundation (NSF), 178–179
Netz, Reviel, 149, 165, 176, 193, 196, 202
Newton, Isaac, 23–25, 46, 53, 90, 138, 144, 162, 196
Newtonian mechanics, 23–25, 41, 45, 47, 53, 66, 144, 162, 174, 193
Novelty, 57, 190–191, 198–202, 230–231
Nussbaum, Martha, 11

Office Space, 1
"Of the Standard of Taste," 93
Oldenburg, Henry, 219
Olenick, R.P. 85
Olesko, Kathryn, 54
"On the Electrodynamics of Moving Bodies," 23
On the Revolutions, 112, 117
"On the Theory of the Energy Distribution Law of the Normal Spectrum," 80
Opticks, 162
Origin of Species, 22, 31–34, 44, 116, 174–175, 192, 199–200
Ospovat, Dov, 32, 192
"Overly Honest Methods," 215

Paradise Lost, 49, 115
Parmenides, 171
Parsing, 122–128
Peer review, 29–34, 198, 207–217
Pennock, Robert, 135
Phage group, 53
Philosophical Transactions of the Royal Society, 223–225
Planck, Max, 80
Plato, 21, 28, 149–150, 168
Platonic dialogues, 130
Pluckrose, Helen, 207
Poincaré, Henri, 61
Polanyi, Michael, 12–14, 50, 58, 180
Positron, 88
Pride and Prejudice, 27, 162–163

Principia, 23, 46, 52, 53, 162, 193, 196
Principle of Humility, 65–67
Professor McInquiry and his dazzling display of wizzbangery, 8–10, 15, 204
Proxemics, 123
Ptolemaic astronomy, 112–119
Ptolemy, 77, 112, 171

Quine, W.V.O., 119

Rawls, John, 11, 48, 66, 102–104, 141, 160
Reasonable Agreement, 53–54, 72–74, 78, 86, 119, 144
Reductio ad absurdum, 130
Reinhold, Erasmus, 112–117
Reisch, George, 55–57
Retraction, 206–207, 217–231
Rey, Georges 125
The Rise of Colleges, 130
Rocke, Alan, 6, 192
Royal Society of London, 219–225
Rudwick, Martin, 3
Ruse, Michael, 43
Russell, Bertrand, 109

Salience, 76–77, 84–108, 117, 121, 130, 135, 137, 143, 146, 150, 153–154, 163, 174, 193
The Sceptical Chymist, 222
Schaffer, Simon, 197, 222–223
Scientific Revolution, 17–18, 94
Scientific Method, 2–4, 9–14, 72, 161
"Second Thoughts on Paradigms," 52–53
Seinfeld, 123
Selleck, Tom, 97–101
Sen, Amartya, 104
Sepkoski, David, 174, 192
Shapin, Steven, 167, 197, 222, 223
Shapiro, Barbara, 197

Sibley, Frank, 91, 131–135
Sincerity, 213–215
Small, Helen, 11, 166
Smith, Lamar, 178
Socrates, 21, 130, 134
Sokal, Alan/Sokal Hoax, 213–214, 227–228
Speculative philosophy, 218–223
Sprat, Thomas, 220–221
Sputnik, 55
Stata, 3
Stichweh, Rudolf, 168
Stokes Law, 79–83
Structure of Scientific Revolutions, 13, 52, 55, 164, 174–176

Tacit knowledge, 13–14, 50–51, 55, 62, 101, 111, 132, 143
Tappenden, James, 162, 197
Theory of Justice, 48, 66, 102–104
Thomson, J.J., 79–81, 101–102
Thompson, Frank, 103
Thucydides, 21, 168
"Tintern Abbey," 104
Tycho, 114–119

Unanimity Condition, 38–39

Van Vleck, John, 13
Veil of Ignorance, 66, 102–105

Wade, Nicholas, 77–79, 84, 109, 118
Weinberg, Steve, 102
Weiss, Bernard, 197
Westfall, Richard S., 193, 196
Wilson, E.O. 7
Wittich, Paul, 112, 117
Wolff, Robert Paul, 7